Living in the Margins in Mainland China, Hong Kong and India

With a range of case studies from Asia, this book sheds light on empirical realizations of marginality in a globalized context using first-hand original research.

In the late 2000s, the financial crisis witnessed the fragility of high levels of market integration and the vulnerability of globalisation. Since then, the world seems to have entered an epoch of anxiety featuring populism with varying degrees of protectionism and nationalism. What is the nature of this populist mood as a backlash against globalisation? How do people feel about it and act upon it? Why should specific intellectual attention be paid to the increasingly marginalised by the recent macroscopic structural changes? These are the questions addressed by the contributors of this book, illustrated with specific cases from mainland China, Hong Kong and India, all of which have undergone substantial populist or nationalist movements since 2010.

A valuable resource for sociologists looking to understand the impacts of globalization, especially those with a particular interest in Asia.

Wing Chung Ho is Associate Professor in the Department of Social and Behavioural Sciences at City University of Hong Kong.

Florence Padovani is Director of the Sino-French Research Centre in Social Sciences, Tsinghua University, Beijing, China; and Associate Professor at Paris 1-Panthéon Sorbonne University, Paris, France.

Margins of Development
Edited by Wing Chung Ho and Florence Padovani

This book series is concerned with the most recent emerging production of margins in different societies. It is about the people who feel, at best, ignored by and, at worst, further or newly marginalized by systemic changes in labour and capital movements and local state programmes and policies. It draws inspiration from sociology and anthropology's overarching aim to explore and better understand the condition of people who feel that they are living on the margins of society under the contours of development. Although sociology and anthropology provide the guiding framework, we invite contributions from related disciplines and fields of study including development studies, human geography, migration and refugee studies, labour studies, leisure and tourism studies, cultural studies, feminist studies.

We want to expand the old boundaries of marginality studies. The actors involved can extend from poor migrants to other actors in society who feel marginalized. The subject matter involved can extend from resource and power distributions to the pursuits of particular cultural values and lifestyles.

Living in the Margins in Mainland China, Hong Kong and India
Edited by Wing Chung Ho and Florence Padovani

For a full list of titles, please visit https://www.routledge.com/Margins-of-Development/book-series/MD

Living in the Margins in Mainland China, Hong Kong and India

Edited by
Wing Chung Ho and
Florence Padovani

LONDON AND NEW YORK

First published 2020
by Routledge
2 Park Square, Milton Park, Abingdon, Oxon OX14 4RN

and by Routledge
605 Third Avenue, New York, NY 10017

First issued in paperback 2022

Routledge is an imprint of the Taylor & Francis Group, an informa business

© 2020 selection and editorial matter, Wing Chung Ho and Florence Padovani; individual chapters, the contributors

The right of Wing Chung Ho and Florence Padovani to be identified as the author of the editorial material, and of the author for his individual chapters, has been asserted in accordance with sections 77 and 78 of the Copyright, Designs and Patents Act 1988.

All rights reserved. No part of this book may be reprinted or reproduced or utilised in any form or by any electronic, mechanical, or other means, now known or hereafter invented, including photocopying and recording, or in any information storage or retrieval system, without permission in writing from the publishers.

Trademark notice: Product or corporate names may be trademarks or registered trademarks, and are used only for identification and explanation without intent to infringe.

Publisher's Note
The publisher has gone to great lengths to ensure the quality of this reprint but points out that some imperfections in the original copies may be apparent.

British Library Cataloguing-in-Publication Data
A catalogue record for this book is available from the British Library

Library of Congress Cataloging-in-Publication Data
Names: Ho, Wing-Chung, editor. | Padovani, Florence, editor.
Title: Living in the margins in Mainland China, Hong Kong and India / edited by Wing Chung Ho and Florence Padovani.
Description: Abingdon, Oxon ; New York, NY : Routledge, 2020. | Series: Margins of development | Includes bibliographical references and index.
Identifiers: LCCN 2020006858 (print) | LCCN 2020006859 (ebook) | ISBN 9780367480783 (hardback) | ISBN 9781003037873 (ebook)
Subjects: LCSH: Marginality, Social—China—Case studies. | Marginality, Social—China—Hong Kong—Case studies. | Marginality, Social—India—Case studies. | Globalization—China—Case studies. | Globalization—China—Hong Kong—Case studies. | Globalization—India—Case studies. | China—Economic conditions—2000- | China—Social conditions—2000- | Hong Kong (China)—Economic conditions. | Hong Kong (China)—Social conditions. | India—Economic conditions—21st century. | India—Social conditions—21st century.
Classification: LCC HN740.Z9 M264 2020 (print) | LCC HN740.Z9 (ebook) | DDC 305.5/68095125—dc23
LC record available at https://lccn.loc.gov/2020006858
LC ebook record available at https://lccn.loc.gov/2020006859

ISBN 13: 978-0-367-51112-8 (pbk)
ISBN 13: 978-0-367-48078-3 (hbk)
ISBN 13: 978-1-003-03787-3 (ebk)

DOI: 10.4324/9781003037873

Typeset in Galliard
by codeMantra

Contents

List of figures	vii
List of tables	ix
List of boxes	xi
List of contributors	xiii
Acknowledgments	xvii

Introduction: why use the concept of marginality today? 1

WING CHUNG HO AND FLORENCE PADOVANI

PART I

Margins in Mainland China: the rural-urban interface 15

1 **Home for fewer people: the demolishment of a farmers' market and its long-term effect on lower-skilled population in Beijing** 17

YULIN CHEN, FEI YAN, YUE YANG, AND HENGYU LIU

2 **Rural *Dama* in China's urbanization: from rural left-behind to urban strangers** 36

JING SONG AND LULU LI

PART II

Margins in Mainland China: Shanghai 53

3 **When a marginal area is transformed into a tourist hot spot: Tianzifang in Shanghai** 55

FLORENCE PADOVANI

vi *Contents*

4 Cemeteries in Shanghai: beyond the margins 75
MAYLIS BELLOCQ

PART III
Margins in Hong Kong 99

5 "My community doesn't belong to me anymore!":
tourism-driven spatial change and radicalized identity
politics in Hong Kong 101
ALEX SIU KIN CHAN AND WING CHUNG HO

6 Surviving the collective subjectivity of Choy
Yuen Village: from multiple marginalizations to
irreversible resistance 126
LINDA YIN-NOR TJIA

PART IV
Margins in India 151

7 Waste in the urban margins: the example of
Delhi's waste pickers 153
RÉMI DE BERCEGOL AND SHANKARE GOWDA

8 Living on the margins of the legal city in the
southern periphery of Chennai: a case of cumulative
marginalities 176
VÉRONIQUE DUPONT AND R. DHANALAKSHMI

Index 195

Figures

1.1	The Sun Palace Farmers' Market and its surrounding markets (July 2016)	19
1.2	Migrant vendors' employment status after the demolition of the farmers' market	23
1.3	Comparison of average monthly income of vendors after the demolishment of the Sun Palace Farmers' Market (Average monthly income in Yuan currency)	24
1.4	Current food-purchasing location choice for residents living in Sun Palace area	27
1.5	Overall impact on the surrounding residents	28
1.6	Impact on surrounding residents according to gender	28
1.7	Impact on surrounding residents according to age	28
1.8	Impact on surrounding residents according to monthly income	29
1.9	Impact on surrounding residents according to living distance	29
1.10	Comparison of different grocery shopping places and Sun Palace Farmers' Market	30
1.11	Residents' preference for where to buy vegetables and fruits	30
1.12	Functions of farmers' market according to the residents' demands	31
2.1	Ningxia and its capital city Yinchuan in China	41
3.1	Evolution of Building Usage from 1997 to 2009	57
3.2	Tianzifang's main entrance 210 Taikang lu, November 2019	65
3.3	The border between touristic and residential area, Summer 2010	67
3.4	Tianzifang before restauration, Summer 2006	68
3.5	Tianzifang on a week day, November 2019	68
3.6	Daily life in Tianzifang, Spring 2005	69
3.7	Visitors in narrow alley, November 2019	69
4.1	Window of an office representing the Binhai guyuan cemetery (M. Bellocq, 2010)	76
4.2	The municipality of Shanghai and its cemeteries	81
4.3	Example of a land saving grave (M. Bellocq, 2012)	84
4.4	Renovated graves in black material (M. Bellocq, 2012)	85
4.5	Displacing graves (M. Bellocq, 2012)	86

viii *Figures*

4.6	Monumental stones in memory of all those whose ashes have been scattered in the sea (M. Bellocq, 2008)	88
4.7	A virtual grave (M. Bellocq, 2015)	90
4.8	Traditional offerings made for the first anniversary of the death (M. Bellocq, 2015)	91
5.1	Hong Kong identity, 1997–2018	103
5.2	Three districts chosen.	106
5.3	San Hong Street & Lung Sum Avenue, in Sheung Shui.	107
5.4	Yan Ching Street & Tak Ching Court, in Tuen Mun.	108
5.5	Tong Lok Street, Sau Fu Street & Castle Peak Road, in Yuen Long	109
6.1	Map of XRL alignment and location of the affected area	131
7.1	At the Car Bumper Sawmill	161
7.2	Bag seller	170
8.1	Chennai IT Corridor	178
8.2	Pedestrian bridge built by the residents of Arignar Anna Nagar over the polluted Buckingham Canal in Chennai (March 2013)	181
8.3	Kannagi Nagar resettlement colony in a floodplain of the southern periphery of Chennai (July 2015)	188

Tables

1.1	Socioeconomic profile of surveyed residents	21
2.1	Basic information about interviewees before and after urbanization	39
5.1	Community, street sections and number of shops involved in Google mapping	105
5.2	Profile of informants	110
5.3	Major change of shops types (≥ or ≤45%) in San Hong Street and Lung Sum Avenue, Sheung Shui	112
5.4	Major change of shops types (≥ or ≤45%) in Yan Ching Street and Tak Ching Court, Tuen Mun	113
5.5	Major change of shops types (≥ or ≤45%) in Tong Lok Street, Sau Fu Street and Castle Peak Road; Yuen Long	113
5.6	Informants and the dimensions their narratives touched upon during the interview	120
6.1	Profile of interviewees	127

Boxes

7.1 Excerpt from interview with Harinder Kumar, the owner of a plastics recycling factory in the Narela industrial estate 164

Contributors

Rémi de Bercegol, PhD, is a research fellow at the French National Centre for Scientific Research (CNRS). He has a doctorate in Urban Planning from LATTS (research group on technology, territories and societies) at ENPC/UMLV, Paris Est, France. He was a Visiting Researcher at the Centre for Social Sciences and Humanities (CSH) in New Delhi between 2008 and 2012. During this time, he undertook research for his book on small towns and decentralization reforms in Northern India (*Small Towns and Decentralisation*, BSpringer, 2017). Beyond the scope of India, his research focuses now on world urbanization and the transformation of cities in the Global South, analyzed principally in terms of their essential services (water, sanitation, waste management and energy).

Maylis Bellocq is Assistant Professor in the Department of Chinese Studies at Bordeaux Montaigne University. Her research interests lie in funeral rites and spaces, Shanghai funeral sector, cultural heritage, tourism.

Alex Siu Kin Chan is a PhD candidate at City University of Hong Kong. Alex graduated from the University of Melbourne, Australia, with B. Envs in Architecture, and a Master of Architecture. He has also obtained M. BLaw from Monash University, Australia. After working in architecture for the past few years, he re-entered academia to focus on urban sociological research. He is currently working on his thesis on identity politics and community change in Hong Kong.

Yulin Chen is Associate Professor at the Department of Urban Planning at Tsinghua University and SPURS fellow at MIT. She received her bachelor's degree of architecture in 2003 and doctoral degree of urban planning in 2010 from Tsinghua University, and then did a post-doctoral research in the Department of Sociology, Tsinghua University. With the background in urban planning and sociology, Yulin studies China's urbanization from the view of migrants' integration and the spatial response. Yulin is the principal investigator of several research projects, including the "Study on Integration of Migrants under the Spatial Perspective" supported by the National Social

xiv *Contributors*

Science Fund of China. Yulin has published more than 30 papers and won many paper awards from the Urban Planning Society of China and the Chinese Sociological Association.

R. Dhanalakshmi is a social science researcher based in Chennai with an academic background in social work. She worked in several Indo-Dutch social sciences research projects for the University of Amsterdam on issues of gender and the labor market, urban waste management and urban governance. She also participated in the international project *Urban Chances – City Growth and the Sustainability Challenge* from 2010 to 2014, and contributed to the work package of this project, which focused on policies and politics to address the challenges of substandard settlements, with an emphasis given to related social mobilization. Her publications include "Governance Urban Environmental Management: Comparing Accountability and Performance in Multistakeholder Arrangements in South India", co-authored with I. S. A. Baud (*Cities*, special issue on Peri-Urban India, 2007); and *Solid Waste Management in Madras City*, co-authored with Shobha Iyer (Chennai: Pudhuvalvu Pathippagam, 1999).

Véronique Dupont is a senior research fellow in urban studies at the *Institut de Recherche pour le Développement* (IRD) – French national Research Institute for sustainable Development, in the CESSMA research unit – the Centre for Social Sciences Studies on Africa, America and Asia in Paris. She was joint director of CESSMA (2014–2018) and the director of the Centre for Social Sciences and Humanities (CSH) of New Delhi (2003–2007). She is associated with the Centre for Indian and South Asian Studies, Paris, and a senior visiting fellow at the Centre for Policy Research, Delhi. Her research focuses on the socio-spatial transformations of Indian metropolises. She is particularly interested in the interrelations between urban policies and residential and coping strategies of the populations in informal settlements. Her recent publications include *Urban Policies and the Right to the City in India* (coedited with M.H. Zérah & St. Tawa Lama-Rewal, UNESCO & CSH, 2011), and *The Politics of Slums in the Global South* (coedited with D. Jordhus-Lier, C. Sutherland & E. Braathen, Routledge, 2016).

Shankare Gowda, PhD, is an urban governance specialist, associated with the Centre for Policy Research (CPR) New Delhi. He is also a collaborator of the Centre de Sciences Humaines (CSH).

Wing Chung Ho is Associate Professor of sociology at City University of Hong Kong and holds a PhD in anthropology from SOAS, University of London. He has published broadly on community studies and social problems in relation to subordinate people in Hong Kong and Chinese societies. His academic articles appear in *The China Quarterly, The China Journal, Journal of Contemporary Ethnography, Journal of Contemporary China, Journal of Contemporary Asia* and *China Review.*

Contributors xv

Lulu Li is a PhD student in Gender Studies Programme at the Chinese University of Hong Kong. Her research interests include gender and work, mate selection, family relations, female entrepreneurship and ICT. Her work has been included in *Handbook on the Family and Marriage in China* (Edward Elgar Publishing, 2017).

Hengyu Liu is a graduate student at the Department of Urban Planning at Tsinghua University. He received his bachelor's degree in engineering from Tsinghua University.

Florence Padovani is currently Director of the Sino-French Research Center in Social Science at Tsinghua University (Beijing). Her research interests focus on internal migration inside China, planned migration in Shanghai municipality and urbanization issues as well as issues on displacement of population from the Three Gorges dam area, dealing with both the first and second generations. Her recent publication is *Development-induced Migration in India and China: A Comparative Look at the Burdens of Growth*, Lexington Books (2016).

Jing Song is Assistant Professor in the Gender Studies Programme at the Chinese University of Hong Kong. Her research interests include gender and family, work and employment, migration and urbanization, and market transition in China. Her studies have been published in *China Quarterly, Urban Studies, Eurasian Geography and Economics, Housing Studies, Population, Space and Place, China Review, Asian Anthropology, Journal of Sociology, Journal of Comparative Family Studies, Chinese Journal of Sociology* and *Social Sciences in China*. Her book *Gender and Employment in Rural China* was published by Routledge in 2017.

Linda Yin-Nor Tjia is a political economist who specializes in infrastructure and logistics development, as well as their impact on society. Her book *Explaining Railway Reform in China* and other book chapters were published by Routledge. She has also published peer-reviewed articles in *Asian Survey, International Social Work* and the *Journal of Social Entrepreneurship*. Tjia received her doctoral degree from the Hong Kong University of Science and Technology, and is currently Assistant Professor at the Department of Asian and International Studies, City University of Hong Kong. Prior to her academic endeavors, she had extensive working experience in the railway and logistics sector in Hong Kong and the mainland China.

Fei Yan is Associate Professor in sociology at Tsinghua University. He received his PhD in sociology from the University of Oxford and completed a postdoc from Stanford University. His research focuses on urban sociology, political sociology and the sociology of development. His work has appeared in *Social Science Research, Urban Studies, The Sociological Review, Social Movement Studies, Oxford Bibliographies in Sociology, Development Policy Review, The China Quarterly, Modern China* and *China Information*. He has been

xvi *Contributors*

awarded the Graduate Student Best Paper Prize by the Association for Asian Studies in 2015.

Yue Yang is a PhD student in the Department of Sociology at Tsinghua University. Yue majored in sociology and economics, with a minor in mathematics at Georgetown University. She obtained a master's degree in contemporary Chinese studies from the University of Oxford.

Acknowledgments

Many people made this edited volume possible. Our thanks go to the organizers and participants of two international workshops. The first was *An International Workshop for Living at the Margins,* and took place in Paris on December 19, 2018, and was organized by the École des Hautes Études en Sciences Sociales. The second workshop, *An International Workshop for Marginality and Internal Migration in Contemporary China,* took place in Hong Kong on October 28, 2019, and was organized by the Department of Social and Behavioural Sciences, City University of Hong Kong. The contributors of this book were mainly participants of these two intellectually stimulating workshops.

We are also grateful to Routledge, in particular Simon Bates who offered unwavering support for this book.

Finally, we have to acknowledge that this book benefited from the financial support of three different grants: (i) French Collaborative Institute on Migration, coordinated by the CNRS (Project No.: ANR-17-CONV-0001); (ii) Research Grants Council of the Hong Kong Special Administrative Region, General Research Fund (*Unravelling Ambivalent Mobilities: The Social Memory, Bicultural Identity and Livelihood Strategies of Young Dam Migrants in Guangdong;* Project No. CityU 9042400); and (iii) PROCORE-France/Hong Kong Joint Research Scheme (*Migrant Mobilization and Economic Opportunities: A Comparison of Young Three Gorges Dam (TGD) Migrants' Experience in Guangdong and Shanghai;* Project No. CityU 9052023).

Introduction
Why use the concept of marginality today?

Wing Chung Ho and Florence Padovani

First of all, we will explain why we decided to devote a whole volume using the old concept of margins. One may say that it is an outdated concept, one that does not fit twenty-first-century societies. But it is still to this day a reference in American sociology. To us it may be seem old, but strangely enough, it is still a very modern concept. We will begin with our reflection on the concept of the "marginal man", a concept borrowed from Park. In the early twentieth century, he was defining marginality as follows:

> a cultural hybrid, a man living and sharing intimately in the cultural life and traditions of two distinct peoples; never quite willing to break, even if he were permitted to do so, with his past and his traditions, and not quite accepted, because of racial prejudice, in the new society in which he now sought to find a place. He was a man on the margin of two cultures and two societies, which never completely interpenetrated and fused. (Park 1928: 892)

The theory framed by Park and his students was somehow ambiguous; however, it did confirm to the reality of the United States at the time of their research (at the end of the nineteenth and early twentieth centuries). Their "typical" marginal man was new in the city either from the countryside or from a foreign county; in a word, he was an outsider trying to obtain a place in American urban society. Before World War II the urban population was booming in the United States and so the main focus of Park and his students was that specific part of the population. To them, these outsiders had to go through "a production of new schemes of behaviour and new institutions better adapted to the changed demands of the group" (Thomas & Znaniecki 1974: 1130). Adaptation can be used in a positive sense and margins can also be positive to a certain extent like the example of health care in Cuba (Spiegel & Yassi 2004).

As Chad Alan Goldberg explains in "Robert Park's Marginal Man: The Career of a Concept in American Sociology" (2012), the theory has taken on a life by itself, and is now being used to analyze issues as different as gender, race and hybrid cultures. The concept went beyond American sociologists and spread over the academic world (Zhou 1997). Goldberg emphasizes that over

2 *Wing Chung Ho and Florence Padovani*

eight decades the marginal man has been present in academia. Such longevity is interesting in itself.

In this present book, the authors test and challenge Park's concept through their fieldwork in mainland China, in Hong Kong and in India, far away from its birthplace. The flexibility of the concept and its ability to analyze different contexts and at different times are putting the marginal man to the test.

Why living-in-the-margins matters?

People being marginalized are different; they do not follow the local norms. Here we mean social norms, economic norms or legal norms. The ones at the margins, willingly or not willingly, do not conform to the majority. Therefore, the margins exist only because there is a normality that most of the citizens comply with. The definition of margins is given in reaction to the main trends. There are margins and periphery because there is a city. We may assume that margins are a social and political construct. All this means that at a given period of time and in a given place margins will be defined in a certain way; they are quite specific. Even if in a global world we tend to have more and more international norms and standards to analyze one society, we should not forget the specificities which cannot be included in general norms. We have the statistics tools to compare inequalities around the world, access to education and so on. But isn't this process of leveling acting like a magnifier either mounting or erasing the margins? The chapters in this volume are going to show quite different case studies, and they will be opportunities to give different definitions of margins.

In the late 2000s, the financial crisis witnessed the fragility of high levels of market integration and the vulnerability of globalization. Since then, the world seems to have entered an epoch of anxiety featuring populism with varying degrees of protectionism and nationalism – Donald Trump's election to the presidency of the United States, Brexit as a referendum outcome in the United Kingdom, Xi Jinping's strong Chinese nationalism with hegemonic characteristics, the rise of ethno-nationalism in Modi's India and the angst of the European Union's collapse, just to name a few.

Spanning the globe has been people's sense of being treated unfairly in the decades of globalization that upholds the *for-all* developmental ideals, such as "a single market *for all*", "democracy *for all*" and "sustainability *for all*". On the contrary, an increasing number of people seem to support an "our country first", "our community first" or "our ethnic group first" mentality with, as Contractor remarks, "skepticism or outright hostility toward multilateral institutions and global trade" and predilection for "leadership styles that emphasize ethnic or group identification, distrust of immigrants, and increased assertiveness sometimes bordering on bluster and aggression" (2017: 163). One should remember that populism here refers to the *purest* strain of democracy, or as Adriaanse (2016: 2; original emphasis) puts it: "a democracy that better reflects the *general will of the people* than the presumably unjust elites represent it".

Introduction   3

Populism thus counterpoises cosmopolitanism which, according to Weiner (2018: 4), is "a transnational universalizing concern and respect for legitimate difference such as cultural diversity, but without condoning cruel and barbarous social practices". What is the nature of this populist mood as a backlash against globalization? How do people feel about it and act upon it? Why should specific intellectual attention be paid to the increasingly *marginalized* by the recent macroscopic structural changes? These are the questions we would like to address in the following sections.

What happened?

To some intellectuals, globalization is the source of the social evils of inequality and poverty. But the past decade proves these intellectuals are only partially correct. It is true that the immense amounts of wealth created after the financial crisis in 2008 have aggravated inequalities in income and knowledge among nations and societies. For example, Alvaderdo et al. observe that:

> the global richest 1% adults captured 27% of total income growth since 1980, that is two times more than the bottom 50% adults, who collectively captured 12% of total growth over the period. The top 1% income share increased from 16% to 20% over the period. (Alvaderdo et al. 2017: np)

Recent economic figures confirm that wealth inequality around the globe is still serious in the aftermath of the financial crisis; on this, Gonzalez-Vicente and Carroll state:

> By 2015, 1% of the global population controlled half the world's wealth, a situation that has only become more apparent with the revelations earlier this year that 8 people have the same amount of wealth as the poorest 50% (or 3.6 billion people) of the world's population. (Gonzalez-Vicente & Carroll 2017: 9)

Alvaderdo et al. (2017) note a break in the trend of global inequality after 2008, but they suggest that reduction in inequality between countries does not mean that inequality within a country is alleviated. Rather, within-country inequality continues to rise in three vastly different regions of the Middle East, Brazil (and to some extent Latin America as a whole) and South Africa (and to some extent sub-Saharan Africa as a whole); they write:

> In spite of their many differences, the striking commonality in these three regions is the extreme and persistent level of inequality. The top 10% receives about 55% of total income in Brazil and sub-Saharan Africa, and in the Middle East, the top 10% income share is typically over 60%. (Alvaderdo et al. 2017: np)

4   Wing Chung Ho and Florence Padovani

What is against the expectation of leftist intellectuals, however, is that globalization-led inequality has not dragged down the poor and made them become poorer. Instead, according to Contractor (2017), globalization has made dramatic decreases in poverty rates around the world since 1980 which have accounted for raising approximately two billion people out of poverty due to foreign direct investment and international trade. Quoting World Bank data, Contractor pinpoints that:

> In 1981, 44 percent [1.98 billion persons] of humankind lived in absolute poverty. With the big increase in global trade and investment since then, even though the world population almost doubled, by 2015 only 9.6 percent [0.71 billion persons], of us were in grinding poverty [which is defined by $1.90 per person per day or lower as income]. (Contractor 2017: 176)

Dabla-Norris et al. (2015) further observe that while poverty has declined in many countries, it is on the rise in advanced economies; they write:

> In many EMDCs, poverty ... has declined, despite rising income inequality in some. In contrast, recent data suggest that poverty rose in advanced [OECD] countries since the 1990s ... particularly in the United States and the United Kingdom. (Dabla-Norris et al. 2015: 14–15)

The portrayal of increasing inequality alongside reducing poverty can be easily understood with Alvaderdo et al.'s (2017) analysis that indicates that though the richest still grasps the most, the economic situation of the poorest has been substantially improved. Specifically, they observe from recent economic data that since 1980, there have been a "high growth at the bottom 50 percent (94%), low growth in the middle 40 percent (43%), and high growth at the top 1 percent (more than 100%)" (Alvaderdo et al. 2017: np).

In parallel with these economic trends, the populist fear of further inequality, precarious job stability and lack of social mobility has grown in the past decade and has taken the form of protectionist trade policies in individual states and societies. For example, Evenett and Fritz (2015: 18) point out that "a total of 539 measures were taken by governments worldwide" that restrict foreign trade and investment in the first ten months of 2015. Other reports indicate that the average monthly rate of imposing new trade restrictive measures by G20 countries since 2009 peaked in 2016, with 21 new measures a month, which outnumbered measures aimed at facilitating trade during the same period (Kutlina-Dimitrova & Lakatos 2017: 1). Analyses show that these measures have harmed international trade as G20 exports have reported an average drop of 4.5 percent since world trade peaked in value in October 2014; 2016 marked the fifth consecutive year, with merchandise trade growth below 3 percent, which was much lower than the pre-2008 financial crisis average of 7 percent growth (Evenett & Fritz 2015: 7; Kutlina-Dimitrova & Lakatos 2017: 1).

Protectionism aside, the increasing global populist sentiment has also led to the rapid resurrection of nationalist and parochial governing rationales that feature what Gonzalez-Vicente and Carroll (2017: 3) call "a discourse of victimhood – from China to Great Britain, from America's rustbelt to Russia – with culprits for pervasive prevarication and inequality sought in distant worlds and cultures". The examples Gonzalez-Vicente and Carroll quote include Trump's "Make America Great Again", Xi's "Rejuvenation of the Chinese Nation" and European countries' right-wing movements to curb immigration, preserve national values and vindicate self-determination (2017: 11). To this, we can add the Indian nationalism, which, according to Kim, refers to "[c]ultural nationalism [that] draws from the idea of a pre-existing Hindu nation and a national identity proud of its linguistic heritage, culture, and territory" (2019). Indian nationalism is very close to Chinese nationalism in its expression.

What has been illustrated above is that the world has recently entered a new era where inequality continues to grow, but with fewer people falling into the trap of absolute poverty. This trend prompts us to think anew about the nature of the backlash against globalization. We endeavor to argue that the recent rise in populism with its attendant protectionism and nationalism is related to people who *feel* they are being increasingly marginalized, or left out in the current globalization process rather than to people who really suffer from the increasing risk of material scarcity. What is then the nature of this marginalization?

How do people feel?

While inequality is not something novel and poverty has actually been improving, why do more and more people seem to be discontented with the emerging global situation and possess a populist sentiment toward it? Former theories have suggested that the main cause of the rise of populism, and, usually, the rise of the right-wing political parties, is due to the collapse of people's trust of the existing local political institutions in dealing with increasing globalization-led wealth disparity, political inequality and/or inbound migration (Eatwell 2003; Golder 2003; Taggart 2004; Mouffe 2005; Mudde 2007). In particular, this points further that job losses and identity threats, due to the influx of foreign products and ideas, have created *Modernisierungsverlierer*, that is, the losers of modernization, who are attracted to right-wing populist ideals of returning to the old, good and stable times of the nation-state by exercising measures of othering *our* "enemies" which are literally whoever defined as "outsiders" (Mudde 2007: 203; see also Adriaanse 2016: 15; Gonzalez-Vicente & Carroll 2017: 11).

Apart from job losses and threats to identity, one important factor which has been interwoven into the fabric of people's anti-globalization spirit in the past decade, as we observe, is the *visibility* of globalization. Specifically, the rampant and rapid capital flows around the globe have created impacts beyond strictly the economic domains of society, such as the closing down of local factories

6 *Wing Chung Ho and Florence Padovani*

or structural change in local job markets, but on people's everyday life in *their* society or community. For example, global real estate property values have appreciated drastically owing to extensive human and capital movements to such an extent that locals' anxiety of losing their rights to the city has increased (Eizenberg 2016; Öz & Mine 2018). Such an increase in the visibility of globalization impacts over the past decade has often been augmented by the influx of outsiders for tourism and trading purposes which has aroused complaints by local people about the disappearance of original ways of life and the lowering of living standards in the receiving societies (Rowen 2016; Müller & Hoppstadius 2017). Contractor (2017: 176) is astute to notice that "various aspects of globalisation such as trade, FDI, the internet, travel, and migration are stitching ... together" distinct peoples from distinct nation-states and cultures.

If the time-honored Veblen concept of "conspicuous consumption" refers to the spending of money on luxury goods and service in order to publicly display the buyer's economic power, what people are increasingly facing is "conspicuous globalisation" through which the presence of migrants, tourists and foreign investors in the developed and the developing worlds has made an impactful public display of the power of capitalism to people at the local level. Rather than suffering from absolute scarcity of materials and food, *new* losers of such conspicuous globalization are bred. They feel increasingly living in the *margins*, or what Weiner (2018: 3) describes that more and more people feel themselves "no longer socially useful", and come to feel themselves becoming "disposable, degraded and humiliated, superfluous, redundant, jettisoned" in their societies or communities (see also Tyler 2013).

In recent years, new economic and social indicators have been created in an attempt to analyze the reality through different angles. Bhutan's Gross National Happiness, the Social Vulnerability Index and a long list of other means are meant to bypass traditional indexes like the Gini coefficient which calculate inequalities in a given society. The social Vulnerability Index might also be called the Social Marginal Index because the population at the margins are also very often the most vulnerable ones.

Back to the context of the present edited volume, people who live in the margins refer to those who find themselves being caught between two different cultures or traditions, and, on occasion, even two different sources of jurisdiction. Simply put, they are to face and cope with two never fully compatible, if not simply antagonistic, lifeworlds: one that features their original, business-as-usual way of life, and one that features atypical thoughts generated directly or indirectly by conspicuous globalization. People tend to suffer from cumulative marginalities as Dupont and Dhanalakshmi explain in their chapter. They feel marginalized because of poverty, because of their social status, because of where they live. This is true not only in India but also in China and in Hong Kong. Consequently, the marginalized people we are concerned with in this book are not citizens whose legal rights are being stripped, or proletariats who suffer from material scarcity; rather, they refer to those who feel unequal and fear of being cast out amid current contours of globalization.

Introduction 7

Scholars have suggested that the ambivalence or even anxiety that marginalized people experience during globalization fails to be soothed by local politics. Smith (2017: 347–348) suggests that the rampant globalization that privileges economic expertise over political public engagement in dealing with local matters has undermined the democratic legitimacy of individual states. Along this line, Adriaanse deems the right-wing populist claim that "things *can* be changed ... [that] [w]e *can* go back to the nation-state, to nativism, to mono-ethnic societies ... is [merely] a false hope" (2016: 14; original emphases; see also Mouffe 2005: 56). On the waning power of local politics in the face of globalization, Adriaanse's illustration is clear; he writes:

> I think that democracy in the globalized world faces a fundamental contradiction: while electoral-democratic systems are more widespread across the globe than ever before in history, the powers of these democracies are increasingly limited and have shifted to global flows of capital, information, goods, money, people, and discourses. (Adriaanse 2016: 9)

With the erosion of power within individual local electoral democratic systems, citizens find various ways of expressing their discontent. This situation is somehow comparable to non-democratic systems where people raise their concerns and try to resist the political power in legal or illegal ways. For example, Kevin J. O'Brien focused on the ways Chinese people are using the right to resist (O'Brien & Li 2006). We are interested in knowing how the marginalized adopt different types of resistance or coping strategies to express their discontent. Central to the chapters incorporated in this edited book is to capture the lives and meanings of people who feel, at best, ignored by, or, at worst, further or newly marginalized due to more recent globalizing trends. In this regard India can put a new light on the situation in China. Comparing two different political systems and analyzing the way marginalized people raise their voices lead to a better understanding of their specificities. Indian people demonstrate in the streets when they want to raise their voices and resist some political decisions. In China, demonstrating in the streets is illegal. When opposing an administrative decision Chinese have to go through petitions or the court.

These different aspects of marginality fit perfectly with the different meanings induced by living at/in/on the margins. We understand that living *at* the margins implies that one is about to slide into destitution poverty; there is a danger of getting there. Living *in* the margins would have a more political and social connotation and has a broader meaning. Living *on* the margins is more a look from the outside. In a nutshell, the three expressions are used in different contexts and have slightly different meaning; all of them are used in this book, but as a general title the editors eventually choose the broader sense as living in the margins. Following Goldberg's (2012) excellent re-reading of Park's concept of the "marginal man" in light of the contemporary intellectual context, we expect to observe that the marginalized people in question will embody not only "maladjustment and disorganization but also ... creativity and innovation" (2012:

8 *Wing Chung Ho and Florence Padovani*

199–200). Their stories will ultimately contribute to a better understanding of the emerging production of margins in the era of conspicuous globalization.

Different cases to illustrate marginality

This edited volume displays different case studies and will shed light on empirical realizations of marginality in the post-globalized contexts of China and India. This book intends to provide first-hand original research to capture the lives of people in these two countries that are ignored or marginalized due to recent globalizing trends, their ambivalent identity between different cultures or traditions, as well as their coping strategies in the face of such a complex environment. Making our case studies in different places, we aim to show how various margins are recently created and what are the strategies adopted by the actors to deal with the marginalization. This also helps avoid the trap of essentialist culturalism that leads to an analytical impasse. We intend to apprehend the phenomenon of marginality through a renewed framework of analysis giving the opportunities to explore the general question of social relationships in a globalized world from a particular angle (Lamont & Thevenot 2000). One should not be surprised that we consider China as the main case of study because it has experienced rampant changes amid the globalization process. To extend our scope to India, however, may require some explanation. One should be well aware that India can be a desirable choice for a cross-analysis with China due to the size of the country and its demography. While the communist party gained the supreme power over China in 1949, India was proclaimed independence two years before. Both countries began their industrial process around the same years, and have been struggling with modernity and nationalism throughout the second part of the twentieth century (Duara, 1995). Transitioning from centrally planned to market-based economic systems, both China and India are notable examples of suffering from rapidly growing within-country inequalities with miraculous per capita income growth in the beginning of the 2000s (Berry & Serieux 2006; Hung & Kucinskas 2010: 1479). And, similar to China, ethno-nationalism in India has been on the rise in recent years. Scholars have attributed the surge in ethnic unrest and conflicts in India to the problems of inequality and political maneuvering in relation to unprecedented globalization (e.g., Priya 2016). Other scholars compare China and India in the ways the two countries have coped with the changes in the post-globalization era, such as the rise of economic reregulation (Hsueh 2012) and technological international co-invention (Branstetter et al 2013). We admit that no perfect comparison is possible with China and India. Both have certain comparable starting points and end points, but have different itineraries (Cernea, 2016). Still, no one can deny that the developments of China and India have been deeply influenced by the same forces of globalization. We deem that the similarities highlighted insofar show the high value of cross-analysis between the two countries. If the term "globalization" is originated in economics and interests the macro-economists, its social impacts on the actors interest us as micro-sociologists. This is the rationale behind we

Introduction 9

pioneer the endeavor to apprehend the phenomenon of marginality in these two countries through the present edited book.

As the readers go through this book chapter by chapter, they will learn that the two chapters based on India bring interesting insights to Chinese scholars. For example, Bercegol and Gowda (Chapter 7) have suggested that the marginalization of waste pickers in New Delhi that was awkwardly contrasted with the symbolization of waste materials as a valuable resource echoes what has been happening in some Chinese cities. Dupont and Dhanalakshmi (Chapter 8) also suggest that the significance of the issues addressed throughout their case study of people who have been affected by large-scale infrastructural projects extends beyond the context of Chennai and other Indian cities. They claim that the relationship between environmental risks and the displacement of the urban poor from precarious settlements is a question that arises in many cities of the Global South. One of the parallel references they quote was the way city dwellers in Beijing were stigmatized and expelled from their habitat by environmental improvement projects at the time of the 2008 Olympic Games.

One will also be quickly aware that two chapters on Hong Kong have been incorporated as part of the illustration of Chinese marginality. To us, Hong Kong is closely related to the mainland of China both geographically and politically. The incorporation of Hong Kong represents an intermediary, between China and India in terms of the legacy from British colonialism. Overall, we consider that China, Hong Kong and India are very much integrated in the current global movement in question and it is relevant to analyze them through the concept of margins. Endeavoring to overcome simplistic essentialist models of national character, we hope that this book will shed new light on the question of marginality that interests social scientists, policy makers, journalists and public intellectuals.

The topics in the following chapters are arranged in four different parts. Parts I and II focus on mainland China. The two chapters in Part I examine the changes in daily life of residents and market sellers in Beijing and that of old ladies being relocated to a city in Ningxia province. Part II concerns the urban development in Shanghai and how the dwellers in question face new problems of marginalization amid the rapid urban development. Part III focuses on how the furthering of the economic integration between the mainland of China and Hong Kong has made the original residents in the community feel being marginalized, if not discriminated. Part IV presents two case studies in India – New Delhi and Chennai – which mainly show the innovative spirit of the marginalized groups.

Chapter 1, by Yulin Chen, Fei Yan, Yue Yang and Hengyu Liu, examines the case of the Chinese government implementing harsh urban planning policies to control the inflows of people and force out lower-skilled populations in recent years. In the context of the regulation of population size in mega-cities such as Beijing, the demolition of the Beijing Sun Palace Farmers' Market in 2013 was a natural policy experimentation to examine the long-term effect of spatial governance and urban planning policies on those who live at the margins of the city.

10   *Wing Chung Ho and Florence Padovani*

Based on in-depth field interviews with previous vendors and residents from surrounding communities in 2016, they find that instead of leaving Beijing, most of the vendors became self-employed again in the newly built farmers' markets within 3 kilometers from the Sun Palace Farmers' Market. However, the demolition still had enduring disruptive effects on their life trajectories and social integration. At the same time, local residents frequently reported that the vegetables sold in supermarkets and community food stations were much less fresh and less diverse compared to those sold in large farmers' markets. As a result, the demolition of the Beijing Sun Palace Farmers' Market and population control policy also had a negative impact on local residents' daily life. This chapter lastly reflects on the spatial displacement and population expulsion policy and makes suggestions on the spatial governance of the planning and designing of farmers' markets for the "lower-skilled population" living at the margins in and of cities.

Chapter 2, by Jing Song and Lulu Li, investigates the understudied group of rural *dama* (middle-aged or old women, or in general married women) in China's urbanization process. Rural *dama* are usually the "left-behind" group in China's modernization process, although their labor and social participation have played an important role in China's rural development. Their inferior position in both socioeconomic and cultural practices, however, has been restructured in the urbanization process. This study uses interviews with relocated villagers who were resettled following land development and urban sprawl in Ningxia, Northwest China. Interviews suggest that *dama* are not only defined by their age and marital status, but also that they feel a sense of being socially useless. These women were deprived of their rural multitasking and mediating roles under the urban economy and governance. Lacking necessary human and cultural capital to navigate their city lives, these women faced low-end or short-term jobs and limited social circles, whereas men and young women tried to distance themselves from this "lagging" group. These women were often considered unattractive and unproductive, and their control over family property and children's life plans declined due to new urban uncertainties. Living at the margins of the city and estranged in family power dynamics, they were trapped between rural nostalgia and the urban dream. Their "otherness" was not new in the patriarchal countryside, but they were further marginalized under new institutions and trends such as urban consumerism. As urbanization reshapes economic activities, family relations and social lives, *dama* face new forms of social marginality when the city comes closer.

Chapter 3, by Florence Padovani, analyzes different forms of marginality in a community located in the former French concession in downtown Shanghai. Tianzifang has been struggling to survive for two decades and this situation affected its residents. As Chad Alan Goldberg underlines, marginality suggests a potential maladjustment and disorganization but at the same time creativity and innovation (2012). This chapter analyzes different forms of marginality where different actors are considered legitimate to raise their voices in favor or against safeguarding the community. In addition to residents, some administrative cadre, developers, academics and artists played an important role in giving

Introduction 11

birth to what is known today as Tianzifang. The link between marginality and legitimacy is key to understanding this particular context. Marginality is not only about human beings (their origin and status) but also about buildings and heritage. Tianzifang is marginal in many ways and this is what saved it from destruction. A Chinese proverb states that the taller the tree the more likelihood it has to be cut. Benefits can be taken out of marginality; this is how being a small area that is quite dilapidated made it possible to create a new model of urban development at a micro level.

Chapter 4, by Maylis Bellocq, examines the issues of urban development and cremation. Although cremation has become generalized in Shanghai since the 1980s in line with the reform launched in the 1950s, the Shanghainese are keen to maintain links with the dead and the grave is the material form of this. So, urns with ashes are, preferably, buried in the earth under a tombstone. But because of the accelerating urban development that Shanghai has undergone over the last few decades, the pressure on the land has increased and this pressure is felt in cemeteries too. Thus, the cemeteries which have left the central neighborhoods since the 1950s are still continually being pushed out toward margins that are increasingly farther away. But today, the municipality no longer wishes to organize spaces dedicated to the dead and is seeking to develop the practice of scattering ashes at sea as well as an online cemetery in order to offer the bereaved a place where they can gather and make offerings. The deceased thus find themselves relegated to the fringes, farther and farther away. This chapter attempts to understand the dynamics at work in the expulsion of cemeteries from towns. The first part will show how the marginalization of cemeteries is linked to both practices around death and political will. In the second part, the cemeteries of Shanghai will be viewed as a mirror of the city and as such the producers of their own margins. The third part will deal with the question of the dematerialization of cemeteries as sought by the authorities of Shanghai municipality.

Chapter 5, by Alex Siu Kin Chan and Wing Chung Ho, empirically examines the changes in the street views of three border communities in Hong Kong in response to tourism-driven spatial changes. The late 2000s in Hong Kong witnessed the emergence of public grievances against mass mainland Chinese tourism and parallel trading. The consequential changes induced to local community landscapes and residents' original lifestyles have brought about a series of unprecedented protests against mainlanders since 2012. Agitated by the fruitless political struggle of Occupy Central in late 2014 that demanded Beijing to give Hong Kong democracy, these "local first" and "my community first" protests have seemingly prompted more locals to self-identify as "Hongkongers" rather than as "Chinese". This chapter aims to examine the tourism-driven changes at the community level and their relation with the emergence of radicalized identity politics in wider society. Empirically examined are the changing street views in three border communities between 2011 and 2017 (by the novel method of "Google mapping") and the meanings that 26 young residents (aged 18–34) gave to these changes. Results indicate that the more the local space is shaped by

12 *Wing Chung Ho and Florence Padovani*

tourism and parallel trading, the more likely that discontent against mainlanders and nostalgia for their original lifestyle were bred among the residents.

Chapter 6, by Linda Tjia Yin-nor, takes a closer look at the case of Choy Yuen Village in Hong Kong. The forced eviction of the old Choy Yuen Village, a small village that gave way to the construction of the Express Rail Link in Hong Kong, has been widely studied in the past ten years. Most of the literature focused on the strategy and trajectory of the social movement, investigating how collective efforts failed to stop the demolishment of the village, but successfully helped the villagers resettle, brought forward an alternative agricultural-led development and sustained a community based on civic engagement. Such empowering discourse, however, has missed out an equally critical discourse of marginalization and irreversibility, in which 47 non-indigenous households had settled in the new Choy Yuen Village with sorrow and much emotion.

Chapter 7, by Rémi de Bercegol and Shankare Gowda, examines the marginalization of waste workers who recover and recycle waste materials. Invisible and invisibilized, the people who handle waste are stigmatized by society; they are seen as different, abnormal and as such relegated to the margins. Why and how does this marginalization manifest itself? Wouldn't it be legitimate to think that these workers should on the contrary be fully involved in the management of waste? Their hypothesis is that it is worth supporting recovery and recycling activities happening in the margins. This could provide a highly efficient solution despite a number of drawbacks, which are partly due to this activity's relegation to informality. To support this claim, they examine empirical materials collected over the course of several field trips in Delhi, India, where waste recovery is heavily stigmatized due to its association with the impurity of waste. The system reveals a rich and complex structure that challenges preconceptions. Finally, the last part discusses how the marginalization of waste recovery workers has also become a political object, with the emergence of discourses that legitimize this work, oppose the reforms or seek to adapt them. Beyond the case of India, this analysis sheds light on the process through which waste recovery is marginalized, while investigating potential courses of action that could help meet the challenges of sustainable urbanization.

Chapter 8, by Véronique Dupont and R. Dhanalakshmi, investigates issues faced by the people living in a precarious settlement located along a river canal in the southern periphery of Chennai, India. This case study shows how living on the urban margins can be understood as a condition that results primarily from economic deprivation and entails cumulative effects. The lack of economic resources pushes people to live in substandard settlements outside the legal sector. Vacant places to occupy are more likely to be available on the outskirts of a city, on non-building land such as the edge of water bodies in low-lying areas. The ensuing settlements are categorized as "objectionable slums", under the constant threat of eviction. Such a geophysical location also exposes their dwellers to environmental risks, especially floods. These dwellers are furthermore stigmatized as encroachers, offenders and polluters, and, hence, are socially marginalized. After eviction, they are relocated to other marginal spaces in another substandard habitat. Lastly, among these multidimensional marginal urban dwellers, some prove to be more marginal than others, namely, the tenants, especially the migrants from the northern states of the country.

Works Cited

Adriaanse, M. L. (2016). *Globalisation, post-politics, and populism: The power shift of neo-liberal postmodern globalisation and its discontents* (Master's Thesis). Leiden University.

Alvaderdo, F., Chancel, L., Piketty, T., Saez, E., & Zucman, G. (2017). The elephant curve of global inequality and growth. *AEA Papers and Proceedings*, 108, 103–108.

Bensebaa, F., & Béraud, P. (2012). Coping with globalization: What are the driving forces of openness and spatial dynamics of innovation? *Journal of Innovation Economics & Management*, 10(2), 3–22.

Berry, A., & Serieux, J. (2006). *Riding the elephants: The evolution of world economic growth and income distribution at the end of the twentieth century (1980–2000)*. Working Paper no. 27. United Nations, Department of Economic and Social Affairs, New York.

Branstetter, L., Li, G., & Veloso, F. (2013). *The globalization of R&D: China, India, and the rise of International Co-invention*. A paper presented at 2012 Asia Pacific Innovation Conference, https://cpbuse1.wpmucdn.com/blogs.gwu.edu/dist/5/1304/files/2018/04/branstetter_li_veloso_paper-sr0g9f.pdf

Cernea, M. (2016). Comparing the Thinking in China and India on Development-Displacement, In F. Padovani (Ed.), *Development-Induced Displacement in India and China – A Comparative Look at the Burdens of Growth* (pp. vii–Liii). London: Lexington Books.

Contractor, F. J. (2017). Global leadership in an era of growing nationalism, protectionism, and anti-globalisation. *Rutgers Business Review*, 2(2), 163–185.

Dabla-Norris, M. E., Kochhar, M. K., Suphaphiphat, M. N., Ricka, M. F., & Tsounta, E. (2015). *Causes and Consequences of Income Inequality: A Global Perspective*. Washington, DC: International Monetary Fund.

Duara, P. (1995). *Rescuing History from the Nation – Questioning Narratives of Modern China*. Chicago: The University of Chicago Press.

Eatwell, R. (2003). Ten theories of the extreme right. In P. Merkl & L. Weinberg (Eds.), *Rightwing Extremism in the Twenty-first Century*. London: Frank Cass.

Eizenberg, E. (2016). *From the Ground Up: Community Gardens in New York City and the Politics of Spatial Transformation*. London: Routledge.

Evenett, S. J., & Fritz, J. (2015). *The tide turns? Trade protectionism and slowing global growth*. The 18th Global Trade Alert Report.

Goldberg, C. A. (2012). Robert Park's marginal man: The career of a concept in American sociology. *Laboratorium*, 4(2), 199–217.

Golder, M. (2003). Explaining variation in the success of extreme right parties in Western Europe. *Comparative Political Studies*, 36(4), 432–466.

Gonzalez-Vicente, R., & Carroll, T. (2017). Politics after national development: Explaining the populist rise under late capitalism. *Globalisation*. doi: 10.1080/14747731.2017.1316542

Hung, H.-F., & Kucinskas, J. (2010). Globalization and global inequality: Assessing the impact of the rise of China and India, 1980–2005. *American Journal of Sociology*, 116(5), 1478–1513.

14 Wing Chung Ho and Florence Padovani

Hsueh, R. (2012). China and India in the age of globalization: Sectoral variation in post-liberalization reregulation. *Comparative Political Studies*, 45(1), 32–61.

Kim, A. (2019). The new Nationalism in Modi's India – Parsing the particular brand of nationalism on display in the BJP's platform. *The Diplomat*, https://thediplomat.com/2019/12/the-new-nationalism-in-modis-india/

Kutlina-Dimitrova, Z., & Lakatos, C. (2017). The global costs of protectionism. *Policy Research Working Paper 8277*. Washington, DC: World Bank Group.

Lamont, M., & Thévenot, L. (Ed.). (2000). *Rethinking Comparative Cultural Sociology: Repertoires of Evaluation in France and the United States*. Cambridge: Cambridge University Press.

Mouffe, C. (2005). *On the Political*. London: Routledge.

Mudde, C. (2007). *Populist Radical Right Parties in Europe*. Cambridge: Cambridge University Press.

Müller, D. K., & Hoppstadius, F. (2017). Sami tourism at the crossroads: Globalisation as a challenge for business, environment and culture in Swedish Sápmi. In Arvid Viken and Dieter K. Müller (Eds.), *Tourism and Indigeneity in the Arctic* (pp. 71–86). Bristol: Channel View Publications.

O'Brien, K., & Li, L. (2006). *Rightful Resistance in Rural China (Cambridge Studies in Contentious Politics)*. Cambridge: Cambridge University Press.

Öz, Ö., & Mine, E. (2018). Problem spaces' and struggles over the right to the city: Challenges of living differently in a gentrifying Istanbul neighborhood. *International Journal of Urban and Regional Research*, 42(6), 1030–1047.

Park, R. E. (1928). Human migration and the marginal men. *American Journal of Sociology*, 33(6), 881–893.

Priya, A. (2016). Ethnicity in post-independent India: A sociological perspective on its causes and manifestations. *IOSR Journal of Humanities and Social Science*, 21(1): 56–61.

Rowen, I. (2016). The geopolitics of tourism: Mobilities, territory, and protest in China, Taiwan, and Hong Kong. *Annals of the American Association of Geographers*, 106(2), 385–393.

Smith, J. (2017). Local responses to right-wing populism: Building human rights cities. *Studies in Social Justice*, 11(2), 347–368.

Spiegel, J. M., & Yassi, A. (2004). Lessons from the margins of globalisation: Appreciating the Cuban health paradox. *Public Health Policy*, 25(1), 85–110.

Taggart, P. (2004). Populism and representative politics in contemporary Europe. *Journal of Political Ideologies*, 9(3), 269–288.

Thomas, W. L., & Znaniecki, F. (1974). *The Polish Peasant in Europe and America*. Boston, MA: Gorham Press.

Tyler, I. (2013). *Revolting Subjects: Social Abjection and Resistance in Neoliberal Britain*. London: Zed Books.

Weiner, R. R. (2018). Abjection, precarity and populist mood. *European Legacy*. doi: 10.1080/10848770.2018.1554392

Zhou, M. (1997). Growing up American: The challenge confronting immigrant children and children of immigrants. *Annual Review of Sociology*, 23, 63–95.

Part I

Margins in Mainland China

The rural-urban interface

1 Home for fewer people

The demolishment of a farmers' market and its long-term effect on the lower-skilled population in Beijing

Yulin Chen, Fei Yan, Yue Yang and Hengyu Liu

Introduction

With the rapid development of mega-cities in China, "urban diseases" such as traffic congestion, environmental degradation and high housing prices are becoming more and more prominent, and strict control of population size has become a core issue of urban governance in mega-cities. In recent years, Beijing, Shanghai and Guangzhou have taken harsh population control measures such as administrative prohibition, industrial replacement and space diversion to control the inflows of people and force out the so-called lower-skilled population. In Beijing, 100 commodity trading markets were dismantled and moved throughout 2014, and 57 were in 2015. An operating area of 948,000 m^2 were involved, and the number of rental stalls were reduced by 21,000 m^2 (Beijing Bureau of Statistics 2016). According to the official urban planning policy, Beijing aims to become a world-class city cluster, and therefore "a decline in urban population growth means fewer traffic jams, less pressure on the housing and public service sectors, and a decrease in urban scale and resource use, which are necessary for sustainable development" (China Daily 2018).

Previous research on the spatial governance of floating and lower-skilled populations in mega-cities in China mainly focused on two major themes. The first theme adopts an elite perspective to examine the effect of government efforts to control the population. The scholarly emphasis in this line has shifted from "whether to expulse the population" to "how to effectively expulse the population". In order to turn mega-cities such as Beijing and Shanghai into global cities, scholars propose specific urban promotion measures such as strengthening household registration management and restrictions, setting minimum standards for rental housing, eliminating low-end industries and business patterns, and adjusting urban spatial patterns to expel the population as the main goal of enhancing a city's global competitiveness (Anttiroiko 2015; Gu et al. 2015; Liu 2015; Yang et al. 2015; Björner 2017).

The second theme adopts a grassroots perspective to investigate the social impact of urban redevelopment on the migrant population and their social

18   *Yulin Chen et al.*

integration. Based on empirical studies on urban villages in Beijing, Shanghai and Guangzhou, scholars found that the mass demolition in the process of urban redevelopment will have an *immediate* impact on the floating population's residence, social relations network and the original informal economic system, forcing them to move to the surrounding or more distant villages in the city (Xiang 2005; Wu et al. 2013; Zhao et al. 2017; Yan 2018; Chen & Liu 2019). However, there is still a lack of in-depth empirical studies and microscopic evidence on the long-term effect of spatial governance and urban upgrading policies on those who live at the margins in mega-cities in China.

To fill this research gap, this research conducted a survey of re-employment status of vendors after the demolition of a farmers' market in Beijing – a typical physical space of the floating and lower-skilled population in mega-cities (Morales 2009, 2011). Essentially, farmers' markets are among the most vulnerable and jeopardized clustering spaces for the floating population and therefore become the main target of industrial disintegration (Chen 2017). In many Chinese cities in recent years, many farmers' markets have been replaced by large, modern supermarkets due to the former's small-scale, low-technologies, safety hazards and disordered environments (Goldman et al. 1999; Hu et al. 2004; Zhang & Pan 2013). In particular in Beijing, since 2006, the Beijing municipal government started to strictly regulate the development of farmers' markets – markets inside the second ring road were banned from further development and could only be converted to other retail forms or relocated outward; new market construction was prohibited within the fourth ring road (Beijing Municipal Commission of Commerce 2006). These regulations further accelerated the demolition of farmers' markets in the city and subsequently had disruptive effects on life trajectories and social integration of self-employed vendors who once worked in the markets.

Meanwhile, the farmers' market is not only the gathering place of the floating population but also the provider of basic services and urban public space of local residents. Previous studies have found that farmers' markets provide a distinctive public platform to build migrant-resident social ties and mutual trust (Yue et al. 2013; Chen 2017). While self-employed migrant vendors can have access to diverse local customers every day to build connections with mainstream society, local residents can also provide migrants with emotional support and information sharing beyond the boundaries of the shopping place. Along this line, this chapter will also investigate the changes in the behavior of the residents of the surrounding communities before and after the demolishment of a farmers' market, so as to fully demonstrate the impact of spatial governance on the floating population as well as local residents in Beijing.

In order to make a comprehensive evaluation of the implementation effect of spatial control measures, we investigated the responses of the floating population in the context of Beijing's industry upgrading and population control policies and trace their self-employment trajectories. We found that most of the migrant vendors became self-employed again in the newly built vegetable markets not far away from the original market instead of leaving Beijing. Though vendors chose to proactively search for new employment by themselves, the demolition still had enduring disruptive effects on their life trajectories and social integration in the host city. At the same time, the demolition of the farmers' market and population control policy also had a negative impact on local residents' daily life. We found that local residents frequently reported that the vegetables sold in supermarkets and vegetable stalls were much less fresh and less diverse compared to those sold in large farmers' markets. In other words, the demand of local residents and the attachment of migrant vendors to farmers' markets still persist during the urban redevelopment and beautification period.

Data and methodology

The case investigated in this chapter – Sun Palace Farmers' Market – was located between the third and fourth ring roads in the northeast of Chaoyang District, Beijing (Figure 1.1). Sun Palace Farmers' Market was at the intersection of Sun Palace Middle Road and Sun Palace South Street, close to Metro Line 10 "Sun Palace Station" and bus station "Xia's Home", covering an area of about 45,000 m^2, with more than 1,000 vendors. It used to be the largest farmers' market between the third and fourth ring roads in northeastern Beijing. The service radius covered areas such as the Sun Palace, Wangjing and Shao Yaoju. On October 16, 2013, Sun Palace Farmers' Market was forced to be demolished

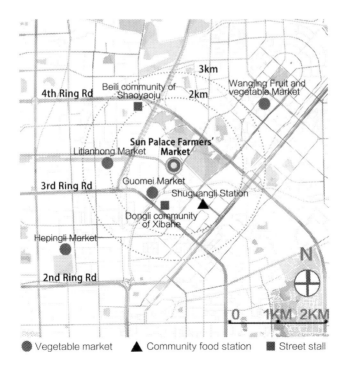

Figure 1.1 The Sun Palace Farmers' Market and its surrounding markets (July 2016).
Source: Author photo.

20   Yulin Chen et al.

in light of Beijing's population size regulation and non-capital function relief policy. There have been many similar markets that were forced to close in recent years, as the municipal government implemented an exclusive policy to remove large-scale farmers' markets from the inner city. In this sense, the demolition of the Sun Palace Farmers' Market provides a natural policy experimentation to examine the long-term effect of spatial governance and urban planning policies on the lower-skilled population in Beijing.

This research will comprehensively analyze the impact of the demolition of the farmers' market on both the vendors and nearby residents. In June 2016, our research team conducted a first-round survey on vendors who once worked in the Sun Palace market. In July 2016, we conducted a second-round survey on residents who used to buy food from the Sun Palace market.

In terms of vendors, as they are highly mobile and spread over a wide range around the Sun Palace area or even areas more distant, we therefore adopted a snowball survey method to find our potential interviewees. Based on clues provided by residents and vendors, our research team finally obtained the contact information of 53 vendors. We first contacted these vendors by cellphone and then went to their workplaces or homes to distribute a questionnaire survey. In the questionnaire, we asked them about current work and life situation/status as well as their level of life satisfaction. Based on the analysis of their answers, we further conducted semi-structured in-depth interviews with 20 vendors who are still working in Beijing to understand their work status, reemployment experience, urban integration and future willingness to stay. Each interview lasted more than one hour. We also traced their previous work experience since arriving in Beijing, seeking to obtain a holistic picture of their economic path and reemployment choice in the process of urban redevelopment.

In terms of local residents, we used the random sampling method to select 13 communities in the 3-kilometer range around the original Sun Palace Farmers' Market. In each community, we randomly distributed ten questionnaires in the morning, evening working hours, and weekend daytime hours and received 110 valid questionnaires in total. The questionnaire return rate was 84.6%. In the questionnaire, we asked questions to learn about residents' current mode of buying vegetables, how the demolishment affects their daily life and their choices of future grocery shopping places.

Among the 110 residents, there were more women, accounting for 61%. In terms of age structure, the average age of respondents was 53, among which the proportion of the elderly was higher, with the group over 60 years old accounting for 41%. Ninety-three percent of respondents are Beijing urban *hukou* or household registration status. In terms of education level, the highest proportion of undergraduate and junior college degrees is 38%, followed by high school (29%) and junior high school (24%). In terms of occupation, most respondents worked as general staff (42%) or workers (26%). From the perspective of personal monthly income, respondents were mainly concentrated in the range of 5,001–7,500 yuan (31%), 3,001–5,000 yuan (25%) and 1,000–3,000 yuan (20%) (Table 1.1).

Home for fewer people 21

Table 1.1 Socioeconomic profile of surveyed residents

	Category	*Percentage*
Gender	Male	39
	Female	61
Age	20–29	5
	30–39	18
	40–49	19
	50–59	16
	60–69	25
	70–79	14
	80–	2
Monthly income	<1,000	1
	1,000–3,000	10
	3,000–5,000	25
	5,000–7,500	22
	7,500–10,000	16
	10,000–20,000	8
	≥20,000	18
Household registration status (*hukou*)	Beijing urban	93
	Beijing rural	0
	Non-Beijing urban	7
	Non-Beijing rural	0
Educational level	Elementary school	4
	Middle school	24
	High school	29
	College	38
	Graduate school and above	6
Occupation	Managers	11
	Technicians	13
	General staff	42
	Business service staff	12
	Industrial transporter	26
	Peasants	4
Overall		100

The emergence of new types of food market

After the dismantling of the Sun Palace Farmers' Market, driven by the demand for food purchases by residents and the employment needs of vendors, a variety of food markets, including vegetable markets, community food stations and street stalls, emerged within 3 kilometers of the Sun Palace area. This new food-purchasing network pattern compensates for the impact of the demolishment of farmers' market, and fully reflects the adaptive strategies of the farmers' market operators, local residents and vendors.

Vegetable markets

Vegetable markets are still the most important places to buy food, but the scale is much smaller than the Sun Palace Farmers' Market, and often provides only

22 Yulin Chen et al.

fresh fruit and vegetables rather than the one-stop service of the integrated market. Most were newly built after the Sun Palace market was demolished. In order to increase their popularity, each small vegetable market adopted its own business strategy. Some markets are equipped with air conditioners to improve the indoor environment. Some markets control the price of vegetables through low booth fees. Some markets operate all day, while others operate just in the morning market. These vegetable markets have different operating conditions and popularity. Some markets are very popular among community residents, while others are not well managed and face the risk of closure. However, all of the vegetable markets are under strict local government regulations and could be closed anytime if there are any urban redevelopment or street beautification projects in the district.

Community food stations

After the Sun Palace Farmers' Market and other vegetable markets were successively demolished, several community neighborhood committees started to respond positively and invited vendors to set up in their community. For example, in Shuguangli, because it was very inconvenient for community residents to buy food, the local neighborhood committee organized consultations and came to an agreement with seven or eight fruit and vegetable vendors. Consequently, a temporary community vegetable station was set up at the entrance of the community, and the stalls were operated every morning. Vendors think that they are welcomed by the community, as long as they do not occupy the road and do not compromise street hygiene. Because these food stations were officially organized by the community, they would not be fined by the city management inspection. Therefore, in the Shuguangli community, this open-air food station has been operating relatively stably for nearly two years (see Figure 1.1).

Street stalls

As the vegetable market was frequently dismantled, some vendors lost confidence in their ability to find a stable job and decided to have a street stall as a "guerrilla seller". The street stalls frequently face the risk of being punishable by urban management, but because of the lack of booth fees and flexible operation, they are also accepted by many migrant vendors. In the Dongli community of Xibahe (see Figure 1.1), there are more than ten vegetable vendors "playing guerrillas" every day: they usually appear in the morning and after work hours, pushing the cart to open along the street at the main entrance of the community. When the city management carries out inspections, these vendors will flee and relocate nearby. After the inspection is over, they will return to their original spot and sell fruit, vegetables and soy products as usual. Such guerrilla operations not only led to an increase in urban management costs, but also undermined urban environmental sanitation. Most guerrilla vendors indicated that they are willing

Home for fewer people 23

to operate in the formal farmers' market as long as they have the right booths, but Beijing's move to dismantle the market has made this possibility increasingly unlikely.

Vendors' responses to demolishment

In mega-cities in China, farmers' markets are characterized by "a spatial pattern of small-scale concentration and large-scale scattering" (Chen & Liu 2019: 126). It is a crucial physical base and public space for the extension of migrants' vending businesses and for incorporating new migrants. According to our survey of 53 vendors, 48 people still remained in Beijing and only five left Beijing. Among the vendors who stayed in Beijing, 38 continued to engage in self-employment, and eight vendors had withdrawn from self-employment and switched jobs, and two were unemployed (Figure 1.2). In other words, more than 70% of vendors continued to engage in self-employment. Therefore, with the demolition of the Sun Palace Farmers' Market, most of the vendors had not left Beijing, and those who stayed were still self-employed.

Self-employed in Beijing

Since the migrant population normally faces formidable institutional, economic, cultural and social barriers in the host society (Wang & Fan 2012), scholars find that self-employed status is more helpful to support migrants to integrate into urban society and is more likely to assist them to permanently settle down in cities (Giulietti et al. 2012; Cao et al. 2015; Liu et al. 2019). In our study, we found that among the 38 people who are self-employed in Beijing, 22 continued

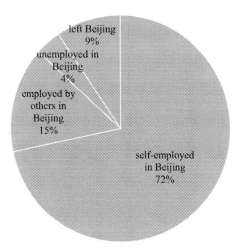

Figure 1.2 Migrant vendors' employment status after the demolition of the farmers' market.

to be self-employed in the vegetable market, another 13 entered the informal space such as street stalls and community food stations to sell food, and three people achieved self-employment upgrades, such as entering a more stable base-shop operation.

Further investigation of the 22 vendors who are now working in the vegetable market shows that most still operate the same business types and sell the same fruits and vegetables as they had done in the original Sun Palace Farmers' Market. In terms of income, most respondents indicated that their current income had decreased from three years ago, the average monthly income being only 4,125 yuan, which is about 33% lower than the original farmers' market level of 6,180 yuan (Figure 1.3). Considering the rising cost of living, selling vegetables alone can only barely maintain their livelihood.

Due to the frequent dismantling of vegetable markets in Beijing in recent years, regardless of whether the market is in good or bad condition, all vendors are worried that the current employment market may be demolished anytime in the foreseeable future. However, despite the potential risks, they still chose to remain in their current place of employment, and did everything they could to secure their job. What it means is that although they are not able to upgrade their business types, they are not willing to give up urban life and so remain in their current employment.

For example, one of our interviewees, Mr. Yan, who sells vegetables in Hepingli vegetable market, has been transferred between six various vegetable markets in the past three years. Selling vegetables in the vegetable market is still his most ideal way of employment. As he said,

> The vegetable market is not easy to find. Once it is dismantled, it will be hard to find a new one. Our market manager (Hepingli vegetable market)

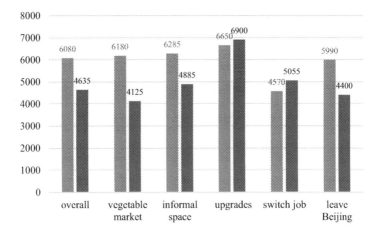

Figure 1.3 Comparison of average monthly income of vendors after the demolishment of the Sun Palace Farmers' Market (Average monthly income in Yuan currency).

is very responsible. He cleans the market every day so that the local government will not use the health excuse to tear down the place.

For 13 vendors who are self-employed in informal spaces such as roadside stalls and community food stations, they have greater operational risks because of the more unstable employment space, but risks and opportunities coexist. With a good relationship with the community and a relatively stable source of customers, the average monthly income for this group of vendors is 4,885 yuan, which is not only higher than that of the vendors operating in the vegetable market, but also only about 22% lower than the previous Sun Palace Farmers' Market level of 6,285 yuan (Figure 1.3). But still, this group finds it difficult to sustain their life and has to stay in Beijing with great adventurous spirit and perseverance.

For instance, another interviewee, Mr. Chang, who sells vegetables at the community food station in Shuguangli neighborhood, indicated that,

> Because the community food station invited us so that we joined their place. It's only a place to eat and drink, there's nothing left, and there's no way to compare the level of earning with the Sun Palace Farmers' Market. But we have to accept the reality. This is our life. If we don't come to community food station but go to other vegetable markets, we might relocate again because those vegetable markets are among the top demolishment targets for the local government.

Furthermore, among the vendors engaged in self-employment in Beijing, three people left the vegetable market and achieved self-employment upgrades. They rented the ground apartment for commercial use to operate on their own business or specialize in wholesale distribution. In terms of income level, this group has the highest income in the original Sun Palace Farmers' Market, with an average monthly income of 6,650 yuan. The monthly income after achieving a self-employment upgrade is even higher than the original level, reaching 6,900 yuan (Figure 1.3). It can be seen that this group often has strong employability and economic strength. The market dismantling not only did not let them leave Beijing, but instead became an opportunity for them to move upward, and finally realize self-employment upgrade. However, only very few people can realize this upgrade and transition.

Switching jobs in Beijing

In addition to self-employment, a small number of people in Beijing chose to start a new career. But this group of people has different career trajectories: those with strong individual ability have chosen careers as retail sellers and have achieved upward mobility in their work, but most have become construction workers, cleaning workers or casual workers. From the income level, this group is the lowest in the previous Sun Palace Farmers' Market, with the average monthly income 4,570 yuan. But after switching to a new job, the average

26 *Yulin Chen et al.*

monthly income has increased, reaching of 5,055 yuan (Figure 1.3). From the perspective of urban integration, it is difficult for them to enjoy many benefits of self-employment, such as flexibility, autonomy or the contact with the public. Respondents mostly said that although "their work is not as comfortable as self-employment, the income level is low, and there is no room for improvement", staying in Beijing is still their priority choice because Beijing has "more opportunities" and they "earn more than at home". As long as they can work in Beijing, they will not leave. Some still expect that if the market environment improves, they will return to the farmers' market to work. It can be seen that market dismantling has the biggest effect on these groups with lower income and weak capacities. However, due to the huge income gap between urban and rural areas, they prefer to stay in Beijing no matter how difficult it is.

Unemployed in Beijing

Of the two unemployed people in Beijing, a young male merchant just finished short-term work and is in the gap before the next job; the other, a female merchant, had just returned from her hometown with her newly born child to reunite with her husband. She said that she has no idea about getting a job in the next year or two, but she will stay in Beijing. However, she admitted that the quality of their life is not very good and that her husband had to work extra hours to support their family.

Leaving Beijing

Among the five vendors who left Beijing, three returned to their hometown in Hebei province either to work as a farmer or to open a small restaurant. Because of the geographical convenience, many vendors from the surrounding areas of Beijing returned to their homes after the farmers' market was dismantled, but they will still return to Beijing to do business as long as they have the opportunity to achieve flexible employment. Such vendors find it the easiest to leave because of the existence of a low-cost exit path and the possibility of returning to Beijing at any time. In addition, a Jiangxi merchant went to Hubei to sell aquatic products, and a merchant who originally sold fruit returned to his hometown in Henan and opened a physical therapy shop. Vendors with additional skills or social resources are also more likely to leave Beijing than those with less employability.

Residents' responses to demolishment

Current food-purchasing "location choice"

For local residents, farmers' markets are an essential place to buy fresh vegetables, fruits, eggs and meat. With the dismantling of the Sun Palace Farmers' Market,

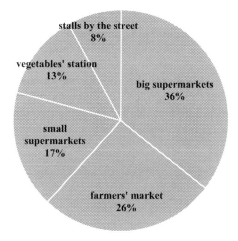

Figure 1.4 Current food-purchasing location choice for residents living in Sun Palace area.

residents in the Sun Palace area had to buy their groceries from supermarkets or community food stations. Our survey found that among the places where residents now buy food, the proportion of large supermarkets is the highest, accounting for 35%, while the proportion of selected vegetable markets is greatly reduced, at only 26%. In addition, many residents go to small supermarkets and community food stations to buy their daily food and their proportion was 17% and 13% respectively (Figure 1.4).

Our survey also finds that most residents (56%) believe that the removal of the Sun Palace Farmers' Market has had an impact on their lives (Figure 1.5). According to gender variable, the proportion of women who felt influential was 60%, which was higher than 45% of men, showing that women were more affected (Figure 1.6). According to age, the group most affected by the market demolishment is mainly the 50–69 age group, while the unaffected groups are mainly concentrated in the younger than 29 age group, showing that the elderly are more affected (Figure 1.7). According to income, the group most affected by the demolishment of the market is mainly those with a monthly income of less than 5,000 yuan, while the unaffected groups are mainly concentrated in the group with a monthly income higher than 20,000 yuan, showing that the low-income people are more affected. (Figure 1.8). Analysis of the distance between the residential quarters and the Sun Palace Farmers' Market shows that residents living farther away (more than 20 minutes' walking) from the area were more affected. These shopping districts had very little to offer, and residents who were willing to "go farther away" were often more sensitive to the freshness and price of the food. Therefore, the market demolishment had a greater impact on residents who lived further away (Figure 1.9).

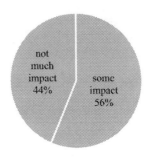

Figure 1.5 Overall impact on the surrounding residents.

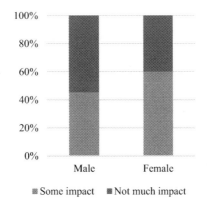

Figure 1.6 Impact on surrounding residents according to gender.

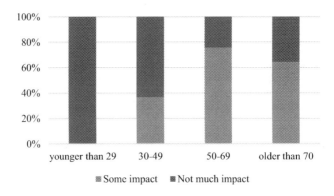

Figure 1.7 Impact on surrounding residents according to age.

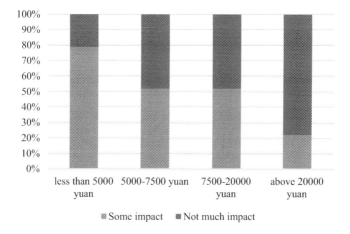

Figure 1.8 Impact on surrounding residents according to monthly income.

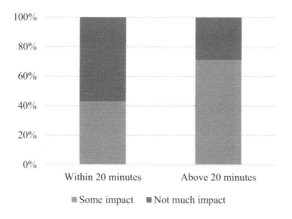

Figure 1.9 Impact on surrounding residents according to living distance.

We further analyzed the specific reasons for where the residents chose to purchase food. We set the benchmark level of Sun Palace Farmers' Market as 0, so that the surveyed residents can compare the existing grocery shops with the original farmers' market, and the scores are +2 from high to low as +1, 0, −1 and −2. From Figure 1.6, we can see that residents generally think that the current grocery shopping area is not better than the original Sun Palace Farmers' Market. Specifically, although the distance and environment have improved, the price, freshness, food types, comparable selection and merchant interactions are not as good as they were in the past, especially the price, which is much higher than that of the original farmers' market.

If we further analyze the residents' evaluations and the types of grocery shopping places they chose, we can find that compared with the Sun Palace Farmers'

Market, the large supermarkets have the best environment, but it also is the most expensive. Small supermarkets and community food stations are not able to compare with the original farmers' market due to size restrictions. Relatively speaking, the original farmers' market can guarantee the freshness of the food because it was purchased daily, and also because the vendors were self-employed, and could negotiate with residents more easily, which is conducive to promoting social integration between the residents and the vendors in the community (Figure 1.10).

Future food-purchasing location choice

Finally, we also investigated the residents' willingness to buy food in the future. The results showed that more than half of the residents chose the vegetable market (52). It can be seen that the farmers' market is still supported by the majority of residents, followed by large supermarkets at 36%, and small supermarkets at 11%. And only 1% of the community food stations were selected (Figure 1.11).

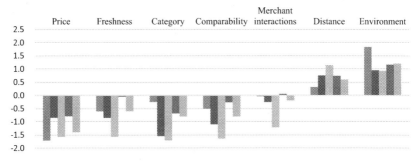

Figure 1.10 Comparison of different grocery shopping places and Sun Palace Farmers' Market.

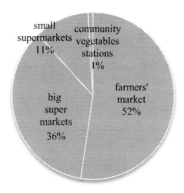

Figure 1.11 Residents' preference for where to buy vegetables and fruits.

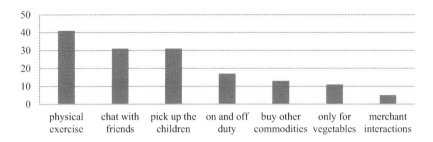

Figure 1.12 Functions of farmers' market according to the residents' demands.

Our survey also found that residents' demand for the farmers' market is more diverse than simply buying food. Many residents think that going to the farmers' market is also a means of taking physical exercise and chatting with friends, and they also can pick up and drop off their children/grandchildren, which they cannot do with other types of grocery shopping (Figure 1.12). In other words, farmers' market also serves as a public space for local residents' daily interactions and community activities.

Discussion

Through in-depth investigation of the demolition of Beijing Sun Palace Farmers' Market, we find that the practice of population control and dismantling of the farmers' market do not achieve the goal of dissolving the floating population and enhancing urban vitality. In contrast, the impact of the large-scale market demolishment is comprehensive and far-reaching, which has a direct and negative impact on the lives of both migrant vendors and local residents, and at the same time affects the normal functions of urban space.

First, after the market was demolished, most of the migrant vendors did not leave Beijing, and a considerable majority were still engaged in fruit and vegetable operations in various formal and informal market spaces that have recently emerged in the Sun Palace area. Their current living conditions and income became worse with lower level of life satisfaction. While upward mobility and economic opportunities seem very rigid and limited, these migrant vendors still insisted on staying in Beijing to earn a basic living.

Second, the dismantling of the farmers' markets also had a great impact on the lives of local residents, especially the elderly, women and low-income groups. Though many new types of food markets and community food stations emerged, they can provide only limited choice for the residents. The overall environment in the supermarkets is decent, but the price of food is such that not many people can afford to buy it. The community food station is supported by the neighborhood committee, and this mode had been endorsed by the municipal government. As an editorial from the *People's Daily* commented, "the vegetable market moved to a distant place, but the residents' stoves are still around" (People's

32 *Yulin Chen et al.*

Daily 2016). However, our survey clearly showed that only 1% of residents selected community food stations as their ideal food-purchasing location. Informal markets such as street stalls are more flexible but have to play the game of "guerrilla selling" under the strict prohibition from urban management forces, further exacerbating the scarcity of vegetable retail space.

Third, the traditional farmers' market also provides a public platform for social and cultural connections between local urban residents and migrant vendors. Essentially, migrant-resident ties can promote migrants' level of subjective well-being with higher economic returns and better social integration (Yue et al. 2013; Wang et al. 2016; Liu et al. 2017). In this sense, a farmers' market is not only a place to buy food and vegetables, but also a unique public space for social communication and intergroup neighboring to help migrant vendors better integrate into urban society.

Policy reflections

A farmers' market is a clustering space to accommodate the floating and low-skilled population and often becomes the primary target of governance due to poor environmental conditions and prominent safety hazards. However, due to the close daily needs of urban residents, the government often faces a dilemma. How to improve the appearance of the city and better serve the local residents through the renovation of such space is an important issue that needs to be solved in China's mega-cities.

First of all, in terms of migrant vendors, it is essential to understand that the farmers' market is an important functional space to help floating and low-skilled population sustain their living in the city. Migrant vendors are the providers of food services to the local community and they also build social networks with urban residents. Even if the farmers' market is dismantled, it will reappear in the form of community food stations and street stalls, but this will increase the cost of urban management. Therefore, the government should try to maintain the stability of the farmers' market in the process of urban redevelopment. If the space is to be transformed, it is necessary to conduct a comprehensive analysis of the interests of all parties, scientifically evaluate the possible impact of space governance and give appropriate guidance in advance. Nonetheless, as our case study shows, the floating population is the group with the strongest willingness to settle in the city. Therefore, it is essential not to expel migrant vendors and food retailers but to retain them and integrate them into urban life.

Particularly in Beijing, the business model of the farmers' market should not be sacrificed in the name of "relieving non-capital function" but should be incrementally upgraded. Comparing Beijing and Tokyo and other big cities in the world, research has found that the proportion of retailers in Beijing is much lower than that in Tokyo, and the gap is greater in traditional wet markets (Yin 2016). If some industries are dismantled without sufficient evaluation, it is likely to cause a serious impact on the original healthy industrial ecology. The development of the farmers' market requires long-term cultivation. Once it is destroyed, it is not easy to recover.

Second, in terms of urban residents, it is essential to care for the elderly, women and low-income groups. As our study shows, these groups frequently reported that the vegetables sold in supermarkets and community food stations were much less fresh and less diverse compared to those sold in farmers' markets. Moreover, in combination with the diversified needs of community residents, such as physical exercise and neighborhood communication, a community food center that integrates various functions such as rest, storage, grocery shopping and public communication could be built to attract more groups to engage in community life. This will not only improve the utilization rate of the public space but also promote the exchange and vitalization of community residents.

Third, in terms of the management of farmers' markets, it is necessary to standardize internal organization and enhance the spatial utilization and beautification. Taking Beijing as an example, many farmers' markets use the form of greenhouses, which have not only a messy appearance but also potential safety hazards. In Singapore, many farmers' markets are among the most attractive landscapes in the city, which not only enhance the surrounding environment but also drive the development of surrounding business districts (Wu & Chen 2017).

Finally, based on the re-recognition of the relationship between "population-industry-city", it is essential to respect the law of urban development and conform to the process of industrial evolution, instead of dissolving the floating population at the expense of downgrading the industry. The government should also adopt a more positive attitude and rebuild the relationship between the population and industry, such as increasing the employment ratio of the local population in the so-called "low-end industries" such as farmers' markets. To achieve this goal, we need to improve the standards, quality and income levels of these industries, so that the industry can cast off the "low-end" status. If the industry is on the verge of being "dissolved" for a long time, it will be difficult to get rid of the state of low quality, disorder and even informality. This is also the goal of providing a better life for the people.

Works Cited

Anttiroiko, A. V. (2015). City branding as a response to global intercity competition. *Growth and Change*, 46(2), 233–252.

Beijing Bureau of Statistics. (2016). *Control and expulsion': Two-pronged planning of a new pattern of collaborative development—information on functional expulsion in cities other than Beijing in 2015*. Beijing Statistical Information Network, 3 March 2016. Retrieved from: www.bjstats.gov.cn/tjsj/sjjd/201603/t20160303_337891.html

Beijing Municipal Commission of Commerce. (2006). *Beijing 11th Five-Year Commercial Development Plan*. (in Chinese). Retrieved from: http://sw.beijing.gov.cn/zwxx/fzgh/ndgh/201912/t20191219_1325626.html

Björner, E. (2017). Urban development and branding strategies for emerging global cities in China. In L. Ye (Ed.), *Urbanisation and Urban Governance in China: Issues, Challenges, and Development* (pp. 135–160). New York: Palgrave Macmillan.

Cao, G., Li, M., Ma, Y., & Tao, R. (2015). Self-employment and intention of permanent urban settlement: Evidence from a survey of migrants in China's four major unbanising areas. *Urban Studies*, 52(4), 639–664.

Chen, Y. (2017). Neighborhood form and residents' walking and biking distance to food markets: Evidence from Beijing, China. *Transport Policy*, https://doi.org/10.1016/j.tranpol.2017.09.015

Chen, Y., & Liu, C. Y. (2019). Self-employed migrants and their entrepreneurial space in megacities: A Beijing farmers' market. *Habitat International*, 83, 125–134.

China Daily. (2018). On way to becoming a world-class city cluster. 5 December 2018. Retrieved from: http://global.chinadaily.com.cn/a/201812/05/WS5c070dfaa310eff30328f129.htmlGiulietti, C., Ning, G., & Zimmermann, K. F. (2012). Self-employment of rural-to-urban migrants in China. *International Journal of Manpower*, 33(1), 96–117.

Goldman, A., Krider, R., & Ramaswami, S. (1999). The persistent competitive advantage of traditional food retailers in Asia: Wet markets' continued dominance in Hong Kong. *Journal of Macromarketing*, 19(2), 126–139.

Gu, C., Wei, Y. D., & Cook, I. G. (2015). Planning Beijing: Socialist city, transitional city, and global city. *Urban Geography*, 36(6), 905–926.

Hu, D., Reardon, T., Rozelle, S., Timmer, P., & Wang, H. (2004). The emergence of supermarkets with Chinese characteristics: Challenges and opportunities for China's agricultural development. *Development Policy Review*, 22(5), 557–586.

Liu, C. Y., Ye, L., & Feng, B. (2019). Migrant entrepreneurship in China: Entrepreneurial transition and firm performances. *Small Business Economics*, 52(3), 681–696.

Liu, R. (2015). *Spatial Mobility of Migrant Workers in Beijing, China*. London: Springer.

Liu, Y., Zhang, F., Liu, Y., Li, Z., & Wu, F. (2017). The effect of neighbourhood social ties on migrants' subjective wellbeing in Chinese cities. *Habitat International*, 66, 86–94.

Morales, A. (2009). Public markets as community development tools. *Journal of Planning Education and Research*, 28, 426–440.

Morales, A. (2011). Marketplaces: Prospects for social, economic, and political development. *Journal of Planning Literature*, 26(1), 3–17.People's Daily. (2016). Don't label the farmers' market as 'non-capital'. 8 June 2016. Retrieved from: http://opinion.people.com.cn/n1/2016/0608/c1003-28419661.html

Wang, W. W., & Fan, C. C. (2012). Migrant workers' integration in urban China: Experiences in employment, social adaptation, and self-identity. *Eurasian Geography and Economics*, 53(6), 731–749.

Wang, Z., Zhang, F., & Wu, F. (2016). Intergroup neighbouring in urban China: Implications for the social integration of migrants. *Urban Studies*, 53(4), 651–668.

Wu, F., Zhang, F., & Webster, C. (2013). *Rural Migrants in Urban China: Enclaves and Transient Urbanism*. London: Routledge.

Wu, J., & Chen, Y. (2017). Learning from wet market development in East Asian metropolis: Cases of Hong Kong, Taiwan districts and Singapore. *Urban Planning International*, 32(6), 91–98. (in Chinese)

Xiang, B. (2005). *Transcending Boundaries—Zhejiangcun: The Story of a Migrant Village in Beijing*. Leiden: Brill.

Yan, F. (2018). Urban poverty, economic restructuring, and poverty reduction policy in urban China: Evidence from Shanghai, 1978–2008. *Development Policy Review*, 36(4), 465–481.

Yang, Z., Hao, P., & Cai, J. (2015). Economic clusters: A bridge between economic and spatial policies in the case of Beijing. *Cities*, 42(B), 171–185.

Yin, D. (2016). Rethinking the dilemma of population control in megacities. *Chinese Journal of Population Science (zhongguo renkou kexue)*, 4, 61–73. (in Chinese)

Yue, Z., Li, S., Jin, X., & Feldman, M. W. (2013). The role of social networks in the integration of Chinese rural-urban migrants: A migrant–resident tie perspective. *Urban Studies*, 50(9), 1704–1723.

Zhang, Q. F., & Pan, Z. (2013). The transformation of urban vegetable retail in China: Wet markets, supermarkets, and informal markets in Shanghai. *Journal of Contemporary Asia*, 43(3), 497–518.

Zhao, M., Liu, S., & Qi, W. (2017). Exploring the differential impacts of urban transit system on the spatial distribution of local and floating population in Beijing. *Journal of Geographical Sciences*, 27(6), 731–751.

2 Rural *Dama* in China's urbanization

From rural left-behind to urban strangers

Jing Song and Lulu Li

Introduction

China has witnessed rapid urbanization. In 2011, the number of urban residents exceeded that of rural residents (NBS 2011). In the processes of urban sprawl and land development, many rural people have been urbanized in a short period of time. It has been extensively studied how villagers fit into the cities and how urban areas accommodate displaced peasants, particularly the poor and the elderly, who have limited life chances after their land is expropriated (Huang 2017). Few studies have examined urbanization from a gender perspective, except for some research on women's rights to land, economic entitlement and participation in communal affairs (Sargeson 2008; Sargeson & Song 2010). This study will focus on how rural women are affected by urbanization, whose position has been defined by the intersection of gender and age in a rural community and reshaped when the city comes closer. They are not only subordinated to the patriarchal gender system but also defined as an unproductive and lagging group, whose multitasking and mediating roles have been undermined in the urbanization process.

This study examines not only these rural women's economic rights but also their family roles and social lives, which are reflected in the stigmatized label *dama*. Although *dama* is not unique to rural women, and many urban women are also defined as *dama*, these rural women have experienced a unique kind of marginality. Similar to the concept of the "marginal man" who is torn between his past and the new society (Park 1928), these rural women are on the margin of the urban-rural divide in the rapidly modernizing China. Compared with their urban counterparts who have been often described as industrial workers, urban citizens or market consumers, rural women are largely an outsider in the nations' industrial growth, urban expansion and consumption-induced development. Compared with rural men, rural women have been less mobile: although many young women are active migrant workers, these factory girls often return to villages when they get older, especially to form and maintain families, and join other left-behind women (Song 2017). Under urbanization processes that subsume villages in an inclusive way, these women are no longer "left-behind". Still, it is to be studied whether the previously left-behind women gain some urban life chances or are further marginalized in the public and private spheres.

Theoretical perspectives

Urban sociology has extensively documented the differentiation and polarization of classes and social groups in modern cities, in which gender is often less visible than class. When land development and urban redevelopment generate huge profits for developers, governments and property owners, the displaced residents are likely to become a new group of urban poor (He et al. 2009). The role of women in the city has been understudied, and less attention has been paid to people's social roles rather than material poverty. A few studies point out how urbanization reshapes people's lifestyles, and thus affects the life of women, but the gender politics underlying their daily life is understudied (Sargeson & Song 2010).

Urbanization in Western societies have reshaped people's lives in fundamental ways through establishing the urban paid employment framework (Adam 1995). Similar processes may occur in these newly urbanized areas in China that have witnessed industrial growth, property development and capitalist investment (Blyton 1985; Blyton et al. 1989; Adam 1995; Huang 2017). In urban factories and companies, time becomes a resource to be managed economically. In Western cities, scholars have found a dichotomy between men's "clock time" and women's "free time", in which women's time is perceived to have low value (Adam 1995). In China's rural areas, women's time management has adapted to their family and work needs, and they often multitask in their agricultural activities, domestic sidelines and household chores (Song 2015a, 2017). In fulfilling these tasks, these women may gain a sense of achievement. But when people's economic contribution is no longer measured using "tasks" but by the efficient use of time (Thompson 1967; Adam 1995), women's unpaid work will be depreciated in the shadow of urban paid work. Further stratification of women's economic and social values occurs due to the biological clock, which could be a replication of the previous dichotomy of young factory girls and older housewives (or the left-behind, in the case of China's rural-to-urban migration).

In spatial terms, the transition from rural to urban settings also redefines the roles of women given the new boundaries of workplace and home (Nelson & Smith 1999). Such a gendered binary division in the urban landscape has led to the development of the Western "sexist" cities (Greed 1994; Darke et al. 2000), in which the separation of public and private spheres reinforces women's subordination and their confinement in domestic arenas (Jarvis 2009; Jarvis et al. 2009). The dichotomy of the inside and outside activities has been regenerated in daily life and also reconstructed over time, but according to post-structural feminists, even if the city has absorbed women into its production system, women are not empowered and liberated (Jarvis et al. 2009). In Western cities, the development of service sectors has created many feminized employment opportunities, usually less prestigious, temporary and low-paid (Somerville 2000; Jarvis et al. 2009). China has similarly witnessed a boom in the service economy oriented toward urban consumption, but due to the rapid urbanization process, it is yet to be examined how production and reproduction systems across the rural and urban boundaries clash, interact and evolve together. On the one hand, the market dynamics is sensitive to gender and age, and women over certain ages may be forced into "mother-friendly" work or "women's" jobs (Jarvis et al. 2009). On the other hand, the urban production and reproduction system may use labels of capitalist modernity and sophistication to reinforce the divides based on age, gender and class (Hanser 2005; Song et al. 2018). This study will examine how such social labels such as *dama* are constructed and practiced at the juncture of the market reforms, the socialist legacy and the rural past.

Many existing studies have focused on Western industrialized cities and the life of marginalized groups in it. In China, a post-socialist society, governments and developers have used land development and urban sprawl to drive economic development, and such modernization campaigns greatly reshaped spatial landscapes and social structures (Guo 2001; Ho & Lin 2003; Hsing 2006; Fan 2008). This study does not only look at marginality in spatial terms but also examines the socially marginalized groups in China's urbanization movement. Such stratification can be a result of the zoning and planning processes that aim to induce capital investment and economic boom, while at the same time relocate residents and distribute development revenues in different ways (Hsing 2010; Song 2014; Huang 2017). Villages may face a display of the power of capital when they are subsumed into cities, which can make local people marginalized and humiliated, even if they do not suffer from absolute poverty (Tyler 2013). However, such effects are not equally experienced across social groups and may lead to further internal inequalities.

Although many studies documented the resistance and disputes witnessed in the affected rural communities (O'Brien & Li 2006; Li & O'Brien 2008), less attention is paid to the gender perspective. A few studies have found the vulnerable positions of women in economic terms after they lost their land (Lou 2007; Wu 2013), but limited research is done on the social construction of their new identities and the related sense of "otherness", due to further differentiation based on the interaction of age, gender, education and access to resources after urbanization. Compared with studies on economic gains and loss, little is known about how "productive" and "lagging" groups are socially constructed, and such discourses have been largely formed based on the gender and age dynamics.

The setting and the people

This study draws on interviews conducted in the resettlement neighborhoods that were recently developed in the sprawl of the municipality of Yinchuan, the capital city of Ningxia (Figure 2.1). This resettlement residential area has accommodated displaced peasants from nearby villages that had been demolished in the urbanization processes mainly in the 1990s and the 2000s. We visited the field site during 2014 and 2015, and interviewed around 100 local people who were relocated into this area following land development. This study draws on interviews with 40 women, aged between 30 and 69 (Table 2.1).

Strikingly, most interviewed women identified themselves as *dama*, a common term for middle-aged or older women, typically married ones. Before urbanization, most had been engaged in a mix of farming and domestic sidelines;

Rural Dama *in China's urbanisation* 39

Table 2.1 Basic information about interviewees before and after urbanization

Number	Name	Age	Education	After urbanization	Before urbanization
1	**Huijuan**	30	Technical secondary school	Street office staff	Studying in school
2	**Majie**	30	Junior high school	Housewife	Running transportation business with her husband
3	**Zhaojie**	30s	Junior high school	Temporary community office staff and then unemployed	Sales clerk
4	**Henqing**	33	Senior high school	Community office staff	Sales clerk
5	**Lujie**	34	Junior high school	Housewife	Clothes sales clerk
6	**Anping**	35	Senior high school	Housewife	Supermarket clerk
7	**Zhenfang**	36	College	Village council staff	Kindergarten teacher.
8	**Jinlan**	36	University	Community officer	Company accountant and then community officer
9	**Lijia**	36	Junior high school	Shopping mall clerk	Supermarket clerk
10	**Zhanglin**	37		Neighborhood janitor	Farming
11	**Juan**	38	Junior high school	Housewife	A shoes store clerk
12	**Xiaogu**	38	Junior high school	Supermarket clerk	Factory worker and then sales clerk
13	**Zhengjie**	38	Junior high school	Property management janitor and then housewife	
14	**Yuqin**	39	Junior high school	Community officer	Farming and raising livestock
15	**Xiuhong**	40	Junior high school	Running a children's clothes stand	Farming and supermarket clerk
16	**Yanxin**	40	Senior high school	Community property management staff	Factory worker
17	**Guanjie**	42	Senior high school	Subcontracting a logistics stand	Factory worker
18	**Yumei**	43	Missing data	Housewife, running a Mahjong stand (2007–2010)	Farming and selling vegetables
19	**Meng**	43	College	Temporary community office staff	Clothes sales clerk, and then running a grocery store
20	**Haichun**	44	Junior high school	Working the family's acupuncture store	Farming
21	**Zhangan**	44	Primary school	Waitress in a local restaurant (2004–)	Supermarket clerk
22	**Xuan**	45	Junior high school	Neighborhood janitor and then unemployed	Farming, raising pigs and occasional migrant work
23	**Chenjie**	45	Illiterate	Helping in a local restaurant	Factory worker

(Continued)

Number	Name	Age	Education	After urbanization	Before urbanization
24	**Xiuhui**	45	College	Company staff	Company staff
25	**Zhenlin**	46	Missing data	Women's officer in the village council (2010–)	Raising livestock
26	**Qianjie**	48	Missing data	Neighborhood janitor	Farming
27	**Ailin**	49	Technical secondary school	Housewife	Farming, working in factories and then raising pigs and helping in the family's restaurant
28	**Qiaohui**	49	Missing data	Community property management staff	Neighborhood janitor
29	**Lijie**	50	Junior high school	Neighborhood janitor and then stay at home, grandparenting, leading square dance	Farming
30	**Xiaopin**	50	Illiterate	Housewife, grandparenting	Farming
31	**Yunxia**	51	Primary school	Housewife, grandparenting	Neighborhood janitor
32	**Jiping**	53	Missing data	Running a Mahjong stand (2003–), grandparenting	Farming
33	**Jimei**	55	Illiterate	Neighborhood janitor, grandparenting	Farming and hospital janitor
34	**Shuhui**	55	Illiterate	Cooking in a company, grandparenting	Farming
35	**Zheng**	56	Illiterate	Housewife, grandparenting	Farming, renting housing to migrants
36	**Guiqin**	57	Junior high school	Gardening work and then housewife, grandparenting	Farming, factory worker
37	**Suan**	58	Illiterate	Housewife, grandparenting	Farming
38	**Cailan**	60	Primary school	Housewife, grandparenting	Village council officer
39	**Xiulin**	68	Junior high school	Housewife, grandparenting	Farming and factory work
40	**Zhenan**	69	Missing data	Neighborhood janitor and then quit the job, grandparenting	Farming

around one third (15 out of 40) had short-term paid work in local factories and stores. After urbanization, around two thirds (27 out of 40) had worked in various urban commercial and service sectors such as cleaning and maintaining residential neighborhoods, but seven had quit their jobs. The remaining women described themselves as "staying at home", mainly taking care of the family and rearing children or grandchildren. In contrast, local men were more visible in running small business (taxi or transportation) or playing mahjong. Some young women were also active earners (teachers, sales clerks, civil servants) in the resettlement area, and they positioned themselves very differently from the stay-at-home middle-aged, or older, women who called themselves *dama* (middle-aged/older women), *ayi* (aunt), *laoayi* (old aunt), *laonainai* (granny), *funu* (women). However, such grouping was not strictly defined by age: it could be induced by the life events of having children or grandchildren (and thus retreating to the caregiver role) or could be exempted due to high education, a decent job, and modern and sophisticated lifestyle. Still, the majority of women felt being "not important" and they strived to make meanings of their new urban lives. This study examines how such gender and age dynamics were formed in resettlement neighborhoods and how urbanization has reinforced or restructured stratification within rural communities.

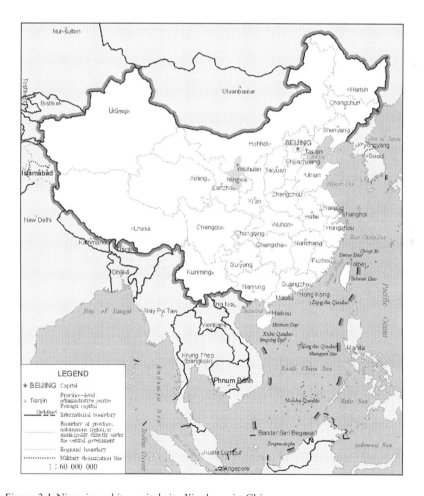

Figure 2.1 Ningxia and its capital city Yinchuan in China.
Source: Ministry of Natural Resources of the People's Republic of China. 2019. Standard map of the People's Republic of China. Map review number: GS(2019)1652.

Unattractive and unproductive labor

The relocated residents were mostly local villagers who have lived on the outskirts of Yinchuan for generations. These rural households used to rely on farming, labor outmigration and family sidelines for a living. Before urbanization, migrant work had not been a major source of family income, particularly for women, and many spent more time in running small family businesses such as raising livestock or selling vegetables to consumers in Yinchuan. Meanwhile, men had been more active in transportation businesses. Although peasants had no "formal" work, they had been kept busy in various tasks. For women, their time had been quite fragmented in multiple productive activities, but their economic contribution had been well recognized by the tasks they accomplished, such as how many pigs and chicken they raised.

After villagers were relocated to resettlement neighborhoods, local governments strictly prohibited raising livestock, in order to "beautify" the expanding city. Many women complained about losing this earning opportunity, except a few who felt relieved. These women were previously considered "weak" and were not the ideal peasants, such as Yuqin (aged 39 when interviewed in 2014). She felt happy that she did not need to raise pigs anymore, and her family also lacked necessary manpower to be more competitive with other families in pig raising. She could not wait for the transformation of the rural village into an urban community, and she found it happier to work as a local community officer, working for the management of the resettlement neighborhoods. But another women Xiaogu (aged 38 when interviewed in 2014) complained that urbanization deprived them of earning opportunities.

> We peasants have no education. We can either go to work in a supermarket or sweep and clean the residential pathways. We can only find this kind of jobs. So when you look at those people who clean up the place and maintain the area, they are all our people, people who can only find such (low-end) jobs nearby. You can rely on your family to look for such jobs, and you only need it to kill time.

Some women used to be proud of their physical strength and ability in taking care of the farm and the family at the same time. But with an education less than required by an urban job, they had to lower their expectations in the urban labor market and were often perceived as "unproductive". When women called themselves *dama*, another implication was that they were no longer young and (sexually) attractive. Similar to what Hanser (2005) found in the service sectors in a northern Chinese city, women's productivity is also closely related with their attractiveness. In the development of gendered job hierarchies, some rice bowls are reserved for young and good-looking girls, whose appearance is related to productivity.

As such, the urban economy led to changes in people's economic value, which was not only about age. In the market-oriented urban economy, older women

Rural Dama *in China's urbanisation*   43

might be squeezed out under other recruitment criteria, as they were usually less educated than young women and often had health issues. They were also considered a less "devoted" group compared with unmarried women due to their family obligations. Even for some women in their 30s, they were also categorized as *dama*, and many found it undesirable to take up the new urban "low-end" jobs, usually the only jobs they could find. They would rather stay at home and be good homemakers, to meet the expectations of women being "good wives and virtuous mothers". Some older women, particularly those who had grown up in the Maoist era, however, found it uneasy to be idle and "unproductive". Becoming unemployed from previous multitasking roles in a rural community, they were eager to find something "to kill time".

Governments also provided "public positions" in local offices for landless peasants, mainly middle-aged men and women who had difficulties in finding other jobs. In the process of urbanization, many new residential neighborhoods were established, and they needed staff to mediate and smooth neighborhood relationships. Zhaojie (in her 30s when interviewed in 2014) was one of them. She had worked on a three-year contract as a local urban management officer, although she felt she was sometimes too "soft" for this new mediating position.

> I worked for it for two years at first, and got renewed for another year, three years in total. Previously, I only worked in short-term jobs in shops and department stores ... My husband earned around 3,000 yuan per month, and my wage was around 1,000 yuan per month in that public position, but my contract already ended. Such public positions were for men above age 50 and women above age 40 who lost land and were allocated by the government's employment bureau ... I was allocated to the urban management office under the campaign of "creating a civilised city" (2011), regulating the street stands and shops. We drove through the streets to see if some were violating the rules and damaging the city's image ... This job was more suitable for a man. Stand owners and petty traders were readier to yield to a strong man; when they saw a woman, they tried to challenge ... I talked to them, and they might follow for this moment, but they came again a bit later ... Because that was the first time the city campaigned to create a "civilised" city, there were a lot of problems to be communicated, and we were hired for this purpose ... I used to imagine I would get a community position. A lot of public positions were community positions ... Every year governments would allocate such public positions twice. I am still waiting for new quotas, and some good positions were quite competitive.

Zhaojie was waiting to get another offer of a public position since her previous contract ended, but she was not optimistic because a lot of people also applied. Such positions were usually popular among women who could not get good jobs in the labor market, and also did not want to do low-end jobs like sweeping floors and collecting trash. But they still curbed their career ambitions by trying to find a job nearby, and were willing to settle for a community office position in their residential area. Some middle-aged women had been active in communal mediating roles, in which they could be somewhat empowered by their age and experience. But the new mediating roles were different from their previous experience, with the new targets of beautifying the city image and cultivating the social stability and "harmony". To avoid being "unproductive" stay-at-home women, some of them redirected their energy following the official narratives and contributing to the disciplining functions of community offices.

But for others who failed to find an external job, either in the labor market or through public allocation, they retreated to their domestic spheres. Due to their education, health status and family obligations, they were disadvantaged in market competition and public allocation of employment quotas, and there was no farm for them to retreat to.

> Previously in the village, someone needed to farm. I could farm until I could not move; when I became too old I passed it on to young people. Now there is no need to farm. Suddenly I have nothing to do. No work, no goal. My heart becomes so hollow. I feel empty inside. (Haichun, aged 44 when interviewed in 2014)

This was also why Haichun felt extended families were no longer needed. When the household was no longer the agricultural production unit, big families were commonly divided into small families. When young people sought earning opportunities outside home, *dama* or middle-aged women were typically "watching" the home.

Family manager from the front stage to the back stage

The common transition from big families prior to land development to small families after resettlement was also accompanied by changes in property structures and family power dynamics. Before land development, the virilocal marriage system in local villages expected parents to help their sons to build housing and get married, and at least one married son would continue to live with parents. Despite women's subordination in a typical rural household with a male household head, women might gain more authority when they became mothers-in-law. But along with the increasing "girl power" given the rise of labor migration and the penetration of urban and Western cultures, not only patriarchal traditions were challenged but also mothers-in-law became more powerless (Yan 2006).

In the field site in Ningxia, such a process has been accelerated by urbanization, which further marginalized middle-aged or old women, who used to be "left behind" in migration and are now "left out" in urbanization. Mothers or mothers-in-law, who used to be the coordinators of the family farming system or domestic sidelines, found their control over the family economy undermined,

Rural Dama *in China's urbanisation*   45

and their mediating roles useless in the context of the emerging urban lifestyle. On the one hand, young nuclear families were separated from extended families when moving into new resettlement apartments, enjoying greater autonomy independence from parents and in-laws. On the other hand, family properties, particularly land, was transformed into a lump sum of compensation, and might be partly controlled by the male household head and partly divided between family members, especially married children (more often married sons). The capitalization of family properties made middle-aged women, usually the previous internal managers of the family, lose the sphere to exert their multitasking skills and mediating agency.

Qiaohui (aged 49 when interviewed in 2014) was a woman who began to work in the community affairs after relocation, but she felt disappointed in her family relationship following urbanization.

> When there was a chance to be enrolled in the rural pension system, I did not pay for it because I needed to invest everything in my children's education. Previously rural people did not rely on a pension system. Instead, they relied on their sons (*yang er fang lao*). Now you could not expect your son to support you. It will be good enough if they stop using your money (*ken lao*) ... My son quit his high school and worked in different jobs. I introduced him into a stable job, but he refused to settle down ... I still needed to pave the way for him, preparing the housing unit for him so that he could get married ... Now people no longer think sons are reliable. They will all go outside and will not stay nearby and come back to take care of you. Who will come back to see their old mothers? ... We (my husband and I) are disappointed ... He would not call back, but we often called him ... We already prepared the housing unit for his marriage, but he needs to find a wife ... Previously we listened to our parents, but not now. Young people have their own ideas.

Qiaohui was among the mothers and mothers-in-law who complained about their distant relationship with the younger generation, particularly after young people moved away for jobs and urban opportunities or moved to their own housing units. When big families split into small families, many young people took it for granted that they would have their share in the household land compensation and the relocation housing units, and the family distribution of property and revenues often led to disputes and resentments. The division of family property and the related family tensions further undermined the bargaining power of middle-aged or older women, who often relied on their husbands as the homeowner and household head, and also had less say over their children's life plans, as they now typically lived separately with their children. However, they were still expected to provide important help to their adult children in housekeeping and babysitting. In particular, grandmothers were often considered as having sufficient time and having nothing to do. Their labor was considered

46 *Jing Song and Lulu Li*

random, fragmented, cheap and unproductive, and within the family, their roles had become less visible as a backstage facilitator.

Guiqin (aged 57 when interviewed in 2014) spent her youth in both farming and rural industries. After her husband passed away in an accident in a rural factory in 1983, she brought up two young children while working on the family farm and in local stores, and got remarried in 1996. She similarly felt that people could not rely on their children to support them after urbanization, and the pension system for landless peasants was more reliable than "having a son". But after urbanization, she had to stay at home because she had to support young people to work outside, while her domestic work was not well recognized and appreciated.

> Previously I was doing some gardening work for our neighborhood but I had to quit this year because I need to take care of my grandson. Every day I spend my time cooking, washing clothes, and watching my grandson. Every morning my son drops him off at my place, and then I prepare three meals. After they finish dinner and pick up the boy, I have time to wash dishes … I feel depressed. And young people are not considerate and they do not help with household chores. Sometimes I lost my temper … I am strong willed and want to go outside to work. When my grandson is older I still want to go outside.

Guiqin's case suggested a typical life history of *dama* embedded in China's social changes: in the Maoist era, working outside was a source of honor and taken for granted by women, and under the market reform, it was more common for housewives or grandmothers to play a supporting role for breadwinners. Guiqin recalled that when she was young, she had been too busy multitasking between work and family, and even had no time to wash dishes. Now she felt tired of washing dishes. Some other grandmothers also complained that in fact they did not enjoy grandparenting tasks, but they had to do so under social expectations that regarded them as "having nothing else important to do".

Due to their positions in the labor market and the family life cycle, *dama* have become the backup laborer, the invisible facilitator and the supporting grandparent to deal with the uncertainties and risks families may face following urbanization. Many of these women used to be the family's internal managers to pool family resources to invest in their children's future. They found that urbanization had deprived them of their bargaining and mediating power and created greater uncertainties regarding the family's life plan and economic prospects. Mothers found that their children were facing a rapidly changing society that they had limited knowledge about and could not predict and intervene. For young people, they enjoyed the new urban exposure, privacy and freedom in their lives, but they still often relied on their parents for living expenses and needed grandmothers for unpaid homemaking and babysitting as in the rural past. The continuing family obligations and the declining say over family resources have made *dama* feel being sacrificed for the sake of others' urban dreams.

Displaced and rootless urban strangers

The transformation from rural villagers to urban residents allowed many to embrace their urban dreams. Now young people did not need to migrate to look for urban jobs; many were employed in the nearby trade centers and industrial parks. But some felt disembedded from the self-sufficient rural lifestyles (Song 2015b). Middle-aged women felt particularly disconnected after moving into urban apartment units, which made it difficult for them to socialize with each other.

> We are still peasants deep inside. You may get an urban job and live as urban people, but when you are detached from these labels, you are still peasants ... Living in apartment units means being restrained. When living in self-built housing, you have a yard and you have freedom. You grow your own food and do whatever you want ... We can look for friends to have a tea and have fun chatting. (Meng, aged 43 when interviewed in 2014)

Villagers echoed that they visited their relatives and friends less frequently, to avoid climbing up floors and worrying about staining clean floors of new homes. Young people particularly disliked frequent mutual visits, because they cherished their privacy and did not want to be disrupted. "Older people used to mingle during the meal time, holding their bowls and talking to each other, socialising and exchanging information. Now people lock their doors first after arriving at homes" (Zheng, aged 56 when interviewed in 2014). Except for a few women who were absorbed into the community management teams and visited residents as one of their duties, most stay-at-home women, who used to take care of family sidelines and manage their courtyards, became more isolated and felt being locked up in apartment units.

Some women became re-connected by joining the square dance activities. These square dance activities were particularly popular among middle-aged women; young women often avoided involving in it as a rustic and tasteless activity, while male participants would be doubted as being too feminine. In contrast, such dances were welcomed by middle-aged and old women as an important way of physical exercise and socialization. Furthermore, for women who grew up in the Maoist era, such collective dancing helped to bring back their memories of the socialist past (Zhou 2014), when women's collective activities in the public sphere were appreciated and praised. Lijie (aged 50 when interviewed in 2014) was one of the women who were forced to stay at home after trying out some temporary urban jobs. Now she became a proud leader of the square dancing group in her residential neighborhood, which became an escape for her from the boring homemaking and grandparenting routines.

> Now I have to stay at home to take care of my grandson, and it is busier than a formal job. Other people can take a break on weekends, but I still need to babysit and cook on weekends ... It is easy to get tired after you watch a child for several days ... I organized them (the dancers) together,

for the sake of our health. It is different from the rural socialization style, that people visit each other's homes ... We start dancing at 7:30 pm until 9:30 pm every evening.

Lijie described square dance as a more civilized and meaningful activity than the previous pattern of rural socialization that people dropped by each other's homes without a purpose. She felt that square dance had a superior purpose and format, which entertained and connected people (mainly middle-aged women) without disturbing others. However, some residents in the neighborhood complained about the noises of the dance music, and they quarreled with the dancers several times. Lijie discovered sadly that she was no longer living in a "community" in which people could use their "face" and emotional attachment to solve disputes, but in an urban neighborhood that people were self-centered and indifferent. At the end, the square dance group decided to dance in a public area far away from the residential neighborhood.

Different from Lijie who were reconnected with her middle-aged female friends through square dance activities, some women (particularly young women) refused to join such activities to avoid being identified as a *dama*. Majie (aged 30 when interviewed in 2014) emphasized that she was a "high quality" person. Different from other relocated villagers who played Mahjong or danced in their leisure time, she read books as a way of self-cultivation. She became a vegetarian, which was exceptional among relocated villagers, and believed she was practicing a healthier lifestyle. She was among the young women who tried to distance themselves from rural *dama*, by embracing the urban lifestyles of sophistication, indifference and modern consumption.

This resettlement area remained quite rural, even if we now live in apartment buildings. Now people visit each other less often, but they like to gather under the buildings. Sitting together and gossiping, whispering about what happened in other families. I never join such gossiping activities. What happened in other families has nothing to do with me. If I have time, I would rather read books.

Majie and some other young women tried to draw a boundary between them and rural *dama*, also because they were more educated and could take part in "superior" entertainment activities rather than the "time-killing" activities. Again, the time of *dama* was devalued and considered cheap, to be mobilized for homemaking and grandparenting duties that usually involved no payment. They were not only marginalized in the labor market and the family life cycle, but also degraded in public affairs and social activities in the residential area.

When villagers strived for their collective interests in negotiating with governments (O'Brien & Li 2006), these women were also represented by their male household heads. As relocation compensation were often handled by male household heads and then divided between the younger generation, middle-aged and older women were rarely involved in spending such family fortune for their own wellbeing or entertainment. After urbanization, mahjong has become a popular entertainment activity among relocated villagers for some time, particularly when local families still had quite a bit of compensation in cash at hand. But according to Jiping (aged 53 when interviewed in 2014) who operated a Mahjong stand at home since 2003, the biggest players were often young men who had flexible working schedules such as insurance agents or taxi drivers, and when old women came, they mainly played with small stakes, or just sat and chatted randomly to catch up with their friends.

Discussion

The Chinese word *dama* can be used to show intimacy to an auntie, respect to an elderly lady or distaste for the outdated knowledge and lifestyle a woman has (Li 2017). This study contextualizes how the negative meanings of *dama* were formed and self-reinforced in a unique developmental setting, in which these women transformed from rural villagers to urban citizens. Although some of them showed a rural nostalgia and others tried to catch up with the more modern lifestyles, they were in general categorized as a "lagging" group in the nation's and the region's modernization campaign. When governments emphasize the goals of social sustainability and harmony in economic development, mass media and the general public have tuned to gender and age terms in stigmatizing the "lagging" groups who do not quite "fit" into the modern and urban dream.

The struggles between their rural past and urban present can be seen as a modern version of the "marginal man" on "the margin of two cultures and two societies" (Park 1928: 892). Living on the margin of the urban and rural societies, these marginal women are considered adapting poorly to China's modernization and urbanization campaign. Similar to studies on the role of women in Western cities, this study finds how the urban economy emphasizes "formal jobs" and punctuality and undermines the productive role of these women. In contrast to their prior multitasking roles, rural *dama* have become a less productive group when the city comes closer. In spatial terms, these women lose their mediating roles in the city's public space as privacy is enshrined and rural connections are undermined. The distaste for "gossiping" among some young and educated people suggests a more complicated internal inequality pattern rather than the dichotomy between urban capital and rural community and points to the multidimensional marginality.

In short, middle-aged or old women have been largely absorbed into low-end jobs, allocated temporary public positions or retreated from their courtyards to the more restrained apartment units. They were perceived as the lagging "others" when the market reform and the urbanization campaign rapidly unfolded. But still, some *dama* tried to carve out their new time and space to be themselves, such as taking up new mediating roles at the community levels and participating in square dance activities, beyond being a low-end temporary worker, unpaid homemaker or free babysitter. As most research on the political economy of China's urbanization and modernization has examined economic rights and

50 *Jing Song and Lulu Li*

entitlements among social groups (Chan 1994; Ma 2002; Wu & Ma 2006; Zhu 2007; Hsing 2010; Huang 2017), this study calls for more research to be done on lifestyles and self-positioning processes of social groups, at the intersections of gender, age and various access to resources. Beyond the locals' anxiety about losing their original way of life and being left out in development (Eizenberg 2013; Rowen 2016), this study turns its attention from absolute scarcity to the relative deprivation and social marginality, or a feeling of being socially useless, as suggested by the investigation on rural *dama*, the former left-behind and the current urban strangers.

Acknowledgments

This study was supported by the Research Grants Council of Hong Kong Special Administrative Region, China (General Research Fund, CUHK14609219), the Worldwide Universities Network, and the Research Committee of The Chinese University of Hong Kong (Direct Grant).

Works Cited

Adam, B. (1995). *Timewatch: The Social Analysis of Time*. 1st ed. Cambridge: Polly Press.
Blyton, P. (1985). *Changes in Working Time: An International Review*. London: Croom Helm.
Blyton, P., Hassard, J., Hill, S., & Starkey, K. (1989). *Time, Work and Organization*. London: Routledge.
Chan, K. W. (1994). *Cities with Invisible Walls: Reinterpreting Urbanisation in Post-1949 China*. Oxford University Press.
Darke, J., Ledwith, S., & Woods, R. (2000). *Women and the City: Visibility and Voice in Urban Space*. London: Palgrave Macmillan.
Eizenberg, E. (2013). *From the Ground Up: Community Gardens in New York City and the Politics of Spatial Transformation*. Surrey and Burlington: Ashgate.
Fan, C. C. (2008). *China on the Move: Migration, the State, and the Household*. Abingdon and New York: Routledge.
Greed, C. H. (1994). *Women and Planning: Creating Gendered Realities*. London: Routledge.
Guo, X. (2001). Land expropriation and rural conflicts in China. *The China Quarterly*, 166, 422–439.
Hanser, A. (2005). The gendered rice bowl: The sexual politics of service work in Urban China. *Gender & Society*, 19(5), 581–600.
He, S., Liu, Y., Webster, C., & Wu, F. (2009). Property rights redistribution, entitlement failure and the impoverishment of landless farmers in China. *Urban Studies*, 46(9), 1925–1949.
Ho, S. P., & and Lin, G. C. (2003). Emerging land markets in rural and urban China: Policies and practices. *The China Quarterly*, 175, 681–707.
Hsing, Y. T. (2006). Land and territorial politics in urban China. *The China Quarterly*, 187, 575–591.
Hsing, Y. T. (2010). *The Great Urban Transformation: Politics of Land and Property in China*. Oxford University Press.

Huang, Y. (2017). Farewell to villages: Forced urbanisation in rural China. In Zongli Tang (Ed.), *China's Urbanisation and Socioeconomic Impact* (pp. 207–227). Singapore: Springer.

Jarvis, H. (2009). Commentary: Gender interventions in an age of disengagement. *Journal of Geography in Higher Education*, 33(3), 369–373.

Jarvis, H., Cloke, J., & Kantor, P. (2009). *Cities and Gender*. New York: Routledge.

Li, L., & O'Brien, K. J. (2008). Protest leadership in rural China. *The China Quarterly*, 193, 1–23.

Li, Q. (2017). Characteristics and social impact of the use of social media by Chinese Dama. *Telematics and Informatics*, 34(3), 797–810.

Lou, P. (2007). A case study on the settlement of rural women affected by land requisitioning in China. *Journal of Contemporary China*, 16(50), 133–148.

Ma, L. J. (2002). Urban transformation in China, 1949–2000: A review and research Agenda. *Environment and Planning A*, 34(9), 1545–1569.

NBS (National Bureau of Statistics). (2011). *Zhongguo tongji nianjian 2011 (China Statistical Yearbook 2011)*. Beijing: Zhongguo tongji chubanshe.

Nelson, M. K., & Smith, J. (1999). *Working Hard and Making Do: Surviving in Small Town America*. University of California Press.

O'Brien, K. J., & Li, L. (2006). *Rightful Resistance in Rural China*. Cambridge University Press.

Park, R. E. (1928). Human migration and the marginal men. *American Journal of Sociology*, 33(6), 881–893.

Rowen, I. (2016). The geopolitics of tourism: Mobilities, territory, and protest in China, Taiwan, and Hong Kong. *Annals of the American Association of Geographers*, 106(2), 385–393.

Sargeson, S. (2008). Women's property, women's agency in China's 'new enclosure movement': Evidence from Zhejiang. *Development and Change*, 39(4), 641–665.

Sargeson, S., & Song, Y. (2010). Land expropriation and the gender politics of citizenship in the urban frontier. *The China Journal*, 64, 19–45.

Somerville, J. (2000). *Feminism and the Family: Politics and Society in the UK and USA*. London: Macmillan Press.

Song, J. (2014). Space to maneuver: Collective strategies of indigenous villagers in the urbanizing region of northwestern China. *Eurasian Geography and Economics*, 55(4), 362–380.

Song, J. (2015a). Women and self-employment in post-socialist rural China: Side job, individual career or family venture. *The China Quarterly*, 221, 229–242.

Song, J. (2015b). Official relocation and self-help development: Three housing strategies under ambiguous property rights in China's rural land development. *Urban Studies*, 52 (1), 121–137.

Song, J. (2017). *Gender and Employment in Rural China*. Abingdon and New York: Routledge.

Song, J., Du, H., & Li, S. M. (2018). Smooth or troubled occupation transition? Urbanisation and employment of former peasants in Western China. *China Review*, 18(1), 79–106.

Thompson, E. P. (1967). Time, work-discipline, and industrial capitalism. *Past and Present*, 36, 52–97.

Tyler, D. I. (2013). *Revolting Subjects: Social Abjection and Resistance in Neoliberal Britain*. London: Zed Books.

Wu, C. (2013). Shidi nongmin zhong de nvxing zaijiuye yanjiu – yige chengjiao cunluo de ge'an chengxian. ("Reemployment of female land-lost peasants – case study of a suburban village.") *Renkou Yu Fazhan (Population & Development)*, 19(5), 17–22.

Wu, F., & Ma, L. J. (2006). Transforming China's globalizing cities. *Habitat International*, 30(2), 191–198.

Yan, Y. (2006). Girl Power: Young women and the waning of patriarchy in rural North China. *Ethnology*, 45(2), 105–124.

Zhou, L. (2014). Music is not our enemy, but noise should be regulated: Thoughts on shooting/conflicts related to Dama Square Dance in China. *Research Quarterly for Exercise and Sport*, 85(3), 279–281.

Zhu, Y. (2007). China's floating population and their settlement intention in the cities: Beyond the Hukou reform. *Habitat International*, 31(1), 65–76.

Part II

Margins in Mainland China

Shanghai

3 When a marginal area is transformed into a tourist hot spot
Tianzifang in Shanghai

Florence Padovani

Robert Park's concept of "marginal man" has great longevity. In 2012 Chad Alan Goldberg explained that it is still relevant today. He underlines that marginality suggests a potential maladjustment and disorganization, but at the same time it also suggests creativity and innovation. Today the notion of marginality is extended to include a broad range of social phenomena well beyond race and ethnic relations, which were the main points developed by Robert Park when he published his article in 1928. This chapter analyzes different forms of marginality through the case of the Tianzifang community in downtown Shanghai. Different actors are considered legitimate to raise their voices in favor or against safeguarding this area. In addition to residents, some administrative cadres, developers, academics and artists played an important role in giving birth to Tianzifang. We will analyze how these actors developed confidence in their legitimacy to negotiate together. The link between marginality and legitimacy is key to understanding this particular context. Marginality is not only about human beings (their origin and status), it is also about buildings and heritage. Tianzifang is marginal in many ways and I would argue this is what saved it from destruction. A Chinese proverb states that the taller the tree the more likely it would be cut down. Benefits can be gained from marginality. This was how it was possible that a small quite dilapidated area could create a new model of urban development at a micro level.

Description of Tianzifang's and Shanghai's *Lilong*

The case study of Tianzifang (田子坊) focuses on a small community in the heart of Shanghai. It is located in the former French concession where many old buildings remain (dating from the end of the nineteenth to the beginning of the twentieth centuries) and whose popularity with tourists is unquestionable. The analysis is based on long-term fieldwork developed through participant observation and interviews from 2005 to 2012.[1] It also relies on official documents and articles published in Chinese and English.

Tianzifang is close to the city center and comes under the authority of Luwan district. The main entrance is located on 210 Taikang Road, but several other entrances were opened during the development of the area (see Figure 3.1).

56   *Florence Padovani*

The community of Tianzifang is squeezed in between Jianguo Zhong Road to the north, a relatively narrow one-way street with two lanes, lined with plane trees and usually busy; the small Taikang Road to the south, a one-way street that was not very popular before Tianzifang's success; Ruijin Nan Road to the west, an important thoroughfare (also one-way, with two lanes and plane tree-lined); and finally the small Sinan Road to the East, also one-way, and comparatively less busy. Sinan Road is famous in communist history as Sun Yat-Sen's and Zhou Enlai's houses are both located there. Both are still a place of pilgrimage. Further south is Zhaojiabang Road, one of the municipality's main thoroughfares with six lanes. It was once an old waterway used for the transportation of goods produced in the small factories that were bordering it. Now covered, it continues to play an important role in Shanghai's transport system.

In the late nineteenth and early twentieth centuries, along the Ruijin Street were some residences and villas and along the Jianguo Street were offices and administrative departments for the French representatives. On the southern part, the river was then called Zaochar Bang. On its banks were shanties and garbage yards. Between the shanties and the administrative buildings, the area was filled with *lilongs*, among which was Tianzifang.

Tianzifang was built during the late 1930s. It consists of a set of small three-floor buildings made of grey and red bricks and a dozen houses called *Shikumen*[2] made of two or three floors. Its original size was 7.2 ha. There was only one lane, but since the 2000s the perimeter has expanded first to the east and then westward, incorporating other *lilongs* under the label Tianzifang, as it can be seen in Figure 3.1.

As Demgenski underlines in his analysis of Qingdao's heritage preservation, there has been a different evolution in architectural style. It reflects the influence of Western architecture in Shanghai and Qingdao, but also an influence of Chinese migrants bringing their own traditions plus the foreign administration regulations as some foreign concessions[3] were established in Qingdao and Shanghai alike. All these influences modelled the *lilong* in Shanghai and the *Dabaodao* in Qingdao (Demgenski 2018: 232). These buildings were demolished, rebuilt, transformed and subdivided to what we can see today.

Due to political instability, wars and rebellions, the situation was very instable in China at the end of the nineteenth century and foreign concessions in big cities like Shanghai appeared as a safe refuge. With the rapid increase of population there was a housing crisis. Some housings were erected quickly in underdeveloped areas of foreign settlements in order to accommodate the influx of refugees. Until the mid-twentieth century people flowed in Shanghai according to the military and economic situation. Ho is even describing some housing which were merely grass huts (Ho 2010: 39).

The *lilongs* were built for basic living standards. It is typical local architecture.

> The word, as an abbreviation of *Lilong* housing neighborhood, is a rich concept that not only refers to the materiality of the dwelling form, but also the vivid social life within and around it, which can be characterised in at least

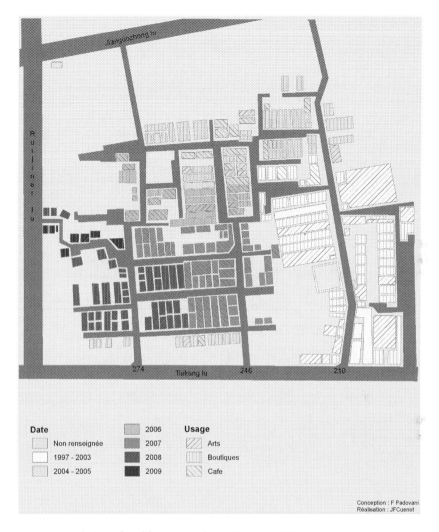

Figure 3.1 Evolution of Building Usage from 1997 to 2009.
Source: Author photo.

three ways: 1/ the physical forms of housing (...) which had shared a similar neighborhood structure, being organized along small alleys; 2/ the social community; 3/ a particular dwelling culture created by the inhabitants.
(Zhao 2004: 50–51)

There are different styles of *lilong* architectural design according to the period when they were erected and the material used for construction. This has changed a little but the important characteristics remain (Fan 2004; Rutcosky 2007).

The buildings are usually made of three floors. They are linked together through alleys and lanes leading to the main gates, which are guarded.

58   *Florence Padovani*

This gives a feeling of safety to the inhabitants and allows them to create strong social ties within a closed perimeter. As a matter of fact, the intensive use of commune areas and a vivid life in the alleys generated a strong sense of community.[4]

In 1949 when the communists took power and founded the People's Republic of China, the *lilong* accounted for 69%[5] of urban dwellings (Fan 2004). These constructions were stopped in 1950 as the new government changed its policy regarding city dwellers. There was no more private property and the State was the only owner. Industries and businesses as well as housing were nationalized. The state provided people working in the cities with accommodation for a very low rent. Part of Tianzifang was then converted into factories and workers were crammed into *lilong* housing nearby.

Since the beginning, a variety of residents lived in Tianzifang. In addition to workers, they included minor officials, artists and teachers who took advantage of the low prices of these buildings to move in. The organizational configuration of the *lilong* induced very important spatial as well as social constraints for their inhabitants. As noted above, it developed a strong feeling of belonging inside a group of people protected from outside. In the early twentieth century one extended family could own one building (especially the *Shikumen* style). During the pre-communist period housing was relatively comfortable for an average size family, but after 1950 it was crowded when several families had to use the same space (Laurans 2005). Each building was re-divided creating small flats which were rented inexpensively to poor families and workers. The kitchen and the bathroom became common spaces. There were no private toilets, so residents had to go to public toilets in the morning, carrying their chamber pots. Another consequence was the degradation of the premises as none of the residents were willing to take responsibility for upkeep of the buildings. In the 1950s, in addition to redefining the space used by individual buildings, several lanes in the *lilong* were demolished to make room for six small factories, which produced watches and spare parts, canned food and so on. The food factory, which housed a photo gallery, Deke-Erh from the 1990s until 2012 (Zhou 2012), has three floors, and the tallest building has six floors. At the turn of the twentieth century, because of its location in the historical center of Shanghai, the area attracted property developers who wanted to benefit from the latest urban transformation policies. When private developers collaborating with local authorities took advantage of the opportunity to launch large-scale modernization projects in the district, Tianzifang was one such project.

Implementation of urban renovation in today's Shanghai

Urban renovation is quite a common phenomenon in major cities vying for international recognition. They all had to face similar problems in relation to urban transformation. The analysis of Istanbul's renovation is very interesting in that regard (Pérousse 2007). Just like in Shanghai, districts that underwent the largest renovations were located in the historical center or its immediate outskirts. There too, urban policies were actively promoted by the authorities, who presented them as necessary for modernizing the city, enhancing its image and improving the living conditions of the inhabitants (Berry-Chikhaoui 2007).

According to Shanghai municipality leaders, the main objective was to eliminate old industrial buildings, dilapidated housings to give a beautiful image of the city connected to the world. Their goal was to transform Shanghai so that it could compete with other global cities (Diglio 2006). As a consequence, the resident population changed and gentrification followed the morphological transformations made to the city.

In this context of high-speed transformations, the issue of historical sites' preservation needs to be addressed. What is to be preserved? How to preserve? Although Shanghai was officially recognized by the Chinese central government as a "national historic city" in December 1986, concerns for historic preservation seemed quite weak[6] compared to the dominant modern architecture being built in business centers, commercial malls and so on. At this point preservation or conservation of cultural heritage in its original stage was not the main goal to be achieved. Heritage should be understood as a process in perpetual change. As Ashworth points out, "Heritage is the usage of the past in the present and that new present will constantly imagine new pasts to satisfy changing needs" (Ashworth 2011: 10). The municipality listed places to be preserved and succeeded to have heritage sites listed at the national level (Yue et al. 2014). By 2006, Shanghai already had 16 key state protective relics, 110 key city protective relics, 21 historic memorial spots and 15 protective sites; altogether there are 400 buildings of historical value (Diglio 2006).

Like many countries in the West which went through urban development and modernization of the cities, it is difficult to find the balance between growth and fast development on one hand and cultural heritage preservation on the other hand (Zukin 2009). An additional point might be that old buildings mainly go back from the concession period and one can wonder to what extent remembering this period of Chinese history is not too shameful (this idea is also shared by Diglio 2006). The ambiguity between the image of a dynamic international city even at an early stage that the Chinese government is promoting and the presence of Western administration in the concessions which is sidelined makes it complicated to preserve the remains of this period of history.

Lastly, the residents of old buildings themselves have a negative perception of these constructions or at least are very ambivalent, feeling they are old-fashioned, not comfortable, too densely populated and so on. None of the people I interviewed raised the issue that the buildings they are living in could be considered as historical heritage. The problem in Shanghai, but it is also valid for other cities in China, is that the massive and rapid destruction, which happened in the 1990s, left small room for discussion and elaboration of a good protection plan (Wang & Li 2009; Ho 2010; Yin 2012; Evans 2014; Demgenski 2018). Basically, it is just a decade later that the issue raised concern and then academics started to publish a lot (Wu 2002, 2015; Ren 2008; Tsai 2008; Yao & Zhao 2009), just to quote the main Chinese authors who publish in English.

60 *Florence Padovani*

To borrow the expression from Lu Duanfang's book: *China Today Is Remaking Its Urban Form* (Lu 2006) and of course while doing so, social relations are also re-ordered while a process of gentrification is taking place. For sure, the expectations from the new group of residents are very different. While some old residents wanted a wet market nearby and some daily-use shops, richer residents preferred leisure activities and luxury shops. After being centered on industrial production (during the Maoist era) Chinese cities are now connected to the market economy (during the post-reform era). Modernization is the main motto. The transformations that happened in Shanghai are the consequences of this new definition of the city.

Here appears a contradiction between what the central State (in Beijing) and even the Shanghai municipality's leaders aim at and what the other social actors dream of. Here we understand social actors as the people who act – or more often react – to policy that they are concerned by. They include residents who do not want to move or who wish to stay in the same area for example. They also include some groups like the artists in Tianzifang who decided to defend their working place. They also include the voiceless, the ones who have no space to speak, the migrants who come for a non-specified period of time and then are supposed to go back to their rural areas, so they have no say. As a consequence, they are the marginalized one. In a nutshell, urbanization is closely linked to socialization and the creation of new identities (Dubar 2000). In Tianzifang, social actors made use of urban planning to their own advantage and they readapted the plan in their own way of imagining sustainable development, meaning that through daily activities they transformed what was decided from above. This way of analyzing social actors is in line with Erving Goffman's work (Goffman 1959). I underline a few elements of his work. Individuals may have different roles in the play. They can change and make choices. The interaction with other actors is led by the sense of a common good to defend.

Two groups of people plus one saving Tianzifang

The three groups of people who were actors in the transformation of Tianzifang were the artists, the residents and the local administration. In addition, a fourth group was present but voiceless: the economic migrants.

All over China at the end of the 1980s, unprofitable state-owned production units were closed. Some were then converted into galleries and artist studios and gradually some restaurants and souvenir shops got there. This phenomenon can be observed in Beijing (e.g., 798 district) but also in several locations in Shanghai like Red House and Suzhou Creek (He 2007; Wang 2009; Zheng 2011). The six small factory work units in Tianzifang filed for bankruptcy in the 1990s. Soon after they were closed. Some artists were then able to rent from the municipality the former industrial sites at very low prices; here they installed their workshops. A community of painters, sculptors, photographers, designers slowly developed. Some of them had studied in the West and were aware of places like Soho in New York City. They considered this a model to be followed and they viewed Tianzifang as a "Chinese Soho". In Shanghai at that time, the idea of converting old factory buildings into artistic venues was brand new.

After 1991, the employees of the state-owned enterprises were given the opportunity to buy their flats at a discounted price. As a result, most of the long term residents in Tianzifang, moved in during the 1950s and chose to buy their flats in 1991. Others were small shop owners and most of this population was on low incomes.

In addition to artists and the residents, there was also the group of the economic migrants. In the *lilong*, different people lived alongside one another. The artists and the older residents did not have much in common and did not have many opportunities to interact in daily life.[7] In fact, the artists did not live in Tianzifang, but only worked there. They paid rent for their studios directly to a government office.

The residents' community in Tianzifang underwent a deep transformation in the 1990s. At that time, longtime residents started to look for new housing, with modern facilities. The ones who were rich enough left Tianzifang. Economic migrants then started to rent available rooms and establish themselves there. They were usually from nearby provinces (Anhui, Jiangsu, Zhejiang), and they came in the hope of earning a better living in Shanghai. The residents and the economic migrants interacted on a daily basis. They jointly used the common facilities and bought their goods in the same wet market. Their income level and their level of education were somewhat similar. In consequence, the two groups had more common interests than they had with the artists. The specificity of the economic migrants is that they are the "voiceless", the ones who are tolerated but who have no rights. Although since 2003 the government abolished the system of forced repatriation, they were never given proper rights to stay in the cities (Zhao & Padovani 2014). So, they were not involved in the creation of Tianzifang, even though they were living there during the time of the negotiations.

The group that we call the artists is made of different types of actors. Some of them have a certain degree of notoriety, like the aforementioned Huang Yongyu, or Chen Yifei, a renowned photographer, one of those with a long stay in North America where he discovered the practice of converting old factories into art galleries. His contribution was particularly significant for the artists who settled in Tianzifang. Some others were just attracted by low rents. Maybe due to their higher level of education, compared with the longtime residents, possibly because they have been abroad and witnessed foreign artists using industrial buildings, or because they made use of their fame to speak aloud; in any case the artists became the defenders of Tianzifang. All these elements gave them legitimacy to defend its preservation. As Demgenski states in the case of Qingdao they are the "old-town protectors" (Demgenski 2016), being very skillful to make use of media and personal connections to pressure the administration to protect Tianzifang.

62 *Florence Padovani*

By 2004, an estimated 1.8 hectares of industrial space had been converted into studios, galleries, artists' studios or interior design offices, occupying almost all of the previously available factory space (Wang 2011). From the start, Tianzifang stood out as different because artists, residents and economic migrants coexisted in the same limited space. In other places where artists have settled in Shanghai, such as Suzhou Creek or Red House, there were often only abandoned industrial structures, thus no inhabitants. The relative harmonious relationship between artists, residents and entrepreneurs is part of the good image on which Shanghai leaders have tried to build. Moreover, there were no protests against eviction and no negative media coverage about the displacement of residents. So, harmonious Tianzifang was put forth as a model to be followed. However, as we will show in the next section the picture is not that rosy.

Fighting for the preservation of Tianzifang

We just mentioned two groups of people – plus one – who tried to save Tianzifang. In addition, the three layers of Chinese administration – the central, the municipal and the district level governments – were involved and interested in the fight for preservation. The last group was made of private investors, who were responsible for financing renovation works. All the groups had their own agenda. The administration and the investors had to negotiate an agreement before any project could commence. Developers obtained urban land use rights and then they went ahead with the project. In this case, in an effort to build a more modern image of Shanghai and to take advantage of an attractive financial opportunity,[8] city authorities made the deal with a Hong Kong real estate company. This company, Shui On Land, was the one that designed Xintiandi and several other *lilongs*. Its plan was to build large luxury residences and a shopping center.

As a consequence of this deal, the economic migrants, the ones who were renting rooms only had to prepare to move further away; they were the silent ones. So when the decision to demolish the area was taken, the occupants could only prepare to move sooner or later.

Amongst the two other groups were the old residents and the artists. The first to react were the artists, who became an important group as the influx of artists seeking inspiration and affordable rents had increased. The mobilization of artists, academics[9] and even political executives took place in various forms to denounce the massive destruction of local heritage. The debate, although sometimes violent, did not receive significant media coverage. It was held in the Luwan district government offices and was not public. Interlocutors suggest that the main argument was that a modern international metropolis needs to keep some historical enclaves. Second, according to people who wanted to preserve Tianzifang from destruction, the experiment of mixing different groups seemed to be working; moreover, the public seemed to appreciate this mix of residential life for the popular classes and artistic flavor. Eventually, Luwan leaders decided to use Tianzifang as an experiment in a new kind of historic preservation. The Asian economic crisis (1997) forced the developers to reduce the scope of their project because of the lack of funds and the fall in real estate prices. So, the Luwan district government took the decision to give Tianzifang some time to show what could be done. It is important to note that the decision was made at the lowest level of the administrative hierarchy. It was a real risk for the leaders because if the experiment failed, they would be responsible for that.

Despite being the first to be affected by the development project, the degree of involvement of longtime residents was minimal. They appeared to be caught in a dynamic that they were not able to stop. Sidelined from the discussions, they were to be evicted for the purpose of adding value to the district. Initiated by the government and by private developers, this huge demolition and development project in Tianzifang, following the model of Xintiandi, was to completely transform the district by reallocating its space. Some people I interviewed said that they were not strong enough to fight against a government decision. They also said they did not want to get into trouble. A very fatalistic feeling was shared by many.

The new Tianzifang

When it was sure that Tianzifang would not be destroyed anytime soon, that negotiations began between the artists, the businessmen and the residents-owners. It was particularly uneasy because on the one hand, state regulations prohibited changing the zoning of land use.[10] On the other hand, because of the large number of owners in such a small area, reaching an agreement thus became a major challenge. One needed the agreement of several private owners in order to get a big enough space to accommodate goods and consumers. Because *lilong* are small buildings with a maximum of three floors, they do not have elevators. It is easier to do business on the first floor or the second one. The third floor is not easily accessible and often not visible from the alley. Therefore, it is more difficult to rent third-floor buildings, and those residents are often likely to stay, even as apartments on the lower floors are rented. So, the social fabric has changed under the pressure of urban renewal. Tianzifang as we know it today was born out of these challenges.

Tianzifang was gaining notoriety amongst Shanghai people and it became quickly a trendy place for young people. But still the situation remained precarious for many of its residents. However, as real estate prices collapsed during the Asian financial crisis of 1997, all major construction projects were either postponed or scaled back. Tianzifang benefited from the situation and, thus, many of its historic buildings, and the people who lived in them, were spared. In 2004, an agreement was sealed between the artists, the government officials and new entrepreneurs, to save Tianzifang. But in return new management structures were created to oversee its development. So far, it was an informal and small-scale committee. The owners were still private ones but most left to make room for shops or galleries. They receive a monthly rent. For the government in order to keep an eye on these transactions they decided to create a management committee to supervise. The main role of the committee was to prevent disputes given the complexity of establishing a lease. The involvement of municipal authorities in the management of Tianzifang marked a turning point in the evolution of the site. One year later, in 2005, Tianzifang was named "Shanghai's most creative industrial zone". This was the final victory for people who wanted to protect the place from destruction because gaining this title meant that it has been formerly recognized as a creative and tourist area that could not be destroyed easily.

If the residents were not fighting on the front line to save their living space, they were the ones who gained economic benefits (at least for the ones living on the ground or the first floor). In 2004, they began renting their property to artists who could not find room in former factories. They also started to rent to entrepreneurs who opened cafes, restaurants and souvenir boutiques. Shops started to be seen everywhere and this was a too good opportunity for residents who wished to move to a less confined environment, to pass up. For those living on the third floor, it was – and still is – quite difficult to find a tenant. Thus, there is the rare situation where residents voluntarily leave their homes and even receive a significant monthly rent, and others who wished that the government had removed them from their homes. These people who usually lived on the second or the third floor would like to move but could not afford to do so if they could not rent out their flat. For M. Zhang, living on the third floor (summer 2010), it was a no-win situation,

> If I move out now without any compensation from the government and without renting my place, how am I going to survive with my little retirement pension? My kids don't want me to stay with them and I don't have anywhere to go. This is really unfair.

They are a marginalized group in Tianzifang even if they contribute to the good image of Tianzifang as a place of social diversity.

Shanghai newspapers reported that the first resident in Tianzifang who rented his flat did a bit of renovation work and, before he had even finished, he was offered 4,000 yuan per month by a fashion designer, who also ended up hiring him as an employee for a salary of 1,500 yuan, which represented more than ten times the worker's former monthly income. Today, prices are continuously increasing, and a 40 m^2 apartment in the main aisle can be rented for up to 40,000 yuan per month (Figure 3.2).[11]

The creativity of Tianzifang and its official recognition brought great vitality to the local community and a substantial increase in income for the residents. Initially, Tianzifang was only one lane located at 210 Taikang Road; subsequently, it was extended to a wider area, and today it encompasses three lanes (210, 248 and 274 Taikang Road). In 2011, the proportion of rented premises was 75% at number 210, 78% at number 248 and only 28% in the third and final section, one that was developed more recently and is located further west.[12] In total, 45% of the families that were surveyed chose to remain there, 37% have rented out their apartments and 17% have become entrepreneurs (1% were not able to answer the questionnaire). Out of the 301 families living there, 114 would like to find a

Figure 3.2 Tianzifang's main entrance 210 Taikang lu, November 2019.
Source: Author photo.

tenant, 34 wanted to leave, 97 wanted to stay and 75 were not sure. These figures show that the development of Tianzifang has had a very significant impact on the residents. Residents who did not have much to say about the transformation of their community, nevertheless, want to take advantage of the development. As people decide to leave their apartment and rent it out, this dynamic will lead to a very different Tianzifang, which likely will look more like Xintiandi. Residents whose income has increased find themselves in a position of choice. However, those with the most choice are those who had ground floor units.

Alongside this transformation, because the resident population density is decreasing, one might expect that the structures should be better maintained. However, the increase in the tourist population and the turnover of entrepreneurs as the rent prices are rocketing have an impact on the maintenance of the buildings. In addition, construction was not planned for shops and restaurants, few inspections are performed, so some fear that the buildings might collapse.

During interviews conducted between 2005 and 2012, some residents, especially those who lived on the second or third floors, complained about not finding tenants. Many were also distressed by the onslaught of tourists, who seemed to consider them as curiosities. Another subject of recrimination was the

66 *Florence Padovani*

disappearance of small shops useful to residents. For example, the large market at the end of Taikang Road, small hairdressers, shoemakers and glaziers have all disappeared to give way to more luxury boutiques. The retired Mrs. Li thus complained in 2010:

> Back in the days, I used to go to the market every morning and we would all meet up, chatting while buying vegetables. Now the new market is smaller, some services are no longer available and then it's much more expensive. Only fashionable shops are left; it is good for young people and foreigners, but not for people like us!

For Mr. Huang, a retired man, the situation is not easier:

> I can only go out early in the morning, otherwise I would have no respite; they all want to take my picture and they make so much noise that my bird becomes frightened. At night, they are shouting and making noise until the late hours. If I could, I would move as quickly as possible. This is not a life!

Ms. Yao (May 2014), who has been living in a nearby *lilong* since childhood and who is selling tea in Tianzifang, is more critical of residents: "People are not sensible; they all think that their small flat on the second or third floor is gold. They are too greedy, so my neighbours underneath are condemned to cope with noise and daily stress". Disputes between residents, bar owners and even customers happen from time to time, forcing the neighborhood committee to intervene. Although residents did not carry out formal demonstrations in front of Luwan's District Committee, some third-floor residents set up banners denouncing the changes they faced (witnessed by the author in April 2008). This shows sporadic resistance, with little impact on the development of Tianzifang.

The departure of residents has only accelerated. There used to be 670 households living in Tianzifang eight years ago; now only 80 remain, most of whom are elderly. Since 2011, street signs in Chinese and English indicating that visitors are not allowed to penetrate further or that photography is forbidden beyond a certain limit have started to appear at the end of shopping aisles. Small booths have been installed at the entrances of the alleys for the security guards[13] on duty; barriers were set to prevent vehicles and even bicycles from entering (Figure 3.3).

At the end of 2012, a survey[14] of the tourists visiting Tianzifang commissioned by Luwan district showed that it was ranked last among the Shanghainese sites (Figures 3.4–3.7). According to the journalist who analyzed the reports, visitors complain that there are too many tourists in the narrow alleys. They also complain about inflated prices for average quality goods. As for the residents, they don't have any more private space where they can meet each other.[15] The businessmen are not satisfied either because the rent is now too high or because there is a tough competition. Some artists left for more attractive places. As an example, Deke-Erh, one of the first famous artists to move to Tianzifang, left for

Figure 3.3 The border between touristic and residential area, Summer 2010.
Source: Author photo.

Suzhou, where the municipality provided him with a large space for a low rent. After eight years of development, there were mixed results. Miss Wu, a Taiwanese, thus explains her feeling (summer 2011):

> During my first visit, while having coffee in an alley, we could see some residents cycling about, carrying the vegetables they had just purchased. This passage of the recent past was quite fascinating. (...) During the past two years, the number of daily visitors has greatly increased. Inside Tianzifang, people have to push and bump into each in order to move forward.

The co-residence of artists and other residents in a single neighborhood now appears to be a victim of its own success. Flat owners are divided among those who enjoy a comfortable income and who have usually left Tianzifang, and others who have to stay and whose quality of life has deteriorated. As for the artists, who allowed Tianzifang to exist, there are also different situations and some left as shown above with Deke-Erh. Rents have become too high, tourists often pass by quickly without making a purchase and competition has become increasingly tough. In this sense, as mentioned above, Tianzifang can be said to be victim of its own success.

Figure 3.4 Tianzifang before restauration, Summer 2006.
Source: Author photo.

Figure 3.5 Tianzifang on a week day, November 2019.
Source: Author photo.

Tianzifang in Shanghai 69

Figure 3.6 Daily life in Tianzifang, Spring 2005.
Source: Author photo.

Figure 3.7 Visitors in narrow alley, November 2019.
Source: Author photo.

70 *Florence Padovani*

When a marginal area is transformed into a touristic high spot

As was bitterly pointed out by some residents, the *lilong*'s surroundings have changed. Until the early 2000s, Taikang Road was a quiet, narrow, one-way road, lined with plane trees. On both sides of this road, from west to east, there were "ordinary" stalls, a glazier, a mattress-maker, a hairdresser who could take care of only a single customer at a time, a covered two-floor market with fruits and vegetables on the first floor, and poultry and live fish on the second, a female vendor of small steamed bread/buns, a watchmaker and a small grocery store. All of these merchants lived at or near Tianzifang. All of them knew each other, and there were strong ties between them, amid an intense community life. It was a *lilong*, like many others in Shanghai on the margins of the modern city. As Tianzifang evolved, the daily-use shops have given way to increasingly upmarket boutiques to please new customers: the visiting tourists. These include many shops selling tea, stylish clothing shops and galleries. This kind of development did not satisfy the residents. The interruption of new actors in their daily life transformed Tianzifang's residents into marginal people in their living space.

Opposite Tianzifang, still on Taikang Road, another *lilong* (Xinxili) was completely destroyed to make way for several luxury buildings and a shopping mall with restaurants, banks, cinemas and boutiques. Here, the residents were evicted by the police and sent to the outer suburbs. At the place of this former *lilong*, a subway station (line 9) was created just before the opening of the World Expo in 2010, with an exit right in front of Tianzifang's main entrance.

The *lilong* of Tianzifang had to invent its own and to fight for its existence. The whole process involved creativity and a particular integration of residents, artists and merchants which is unique to Tianzifang and contributes to its attractiveness. Tourists, who are mostly Chinese, come to walk through the streets and make a selective reading of local history through a sanitized reconstruction of a place that we have previously described as lacking any form of modern comfort. However, this success is not without its problems. At a certain point, sustainable development, one that would allow social and economic development as well as historic preservation, appears to have become untenable.

Tianzifang is different from the other Shanghai redevelopment projects in many respects: first because of the long and difficult struggle for survival that took place between the different actors, second because of the manner in which it escaped demolition[16] and finally because of the fact that it later became a model in terms of urban renewal. After 2005, when Tianzifang was proclaimed "Shanghai's most creative industrial zone", its status changed and it is from then on that it was seen as a model to be emulated. But, to my knowledge, up to this date no area in China claims to have emulated it. It was initially saved by a spontaneous congregation of artists and other actors who felt the need to get involved, but the artists are starting to leave now, joining the residents who already left; both have been progressively replaced by shopkeepers. The alleys have become saturated with waves of tourists gradually altering the unique character of the area.

Buildings have undergone a number of changes intended to allow the creation of galleries and boutiques. Housing have been transformed into restaurants, galleries and shops. Today, Tianzifang is a victim of its own success, and it is becoming, step by step, similar to other "historic villages" and enclaves in China, a reconstructed leisure area with an obsolete fragrance where you can buy the same souvenirs as elsewhere. What was making the uniqueness of Tianzifang – the cohabitation of residents, artists, shops and tourists – is fading away.

In other words, the ultimate goal of the leaders of the Luwan district, with the approval of higher authorities – which was to reshape the urban landscape and to modernize it while at the same time protecting Tianzifang as an enclave – seems to work beyond expectation. At the same time, taking advantage of the opportunities available to them, the artists and the residents reorganized the space in terms of function, thus reshaping its social fabric as well. In Tianzifang, residents were not evicted but gradually moved away, and gentrification inexorably continues. This enables the fabrication of citizens seemingly corresponding to the standards of a truly international city, and it is used to display a flattering image of Shanghai. In a way one might say that Tianzifang's uniqueness is fading away and it seems to be marginalized as it did not manage to become a model for urban development in China.

Notes

1 For this chapter I used 25 interviews: 5 with people from the administration and 20 with people living in Tianzifang.
2 They have a front yard protected from outside by a wall and high wooden gates. On each side and above there are carved stones which give its name to this style of house.
3 At the end of the opium wars some "unequal treaties" as they are called were signed between Western countries (plus Japan) and China. This was how France gained a concession in Shanghai in 1849 and Germany in Qingdao in 1898.
4 This is well described by the Shanghainese writer Qiu Xiaolong (2010).
5 Even in the 2000s before the urban renewal, *lilongs* were the most common type of housing in Shanghai.
6 Article 14 §1–2:

> The development of new urban areas and the redevelopment of old urban areas must be integrated in a unified plan, must be planned and arranged rationally, must pursue a course of comprehensive development, and must give priority to the construction of auxiliary, complementary projects and of infrastructure works, and construction work must be carried out with a relative concentration of resources. The redevelopment of old urban areas must be integrated with the restructuring and redistribution of industries, must rationally readjust the use of land, must keep a check on the building of high-rises, must lower building density, must increase public green space, must help improve urban traffic, must further improve urban infrastructure, and must strengthen the multifunctionality of the city. (…) *Regulations of Shanghai Municipality on City Planning*, 1995

7 Ms. Li (summer 2010):

> When Chen Yifei died many famous people came to his studio and they wanted to see what Tianzifang looked like but nobody spoke to us, they stayed together. TV was there. (…) afterwards some artists came back here but it was their business.

72 Florence Padovani

8 "In China, in 2010, revenue from trade in real estate accounted for 1/3 of national revenue" (Yu 2014: 24).

9 Like Chen Yingfang, then Professor of Sociology at East China Normal University. She published two books in Chinese about slums in Shanghai and social problems with urban development (2008, 2009).

10 Article 45:

> The use of an architectural structure must conform to the function designated and approved for it in the Permit for Planning of Construction Project. Any change in the designated function of an architectural structure must be reported to the Municipal or Area/District/County Administrative Department in Charge of City Planning that originally handled the examination and approval procedures for approval. *Regulations of Shanghai Municipality on City Planning*, 1995.

11 This figure was given by several people during interviews in May 2014. There is no set maximum price; rather prices are set by negotiation between parties.

12 Results of a public poll ordered by the local committee from Luwan district in 2010. The survey interviewed 671 families in Tianzifang. The whole survey has not been published, but some abstracts are available (Xu 2011).

13 They are paid by the management committee. In China one can see those at the entrance of gated communities and in most public spaces. In that sense Tianzifang is not an exception.

14 Report of the survey in the following article (in Chinese) (Zhou 2013).

15 The role of the *Lilong* traditionally was to get a community life inside and shops outside with a few alleys opening to the outside. Now it is the opposite; inside the *lilong* is full of outsiders and there is no more community life.

16 Some other projects were put on hold but the difference is that the *lilong* was first demolished before a new allotment would be defined.

Works Cited

Ashworth, G. J. (2011). Preservation, conservation and heritage: Approaches to the past in the present through the built environment. *Asian Anthropology*, 10, 1–18.

Berry-Chikhaoui, I. (2007). Les citadins face aux enjeux d'internationalisation de la ville. Casablanca et Marseille: Où est le Nord, où est le Sud? *Autrepart*, 1, 149–163.

Chen, Y. F. (2008). Actual crisis of urban development and rationalization. *Sociological Research*, 3, 16–28 (Chinese).

Chen, Y. F. (2009). Légitimité, rationalité et stratégies politiques: Les fondements du miracle urbain chinois. *Terrains & Travaux*, 16, 97–135.

Demgenski, P. (2016). Urban renewal in Qingdao: Creating scenic neighbourhoods, but for whom? *Asia Dialogue* (online) http://theasiadialogue.com/2016/08/10/urban-renewal-in-qingdao-creating-scenic neighbourhoods-but-for-whom/

Demgenski, P. (2018). Living in 'the Past': The effects of a growing preservation discourse in contemporary urban China. In D. Yannan, M. Marinelli, & Z. Xiaohong (Eds.), *China: A Historical Geography of the Urban* (pp. 225–247). Cham: Palgrave Macmillan.

Diglio, S. (2006). Continuity, Transition and Transcendence: Urban Reform and Development in China. RGS-IBG Annual Conference 2005 (London, August 31st – September 2nd, 2005).

Dubar, C. (2000). *La Socialisation, Construction des Identités Sociales et Professionnelles*. Paris: A. Colin.

Evans, H. (2014). Neglect of a neighbourhood: Oral accounts of life in 'Old Beijing' since the eve of the People's Republic. *Urban History*, 41(4), 686–704.

Fan, W. B. (2004). *The Conservation and Renewal of Lilong in Shanghai*. Shanghai: Shanghai Science Publishing Company (Chinese).

Goffman, E. (1959). *The Presentation of Self in Everyday Life, Doubleday in Garden City*. New York: Doubleday Anchor Books.

He, S. J. (2007). State-sponsored gentrification under market transition The Case of Shanghai. *Urban Affairs Review*, 43(2), 171–198.

Ho, W. C. (2010). *The Transition Study of Postsocialist China – An Ethnographic Study of a Model Community*. Singapore: World Scientific Publishing.

Laurans, V. (2005). Shanghai: Modern conveniences as an argument for displacing residents. *China Perspectives*, 58, March – April 2005. Retrieved from: http://journals.openedition.org/chinaperspectives/459

Lu, D. F. (2006). *Remaking Chinese Urban Form – Modernity, Scarcity and Space 1949–2005*. London: Routledge.

Park, R. E. (1928). Human migration and the marginal man. *American Journal of Sociology*, 33(6), 881–893.

Pérouse, J. F. (2007). Istanbul, entre Paris et Dubaï: Mise en conformité « internationale », nettoyage et résistances. *Villes Internationales* (pp. 31–62). Paris: La Découverte – Recherches.

Qiu, X. L. (2010). *Years of Red Dust: Stories of Shanghai*. New York: St Martin's Press.

Ren, X. F. (2008). Forward to the past: Historical preservation in globalizing Shanghai. *City & Community*, 7, 1, March.

Rutcosky, K. (2007). *Adaptive reuse as sustainable architecture in contemporary Shanghai* (Master's Thesis). Lund University.

Shanghai Municipality. (1995). *Regulations of Shanghai Municipality on City Planning*. Retrieved from: www.asianlii.org/cn/legis/cen/laws/rosmocp507/

Tsai, W. L. (2008). *The redevelopment and preservation of historic Lilong housing in Shanghai* (Master's Thesis). University of Pennsylvania.

Wang, J. (2009). Art in capital: Shaping distinctiveness in a culture-led urban regeneration project in Red Town, Shanghai. *Cities*, 26(6), 318–330.

Wang, J., & Li, S. (2009). *The rhetoric and reality of culture-led urban regeneration – A comparison of Beijing and Shanghai, China*. The 4th International Conference of the International Forum on Urbanism, Amsterdam.

Wang, W. H. (2011). Commercial gentrification and entrepreneurial governance in Shanghai: A case study of Taikang road creative cluster. *Urban Policy and Research*, 29(4), 363–380.

Wu, F. L. (2002). China's changing urban governance in transition towards a more oriented market economy. *Urban Studies*, 39(7), 1071–1093.

Wu, F. L. (2015). State dominance in urban redevelopment beyond gentrification in urban China. *Urban Affairs Review*, 52(5), 631–658.

Yao, P., & Zhao, Y. (2009). How to protect and utilize historical heritage: A case study with Xintiandi shopping mall in Shanghai. *Journal of Liaoning University, Natural Science*, 16(1), 75–84.

Yin, X. T. (2012). *Trends of Preserving Historic Districts, Communication 48th ISOCARP Congress* (not published, transmitted to the author).

Yu, H., Chen, X. M., & Zhong, X. (2014). Communal entrepreneurship in old neighbourhood renewal: Cases studies of Shanghai Tianzifang shopping district. *Global Urban Studies*, 7, 15–38.

Yu, Y. C. (2011). *Tianzifang Yesterday and Today* (Chinese). Retrieved from: http://blog.sina.com.cn/s/blog_517081ff0100 pgnr.html (Accessed 17 February 2011).

74 Florence Padovani

Yue, W. Z., Fan, P. L., Wei, Y. H., Dennis, et al. (2014). Economic development, urban expansion, and sustainable development in Shanghai. *Stochastic Environmental Research and Risk Assessment, 28*(4), 783–799.

Zhao, C. L. (2004). From Shikumen to new-style: A rereading of lilong housing in modern Shanghai. *The Journal of Architecture, 9*(Spring), 49–76.

Zhao, Y. Q., & Padovani, F. (2014). Expulsion des résidents d'habitats délabrés (penghuqu) et reconstruction de la vie des nouveaux migrants à Shanghai. *L'Espace Politique, 22*(1). Retrieved from: http://journals.openedition.org/espacepolitique/2984

Zheng, J. (2011). 'Creative Industry Clusters' and the 'Entrepreneurial City' of Shanghai. *Urban Studies, 48*(16), 3561–3582

Zhou, P. (2012). Famed artist to leave Tianzifang. *Global Time.* Retrieved from: http://www.globaltimes.cn/content/737539.shtml.

Zhou, S. L. (2013). Why Tianzifang has been transformed into the AAA level area the less satisfactoryone? *Jiefang Daily,* 22 March 2013 (Chinese).

Zukin, S. (2009). *Naked City: The Death and Life of Authentic Urban Places.* Oxford: Oxford University Press.

4 Cemeteries in Shanghai
Beyond the margins*

Maylis Bellocq

Every year, over 100,000 deaths are registered in the municipality of Shanghai, which means that this is the number of bodies to be managed and dealt with.[1] In nearly every case, the dead are cremated, in line with the first funerary reform adopted at the end of the 1950s.[2] Once the cremation is over, the families then recover the ashes of their loved one which they place not in an urn, but in a small funerary box in the shape of a miniature coffin. The remains of the dead person will therefore be kept preferably in a grave of limited size. The spread of cremation as a practice in large Chinese cities has been driven by a wish to conserve raw materials and to preserve real estate and thus to combat the loss of arable land and plots of land needed for urban development. (Whyte 1988: 293–294; Fang & Goossaert 2008; Henriot 2016). Thus, graves and cemeteries have been viewed by the authorities as being a great waste and it has become absolutely necessary to limit them. While this first funerary reform did not remove all cemeteries, it nevertheless helped to reduce the impact on the land space, thanks to the miniaturization of coffins and graves. However, despite these first results, cemeteries are still often in the sights of the municipality of Shanghai who would like to see them disappear once it has managed to remove them outside the central areas (Henriot 2016: 143–194). In fact, from the 1950s onward these necropolises were banned from the city center of Shanghai (Henriot 2016: 189). From the 1980s, cemeteries were developed in the outlying districts of the municipality (Aveline-Dubach 2012). The most recent ones have been located on sites that are ever further from the city center. Only the Martyrs' Cemetery remains in the central district of Longhua near the temple of the same name.

In the central districts of Shanghai, like in many Western countries, there is an invisibilization of death that is taking place and here it is favored not only by political will but also by urban renovation on a grand scale. Cemeteries had definitively left the city by the 1950s and the eight central districts have only two funerary centers: Longhua and Xibaoxing. Traditional funerary shops are now tending to disappear as old neighborhoods are renovated. The only traces of

---

* The author would like to acknowledge that this book chapter was translated from French by Moya Jones.

death that are still possibly visible in the city center, yet which are being dissolved or absorbed into the urban landscape, are offices representing the cemeteries whose appearance is very similar to that of estate agents (Figure 4.1).

This invisibilization is not totally dissociated from the rapid development that Shanghai has undergone over the past few decades, leading this megapolis to become a world-ranking city. Many sizeable renovation programs have reconfigured the city. The real estate market has undergone exponential growth with significant speculation generating record prices per square meter. In such a context, cemeteries represent so many lost spaces, or at least spaces that cannot be rented. The old neighborhoods where "traditional" funerary shops were located have been razed as have the small businesses set up more or less legally along certain streets. Thus, the funerary shops which gave death a certain visibility within the city are disappearing. This is the case, for example, of dozens of small shops specializing in funeral services which even a few years ago were to be found close by the Xiahai temple and the Xibaoxing funerary center. Today, only a few of them still exist but in a much standardized form.

The invisibilization and the denial of death in modern societies are popular themes in funerary studies (Ariès 1975; Thomas 1991, 1994; Urbain 2005). Invisibilization occurs when the dead person disappears from people's daily lives: nowadays people generally die in a medical institution, no longer taken charge of and cared for by relatives but by professionals. The dead no longer resemble the dead (Urbain 2005: 51) and cemeteries are expelled to the peripheries of towns and villages. Chinese

Figure 4.1 Window of an office representing the Binhai guyuan cemetery (M. Bellocq, 2010).

Source: Author photo.

megapolises have not avoided this state of affairs. Cemeteries, the dead, or at least their concrete, material representation which is to say the corpse or mortal remains, finally "the only trace of our existence in the world and in language" (Foucault 2004: 16), are ejected from the community of the living to the fringes of the city.

In this chapter, in order to analyze the place reserved for cemeteries today in Shanghai the idea of margins will be tackled in both a spatial and a social dimension, as the two share a correlation anyway. We will take into account the spatial dimension, on account of the cemeteries being relegated to places that are ever further from the center of the city and the city itself, and the social dimension insofar as the deceased is not just limited to their mortal biological remains; he or she remains a social being because of the reciprocal link maintained with the living in the context of the exchanges in which he or she participates (Brossat 2011).[3] The deceased are thus biologically dead but socially alive (Hallam et al. 1999).

The cemeteries of Shanghai can, from this point onward, be considered as so many marginal territories, places displaced to the periphery which contributes to the sidelining or the marginalization of a "population". The cemeteries of Shanghai thus seem to be able to be inscribed partly in urban fringes as defined by Sierra Alexis and Tadié Jérôme (2008: 3):

> as a location for sidelining, arising from official policy supported by the majority, integrated by the leading urban actors ... Margins are established in a relation - or even a tension - that is sometimes dichotomous, between formal and informal, power and counter-powers, between recognition and denial.

The planning for cemeteries in Shanghai is to be found in this desire to push them aside, as decided by the political authorities but also in the relations between formal and informal when we refer to funerary practices themselves, between recognition and denial, when it comes to a dead person or to death. But, more than a denial, here it is more a case of invisibilization. These two authors (2008: 11) also highlight the fact that invisibility, which can characterize the margins to different degrees, does not prevent them from having a dynamic function because of the movements and the circulation that they generate. They "are generally the sites of interaction linked to the rest of the city" (Sierra & Tadié 2008: 5). This is a reminder of the definition of a cemetery put forward by Foucault (2004: 16):

> The cemetery is certainly a place unlike ordinary cultural spaces. It is a space that is however connected with all the sites of the city, state or society or village, etc., since each individual, each family has relatives in the cemetery.

This chapter will try to understand the dynamics at work in the expulsion of cemeteries from towns. The first part will show how the marginalization of cemeteries is linked to both practices around death and political will. In the second part, the cemeteries of Shanghai will be viewed as a mirror of the city and as such the producers of their own margins. The third part will deal with the question of the dematerialization of cemeteries as sought by the authorities of Shanghai municipality.

78 *Maylis Bellocq*

The field work on which this chapter is based began in 2009 and aimed at a better understanding of funerary practices and spaces in Shanghai. Firstly, in order to gain an overall view of how funerals took place in Shanghai, I carried out semi-directed interviews with Shanghainese acquaintances and friends as well as with managerial staff at the Institute for Studies of Funerary Culture in Shanghai with whom I had been in contact through the ANR FunérAsie program. This is how I came to meet two cemetery managers and two retired members of the Civil Affairs Bureau. Afterward, when I had a clearer idea about the funerary sector in Shanghai, I visited three funerary centers in central districts – Longhua, Yishan and in particular Xibaoxing – where I carried out a series of interviews with employees (e.g., salespeople, ceremony officiants, embalmers, hearse drivers) and managers. These different interviews were followed up by an exhaustive visit round the centers. In addition, some of my special informers arranged for me to attend about 15 ceremonies. At the same time, I was visiting 14 Shanghai cemeteries where I was able to observe how the space was organized and the shape of the graves. I was also able to attend ceremonies for burials or for making offerings and I carried out semi-directed interviews with families, with cemetery staff and, when possible, with cemetery directors. The temples (Yufo, Longhua, Jing'an, Xiahai and Ji'an) are some of the other sites where I could carry out my observations in order to understand better the order of the ceremonies organized by the families in memory of their deceased relation.

Another part of my research concerned the small funerary shops whose owners offered a funeral service called *yitiaolong fuwu* (full service). This could range from declaring a death to purchasing a grave and even going as far as organizing commemoration services for the deceased. These little shops were a fruitful and efficient entry into this world allowing an understanding of funerary practices as a whole. In fact, most Shanghainese use them when they are facing the death of a relative. I carried out 20 or so interviews in these shops, and two of the people I spoke with became special informers who, when I am in Shanghai, call me as soon as they are approached to organize a funerary ceremony, whether this be a funeral, the end of mourning or commemoration of the deceased.

The progressive expulsion of the dead from the city

In order to understand the link between the living and the dead in China and to better comprehend the social role played by the deceased, as mentioned in the introduction, it seems important to remember that according to the Chinese conception of death there is no clear distinction between the world of the living and that of the dead. These two worlds share many interactions which link them, and they constitute a universe which is one and the same. On this topic, Thoraval (2014: 208) prefers to speak of two dimensions of one world. In fact, because of the Chinese ancestral cult, the living and the dead are united by a link of reciprocity. This relationship of give and take constitutes a social link. Even today in Shanghai, the living offer gifts to their ancestors on different occasions (anniversaries of birth or death, Festival of the Dead, etc.) and these gifts can be made at home, in the temple or at the cemetery depending on circumstances.

Cemeteries in Shanghai: beyond the margins   79

According to Chinese beliefs, death is the moment of separation between the Yin and the Yang principles which constitute an individual. The Yang element goes to settle in the commemorative tablet placed on the home altar, while the Yin part remains attached to the remains and is therefore buried with them (Cohen 1988: 182; Thoraval 2014: 220).[4] These are funerary rituals which allow the parts of an individual to successfully find their place after death. A ritual which is not carried out properly means there is a risk of disorder in that the souls of the dead, finding no place for themselves, are likely to come and disturb the peace of the living. It is therefore necessary to obey the prescribed rituals associated with funerals so that "order", such as it is understood by Douglas (1992), is maintained and is not troubled despite the potential disorder which the departed might create within the community. By analyzing the practices and the different systems which, in societies, allow the pure and the impure, the soiled and the clean and the idea of pollution to be grasped, Mary Douglas shows that dirt, impurity, death and everything which relates to pollution are associated with disorder, in other words with whatever is not in its right place and which might thus represent a threat to the smooth running of society. One of the functions of the funerary rituals is precisely to put dirt, impurity and pollution in their place and to push out to the symbolic fringe those elements that disturb order. Another effect is that order is reinforced by reaffirming the cohesion of the group.

Watson (1988: 12) has shown that in China the funerary ritual consists of two series of rites: those linked to the funeral, which take place between the moment of death and the expulsion of the deceased's body, sealed in a coffin, from his or her village or town or neighborhood. It was/is primordial that during this ritual sequence the souls of the dead remain associated with the body in order not to become evil spirits. Then come the rites linked to the expulsion of the coffin from the community, in other words the burial or cremation rites.

At the close of these ritual sequences, the souls that make up an individual can, according to their nature, find their place (tomb, household altar or tablet in the hall of ancestors) (Watson 1988: 9). These rites are concerned with the separation of the deceased's spirit from the community of the living and its reintegration therein as the spirit of an ancestor as well as the expulsion of the mortal remains from the community of the living. The disorder caused by the death of one of the community's members is thus neutralized when through a series of rituals it is granted a place. The deceased therefore becomes an ancestor who is no longer part of the community of the living, strictly speaking, but who plays an important part on the fringes of life. The deceased, now an ancestor, thus finds a place at the meeting of two worlds, that of the living and that of the dead, a situation which is a reminder of the "marginal man" proposed by Ziller et al. (1969: 490) and cited by Goldberg (2012: 207): "The greatest potential asset of the marginal man to management is his ability to assume an intermediary role between two groups, coupled with his objectivity". The power of the ancestor thus lies in this intermediary role between the world here below and the world beyond, and this allows the ancestor to intercede in favor or not of his or her descendants.

Douglas (1992: 114) wrote: "Being on the margins means being linked to danger and touching the source of some kind of power". In fact, the deceased,

80 *Maylis Bellocq*

the ancestor or rather whatever is symbolically invested in their representations takes on a positive or a negative power according to the devotion coming from his or her descendants. The imperial state already took an interest in funerary ritual (Watson 1988) and made sure that "the dissemination of beliefs and of correct practices when dealing with death is the occasion when certain values that were at the heart of its conception of social and cosmic order should be re-affirmed" Thoraval (2014: 225). The funerary reform that started in the 1950s is a continuation of this concern but the worries of the communist government were of a different kind. In fact, funerals must be the occasion to reaffirm social order but a social order that conforms to communist values. Besides aiming for the generalization of cremation, the reform which was launched in the 1950s tackled funerary practices and beliefs which was tantamount to attacking a traditional order founded on the power of family clans where ancestor worship is one of the pillars. This was a question of believing in the values of communism and no longer in the power of ancestors. Death and the beliefs and rituals linked to it were then banned from the public sphere and partially from the city center. During the Cultural Revolution cemeteries were vandalized by the Red Guards and commemorative tablets were burned (Henriot 2016: 190). The dead seemed to become the object of an increasingly significant marginalization.

However, the spatial marginalization of death has not always been so marked. In some cases, once the coffin was sealed, that is, once the first sequence of rituals described by Watson (1988) had been accomplished, the remains could stay some time, anywhere between a few months and even a year, close by the living as a sign of respect for the deceased (Watson 1988: 15). In Shanghai, while waiting for a decision from a *fengshui* specialist or a Daoist master regarding the place and the date when the burial could take place, the body sealed in the coffin could be kept in a temple or placed in a field where the dead had already been buried (Henriot 2016: 146–147).[5]

In the city of Shanghai the distancing of the dead has gone on increasingly throughout the twentieth century and particularly since the 1950s, whereas up until then death had been part of the urban landscape: funerals were public, funeral processions wound through the city and coffins traveled through the streets waiting to be delivered. Some cemeteries had still not been transferred outside of central districts and bodies might even be abandoned in public places. These bodies were generally those of tramps who had died in the street or of children or people placed in coffins whose impoverished relatives could not afford to bury them (Henriot 2009, 2016).[6]

In Shanghai there was therefore a certain proximity between the living and the remains of the dead. But with the reform all funerary practices came under the control of the authorities and could take place only in defined places and in a sober manner: no more ostentatious corteges which were the pretext for the demonstration of the power of the family line. From the 1980s funerary ceremonies took place in confined places, in funeral centers (*binyiguan*); cremation was generalized and ashes were stored in funerary centers and then in cemeteries that offered different types of sepulchers.

Today the specialists and the actors in the funerary sector in Shanghai estimate that after 40 years of effort, the municipality has finished the first part of the funerary reform, focused on the spread of cremation, which they call "the first funerary revolution" (Gu et al. 2003; Gu 2004; Wang 2004). The second part of the reform concerning the non-conservation of remains should soon be accomplished in the near future. The first part was about the desire to protect natural resources and land and was brought about thanks to a long campaign of information or even propaganda and to the excesses of the Cultural Revolution (Goossaert & Fang 2008: 59; Henriot 2016: 309–338). Afterward this was accomplished thanks to investments which have led to the setting up of a network of funerary centers and crematoriums. By the 1980s cremations were at about 95% and today this figure is almost 100% since burial is still authorized for the Muslim Hui minority.

Except for the Cemetery of the Martyrs and Heroes of the Revolution, there is no longer any cemetery in the city center. There is a possibility for the martyrs of the Communist Revolution and ranking members of the Communist Party to lie there, but ordinary citizens, once dead, must leave the city and occupy the cemeteries on the ever more distant peripheries.[7]

The deceased finds him- or herself marginalized at three levels: symbolically through ritual, socially because of the place that she or he occupies as an ancestor, and spatially due to the fact that cemeteries are expelled out of town and because of the funeral ceremonies which are now held in enclosed, controlled

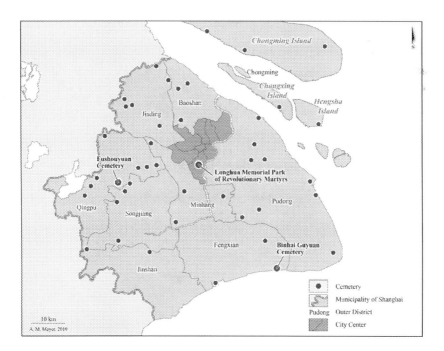

Figure 4.2 The municipality of Shanghai and its cemeteries.
Source: Author photo.

82 *Maylis Bellocq*

spaces.[8] The cemeteries of Shanghai are now on the outskirts of the city, and these fringes are moving further and further away. And, as the next part will demonstrate, the cemetery as a *mise en abyme* for the city has produced its own margins (Figure 4.2).

The cemetery: a city on the edges of the city and producer of its own social and spatial margins

After having come up against the Shanghainese lack of enthusiasm for cremation, the continuing application of the funerary reform, which consists in minimizing the impact of cemeteries and graves on the land and even to make them disappear altogether, now faces a fresh obstacle: the importance that Shanghainese give to the grave in the relationship that they maintain with their deceased family members. Although cremation has become a completely accepted practice, the conservation of the ashes, preferably in a grave, remains deeply rooted in the culture of the Shanghainese. The cost of graves has been kept high deliberately but this does not incite people to give up on this choice, nor does the distance between the cemeteries and the central districts of the city. In Europe, and particularly in France, there is a similar phenomenon; fewer and fewer visits are made to cemeteries and yet the habit of paying out large sums for the purchase of a tomb still persists (Urbain 2005: 269).

Despite the persistence in the use of graves, between 1985 and 2006 cremation led to the saving of 400 hectares of land. But today, fresh difficulties arise where cemeteries are close to full capacity. In fact, demographic pressure weighs heavily on funerary spaces since the number of deaths each year in Shanghai rose from 86,000 in 1990 to 124,000 in 2015.[9] With an ageing population by the 2030s there will be about 170,000 deaths per year and 240,000 in the 2050s (Gu et al. 2003: 31). However, according to estimates published by *The People's Daily* in 2014 there were only 100 or so hectares available in the city's 44 cemeteries whose total area covers 500 hectares.[10] This lack of land is more or less severe depending on the cemetery. According to Gao Jianhua, director of the office of funerary affairs in Shanghai, more than three quarters of the cemeteries in Shanghai find they are almost full and most of them have no chance for extension. The funerary sector of the municipality is trying to respond to these different constraints by promoting new forms of final resting place. Among these are burial plots with an area of under 1 m^2 (Gu et al. 2003: 35; Aveline 2012: 89). We are also seeing the miniaturization of graves and a verticalization of mortuary spaces which recall the high-rise accommodation blocks in the center of Shanghai.[11] Moreover, these different solutions for tombs mean that funeral services and costs can be diversified, although this diversification signifies a kind of social marker and the creation of margins within the cemeteries themselves.

When one examines the development and management of cemeteries in cities today, and in particular in Shanghai, it is quickly obvious that the problems, the issues and certain dynamics of marginalization which characterize urban transformations can be found in the spaces set aside for the dead. Two cities exist

Cemeteries in Shanghai: beyond the margins 83

side by side, that of the living and that of the dead, circumscribed in peripheral and confined spaces (Urbain 2005). Foucault (2004: 17) in fact spoke of the cemetery as "the other city, where each family possesses its *dark* resting place."[12]

The first similarity which we find in Shanghai relates to the cemeteries being opened up to the market economy, as was the case with urban spaces in the 1990s. From the mid-1980s in Shanghai private capital was mobilized, generally in a public-private partnership, for the development of cemeteries (Aveline 2012: 79–82). An immediate consequence of this liberalization was the sale of graves whose prices varied according to the site, the model, the surface area and the cemetery where they were located. The cemeteries' list of tariffs specifies the price of graves taking into account different criteria such as the sector, the grave's size and the yearly or ten-yearly costs. Graves located in the first row of one of the cemetery square grids are 10% more expensive, while those set at the end of a row have costs raised by 5%. In the columbariums, the cost of alcoves situated on the fourth row is nearly three times more expensive than that of niches on the bottom row.[13] Like for apartments, the prices vary from one story to another. This parallel with real estate buildings is extended by the presence of funeral services offices from the central districts which look like estate agents' offices or those of real estate promoters.[14]

Just as for housing, the Shanghai municipality has two kinds of cemeteries: public cemeteries (*gongyixing gongmu*) located in the villages around Shanghai and destined only for the residents of these villages;[15] and more commercial cemeteries (*jingyingxing gongmu*), of which there are 44 as well as 10 columbarium parks. The commercial cemeteries have services which vary widely from one place to another. At one extreme, there are landscaped cemeteries like Fushouyuan and Binhai Guyuan, and at the other extreme there are cemeteries like Ansi Lingyuan located in the industrial district of Baoshan. The price of a tomb varies therefore from 1,000 yuan to over 100,000 yuan according to the cemetery and the elements already detailed. The distance from the grave to a water source or a little hill can also be taken into account in the calculation of the price because even though *fengshui* no longer has a role in Shanghai cemeteries, certain principles are nonetheless respected with, in some cemeteries, the presence of a water source and little mounds. The graves themselves are systematically oriented toward the south

The social division of the space is marked not only from one cemetery to another but also within a cemetery and may be reinforced by the layout. For example, the Binhai Guyuan cemetery has zones that are defined according to the social status of those who are deceased. Thus there is a zone for celebrities; another for senior cadres (party or administrative); one for teachers, model workers, Christians, children, martyrs and heroes, ordinary people; and finally a zone marked out for "graves of public interest", "social graves" (*gongyi zang*), almost like rent-controlled public housing units (Urbain 2005: 163). During an interview in 2009 with the director of one of the cemeteries, on the topic of this division of space, he explained that "buying a grave is like buying a dwelling, one likes to know who one's neighbours are". Other cemeteries in the municipality have planned development in order to accommodate "social graves". Very often these consist of columbariums with alcoves where the price is around 1,000 yuan. These are graves which are very economical in terms of land use and for this reason their exact name is "land saving graves of public interest" (*gongyi jiedi zang*) (Figure 4.3) which is less stigmatizing.

Real estate speculation is another point where we can find a parallel between city and cemetery in Shanghai. In fact, the liberalization of the real estate market in the 1990s gave rise to an increase in speculation which did not spare cemeteries or more specifically graves. Over the last couple of decades the cost of graves has not stopped rising and increased by 167% between 2008 and 2011.[16] This price increase can be explained by the amazing improvement in the standard of living for certain categories of Shanghainese who now have the financial means to conform to the practices traditionally associated with death by offering the dear departed lavish funerals. But this increase is also widely linked to the rarity of available spaces for the laying out of new graves as well as to speculative practice. In order to combat this, as early as 2008 the Shanghai municipality adopted a regulation to control the acquisition of graves: the presentation of a death certificate would now be necessary. However, people aged over 80 or with an incurable disease or isolated old people with no children were authorized to purchase a grave while still alive.[17]

Another urban phenomenon to be noticed in Shanghai cemeteries is that of renovation. In fact, cemeteries which are unable to extend have found new economic ideas inspired by practices linked to ancestor worship. To those families who wish it the offer is made to renovate the graves of their loved one. Just like

Figure 4.3 Example of a land saving grave (M. Bellocq, 2012).
Source: Author photo.

in the city for dwellings deemed insalubrious, "old" graves can be destroyed and then rebuilt on the same spot with more modern materials and in a more modern aesthetic style. This is usually an important event for a family as is shown by the reconstruction date that figures on the renovated gravestones (Figure 4.4). It is a chance for the family to get together and in fact it is quite common that in parallel a ceremony is organized at a temple in the city. In the past, when one wished to thank one's ancestors for their benevolence or when the benefits were a long time coming, the orientation of graves could be modified according to *fengshui* principles. Then it became a question of improving the ancestor's comfort by supposing that this would be beneficial to the living descendants (Ahern 1973). Today families renovate their relations' graves for similar reasons and they are thus showing filial piety.

While during grave renovation at the family's request, the remains of the dead are not moved, in some cemeteries, however, there are spaces reserved for a "displaced population", like for example at the cemetery of Tianzhang. These are "public interest" village cemeteries swallowed up by urban development. Once they have been destroyed to make way for infrastructure development each deceased person's name is engraved on a plaque which is then placed in one of the cemeteries in the district (Figure 4.5).[18]

This procedure is a kind of echo of the renovation programs carried out in old neighborhoods in the central districts which entail the displacement and the rehousing of inhabitants in collective housing located on the city periphery. This

Figure 4.4 Renovated graves in black material (M. Bellocq, 2012).
Source: Author photo.

Figure 4.5 Displacing graves (M. Bellocq, 2012).
Source: Author photo.

kind of operation, whether it is in town or in a cemetery, allows an undeniable optimal use of plots of land.

In the city, the renewal of the population, which seems natural, is framed by a series of laws and regulations which define fecundity, place of residence and the ways of handling the dead. It is the same thing in cemeteries where rules determine the welcome and the residence of the "newly dead" and also attempt to define norms so that "the old dead give way to the new dead".[19] This last point has not been entirely resolved in Shanghai but the cemeteries are encouraged to favor the scattering of ashes found in the oldest graves and whose families no longer pay the yearly or ten-yearly charges. Although this is linked to the desire to reduce the duration of concessions, it is still largely insufficient to meet the pressure on land space. Cemeteries are therefore obliged to become vertical and graves to become miniature. But without the development of supplementary spaces these strategies will not suffice to deal with an ageing population which in a cemetery is synonymous with a growing population. Thus, funerary authorities in Shanghai want to push the reform even further and arrive at the non-conservation of remains, thereby avoiding space constraints.

The practices and beliefs concerning cemeteries that we have been able to observe here feature in a continuity of those which used to occur before 1949. Then, as now, the burial place was an important social marker. Before 1920, in Shanghai, the dead could be buried in family cemeteries for the better off, or in individual graves situated on preferably non-arable land around the city or else in charity cemeteries also situated on the city margins. This last category of cemeteries was for the burial of the most destitute and the unclaimed or abandoned dead. These three methods of burial corresponded to different social statuses for it was out of the question to be buried close to someone of a lower social order. From the 1920s onward public and private cemeteries began to develop. These cemeteries and in particular the public ones suffered at one point from the negative image which was associated with the charity cemeteries, which are the predecessors of the modern cemetery (Henriot 2016: 152–170). The social divisions which can be seen from one cemetery to another and even within some of them are thus not a new feature but they are tending to become more diversified. Moreover, throughout the first half of the twentieth century graves and cemeteries were regularly displaced notably on account of urban expansion. In 1949 the space still available in the 41 private cemeteries around the city was already very limited (Henriot 2016: 178–192). In order to remedy this, the Shanghai municipality encouraged the practice of cremation before this was imposed during the Cultural Revolution following the destruction committed in cemeteries by Red Guards (Henriot 2016: 184). Today, faced with similar difficulties, the Shanghai municipality is encouraging the scattering of ashes at sea and the material traces of death seem destined for even more invisibilization and are destined to lose their spatial footprint.

Beyond the fringes: the dematerialization of cemeteries

Despite a few regulatory adjustments which aim to reduce the footprint of graves, the pressure on cemeteries remains strong. The interment of ashes and the new forms of graves that are economical in land use are presented by the municipality as transitory measures leading to the second phase of the funerary reform where the aim is the non-conservation of remains (Gu et al. 2003: 9–10, 29–37, 233; Gu 2004: 308; Wang 2004).

When they examine the "second funerary revolution", Gu (2003, 2004) and Wang (2004)[20] refer to the thoughts of Zhou Enlai on the topic, but they give no specific references.[21] The first "revolution" consisted in the transition from preserving remains to not conserving them, while the second funerary "revolution" will be even more radical with the passage from the keeping of ashes to their non-conservation.[22]

As is pointed out today in publications by the funerary sector in Shanghai, the first "revolution" or stage is in fact only a preparatory phase for the second "revolution" or stage. This is an unavoidable transition because it would have been unthinkable to go directly from keeping bodies to the non-conservation of remains.

Shanghai city council began promoting the scattering of ashes at sea (海葬 *haizang*, a sea grave) in 1991. This is done collectively in a regulated fashion during gatherings on boats freighted by the Funeral Interment Service (FIS) (photo).[23] Between 1991 and the end of 2017, the contents of 40,520 urns were thus scattered at sea and according to the figures available for 2016, the ashes from 3,000 urns were cast into the sea that year. These figures seem to be fairly low considering the number of deaths each year in Shanghai but they do seem to be on the rise, as is the Shanghainese' favorable opinion of "sea graves". The results of an enquiry carried out by Ligong University in 2016 revealed that 24.7% of Shanghainese were in favor of sea graves compared to only 4% in 2003.[24]

Despite the increase in the number of scatterings at sea this practice still clashes with the concept that the Shanghainese have of death and the importance that they attach to the grave in their funerary practices. In order to palliate this, since 1998 in Binhai Guyuan cemetery, the FIS has erected a big monumental stone on which are inscribed the family names and first names of all those whose ashes have been scattered at sea. The names are gathered together on the stone according to the date of the scattering (Figure 4.6). The cemetery thus provides families with a place for meditation or for offerings, in particular on Tomb Sweeping Day, *Qingming*.

However, there are problems because space is restricted and this means that certain ritual offerings cannot be made. Thus, to mark the day of the dead *Qingming* (清明), the cemetery organizes a collective offerings ceremony. This is held on the last Saturday in March which does not correspond to the Memorial Day at all (Zhou & Gao, 2017).

In order to encourage the scattering of ashes at sea, the Shanghai municipality has gone even further and since 1999 it has set up a system of subsidies for

Figure 4.6 Monumental stones in memory of all those whose ashes have been scattered in the sea (M. Bellocq, 2008).
Source: Author photo.

families. In 1999, 150 yuan were granted to families who chose a sea grave for one of their relatives. This rose to 400 yuan in 2007, 2000 yuan in 2012 and 4,600 yuan since 2018. Today, out of these 4,600 yuan, 3,000 yuan are given directly to the family and the remaining 1,600 yuan go to organizing the scattering of the ashes on the boat chartered by the FIS.[25]

Several issues are raised here. The city council's investments to encourage the scattering of ashes at sea reveal the determination to develop rapidly this form of final resting place. But this system of subsidies runs counter to the notion of filial piety and the ancestor worship of the Chinese. A funeral, preferably very costly, was the means to pay back one's parents and to ensure their benevolence when they became ancestors. Since the 1950s and the reform which aimed to thoroughly transform funerary practices, less sumptuous funerals have in principle been more or less accepted by the people but from that to accepting payment on the occasion of a loved one's funeral.[26] Moreover, around *Qingming*, the day of the dead, the Chinese press regularly publishes articles on the high cost of funerals and often the title of the articles contains a phrase meaning "cannot afford to die" (活不起, 更死不起, to not have the means to live and even less to die).[27] In Shanghai, the funeral center chosen, the kind of grave, the cemetery and the plot selected for the grave are all potential social markers.[28] According to my informers from among those proposing funeral services, two types of family turn toward the scattering of ashes at sea: families in financial difficulties and progressive families or persons, even party cadres, who are responsible for setting an example.[29] Some of my interviewees seemed to think that the scattering of ashes is not very widespread for questions of *face*.[30] This is because it is a form of burial which is in contradiction with the precepts of filial piety and above all it is stigmatizing and, for the poorest, is only a second-best solution.

One of the constraints of burial at sea lies in the fact that once the ashes are scattered, apart from the certificate testifying to their dispersal and the name of the departed engraved on the collective memorial stone in Binhai Guyuan cemeteries, the families have nothing to hold onto. There is nowhere for them to go and pay their respects or make offerings on the day of the dead or other occasions. Seeing that the number of burials at sea is so low, the great stone erected in Binhai Guyuan cemetery is not sufficient to remove all the forms of resistance present among the populations regarding funerals at sea. Starting in the 2000s, documents began circulating in the funeral sector that made progressive mention of the potential interest of the internet for the provision of a medium for memorials. These could be a substitute for graves once the ashes had been dispersed or could be a complement to any other kind of grave. In the documents, stress is laid on the unlimited space that the internet provides as opposed to the limited areas available to the municipality (Shanghai Binzang Wenhua Yanjiusuo nd: 445–452).

With this in view, since March 2000, the FIS has offered a virtual cemetery on its website. The particularity of this cemetery is that it is the result of an institutional initiative unlike other cemeteries of the same type which have been set up by specialized companies, or associations or even by "real" cemeteries which offer an extension of their services on the net (Bourdeloie 2015: 3; Georges 2014: 505).[31]

In Shanghai, families who have scattered the ashes of a relative have the chance to create a virtual grave on the FIS site in order to compensate for the absence of any space, apart from the collective memorial in Binhai Guyuan cemetery, where they can go to worship.

The home page of the online cemetery proposes a search engine which allows one to locate the "grave" of a loved one. It also has tags with the photo and the name of the different people who have their grave on the site. A click on one of the tags brings up the virtual grave of the deceased (Figure 4.7), and a tab allows access to a presentation of the deceased and all his or her qualities and the events that marked his or her life. Another tab takes you to a page where there are up to ten photos of the deceased, at different ages. Finally, a third tab gives access to a page where it is possible to make virtual offerings: bunches of flowers, pieces of music, alcohols. No traditional offering such as paper money or even incense is on offer.

When the relatives make an online offering, they have the chance to leave a dated, written message and they have to specify their link to the deceased. These messages are often the moment to pass on family news, the health of family members, a birth announcement, a change in professional situation and so on. Some of them also describe the offerings that were burned on *Qingming* day – the Day of the Dead. The dates given at the top of the message show that most of the virtual offerings are made at times which would ordinarily have justified a visit to the grave: the Day of the Dead, winter solstice, anniversary of death or birth.

The little messages which accompany the virtual offerings and which often describe the ritual offerings made in the home prove that the traditional

Figure 4.7 A virtual grave (M. Bellocq, 2015).
Source: Author photo.

practice of burning votive papers still endures. The virtual grave has not necessarily driven out traditional practices and it even has a tendency to complement them. Gamba (2016: 54) defines the digital rituals as "parallel rituality". But in the case of the virtual cemetery set up online by the Shanghai municipality it is a question of both a substitute rituality, insofar as this cemetery has been created in order to replace material tombs, and a "parallel rituality" in that the rituals that should have been carried out at the grave are in fact done at home in their traditional form, while online it is a click on an icon.

However, the offerings rituals that the site proposes correspond to the aims of funerary reform insomuch as they control funerary practices and ancestor worship. Article 36 of the Regulation for the Management of Funerary Affairs (2018) stipulates that the manufacture and sale of "superstitious funerary objects" are forbidden.[32] Other documents circulating within the Shanghai funerary sector advise recourse to science and to the humanities for the reform of "funerary practices handed down over several millennia" (Gu et al. 2003: 3). The internet cemeteries are even presented as a way to progressively eliminate "bad traditional funerary habits" (Shanghai Binzang Wenhua Yanjiusuo nd: 449). On the Shanghai online cemetery, incense and votive articles usually represented in paper form and destined to be burned (money, house, car, etc.) are not included among the offerings proposed (Figure 4.8).

Figure 4.8 Traditional offerings made for the first anniversary of the death (M. Bellocq, 2015).
Source: Author photo.

92 *Maylis Bellocq*

The internet cemetery has allowed the funerary reform to progress in that it facilitates, in principle, the non-conservation of bodily remains indirectly and targets indirectly the funerary practices associated with ancestor worship and linked, according to the Chinese Communist Party's terminology, to "superstitions". Different texts published in the Report on Funeral Development of China (2014–2015 and 2016–2017) examine the issue of online offerings and underline the advantages that these have; they are simultaneously "civilized" (*wenming*), an expression used in opposition to any superstitions, and ecological insofar as they mean the practice of burning can be avoided as well as problems with traffic flows toward cemeteries during the festival of the Day of the Dead (Huang, 2015; Ma et al. 2017; Qi & Zhu 2017).

Nevertheless, a parallel can be made between the practices linked to ancestor worship in real life and those proposed on internet. In real practices, fire and smoke allow words and paper votive objects to be transmitted to the deceased. On internet, the click can be linked to the lighting of a flame which will allow messages and offerings to be transmitted to the departed on the other side, the world of the dead, the virtual worlds, in the *cloud,* which makes the distant stockage of data a periphery or margin of our computing equipment. As far as embodiments go, this seems to work. Moreover, some promoters of virtual cemeteries in China go so far as to evoke the "magic" of the mouse and the click when one makes an online offering as well as a digital existence which allows the dead to become immortal (Shanghai Binzang Wenhua Yanjiusuo nd: 447).

These new practices, which the Shanghai municipality is trying to spread, also enable a response to be made to the new ways of life marked by geographical mobility. This "second funerary revolution", which aims to push cemeteries further and further toward the fringes of the city and even beyond and which also seeks to combat certain habits and funerary practices, is also contributing to a renewal of rituals and perhaps also, as Gamba says (2016: 69), to "a dissolution of rituals in daily activities". The virtual cemetery in fact is accessible at any time from any place. Thus, by dint of being pushed further and further away, maybe the cemetery will end up occupying a central place despite its invisibilization.

Conclusion

The dynamics at work that we have been able to observe and which today characterize the cemeteries in Shanghai are inscribed in a historical continuity as described in the works of Henriot (2016). As was the case during the first half of the twentieth century, cemeteries are social markers. In fact, they display socio-spatial divisions generated by a commodification of space, similar to those in the central districts. The most "vulnerable" dead are often relegated to the least prestigious cemeteries and/or to the less desirable spaces within burial grounds, and it sometimes happens that there is no place for them.

The cemeteries of Shanghai have been pushed incessantly to the fringes of the city and henceforth it is a question of pushing them even further beyond these margins. In fact, the funerary authorities of the city are looking to promote the non-conservation of remains and to replace real graves with virtual tombs. So, is it not the case that cemeteries, which seemed destined to lose all kinds of visibility because of their dematerialization, are now going to occupy a kind of central place in that they will allow the deceased's loved ones easier access?

The hurdles to be overcome before the non-conservation of remains becomes generalized still seem to be of some importance. At first sight, this perspective may not seem very realistic or even reasonable. But there can be certain positive aspects when one thinks about the fact that

> digital tools liberate us from all physical constraints and considerably widen the users, the space and the time possible for rituals: computers, tablets, mobile phones … the cemetery is no longer the only and the necessary place for paying respect. (Le Breton 2016: 10)

Moreover, in the past, China has been in a position to set up unpopular reforms or laws in total opposition to Chinese traditions. For example, this has been the case with the generalized spread of cremation, whereas Confucian teaching tells that preserving the integrity of the body of one's parents is an act of filial piety. Another example is the one-child policy. So maybe one should not underestimate the country's ability, or at least the capacity of the Shanghai municipality, to see through the "second funerary revolution". The documents and reports produced by the funerary sector in China and in Shanghai reveal a firm determination to pursue the transformation or practices surrounding death and in particular methods of burial, but major obstacles still remain. In fact, as some figures show, the Shanghainese remained very attached to graves: on average, each year, 70% of the dead have their ashes interred in a grave and for 80% of them this has an area that is less than 1 m^2; 28% of the dead have their remains placed in columbariums or other forms of sepulchers which are economical in terms of land use, and the ashes of the remaining are scattered at sea (Zhou & Gao, 2017: 39). These figures bear witness to a certain development toward the miniaturization of graves which in the long term could lead to their disappearance. Also, a new argument has come to motivate the authorities' pursual of this marginalization of the remains of the dead: ecology. In the same way that a sanitary argument had been able to justify the rearrangement and the displacement of cemeteries in the municipality of Shanghai throughout the first half of the twentieth century, today graves which are undemanding in terms of land use and even disappearing in favor of the internet are being encouraged for ecological reasons. The recourse to virtual graves allows the land to be preserved when the ashes are scattered at sea and online commemorations are a way to limit road traffic toward the cemeteries at the time of Qing Ming and also the burning of paper offerings. Zhou & Gao (2017: 40) underline in the conclusion of their article, which appeared in the Report on Funeral Development of China (2016–2017), that here there are important factors in the reconfiguration of funerary activities in conformity with the standards of a world-class city like Shanghai.

94   Maylis Bellocq

In the long run, what will be the impacts of such a marginalization of the deceased and their remains? The answer probably lies in the hands of the young generations. Being hyper-connected they will doubtless be more likely to appropriate these new forms of rituals. Because of the easy accessibility of virtual cemeteries, will there be a new relation or even dialogue with the dead? Today internet rituals are practiced alongside traditional rituals but what will happen in the future? Will these be carried out in an individual way within a virtual community and no longer in a collective manner? These questions are becoming more salient since the urban development of Shanghai entails the disappearance of the little funerary shops which allow the Shanghainese to organize funerals and all of the rituals linked with death in a manner that conforms more or less to tradition and to certain beliefs.[33]

Notes

1 In 2010, 108,700 deaths were registered in Shanghai and 124,200 in 2015. www.stats-sh.gov.cn.
2 The burial of bodies is allowed only for Muslim minorities. There is a Muslim cemetery in the municipality (Hui).
3 On this topic Alain Brossat wrote:

> A cemetery is thus a place where the dead dwell and it is not peopled by cadavers. They are the dead that you can frequent, whose relations visit on the Day of the Dead or everyday – there are even visits made by those who suffer endlessly from their loss who come to talk, to confide their pains and their secrets- the 'living dead' therefore, in a kind of manner. (Brossat 2011: 126).

4 As Watson points out (1988: 8): "There is a considerable debate regarding the exact configuration of the soul, but most observers accept a dual (*hun* versus *po*) or tripartite (grave, domestic shrine, hall tablet) division".
5 As C. Henriot highlights, it was perhaps also an economical way of dealing with the remains.
6 The abandoning of children's bodies in public places could be explained by an ancient tradition whereby children who died before the age of ten were not buried. Their bodies were simply rolled up in a carpet or in paper and left by the side of the road on the outskirts of a village. These children were not considered as complete members of the family and they could even bring bad luck to their relatives. For these reasons, they were not buried with other family members.
7 One other famous dead person enjoys this privilege: Mao's embalmed remains lie in a mausoleum situated in the very heart of Beijing on Tiananmen Square.
8 Since the 1980s, with the relaxing of the fight against superstition, death rituals have returned, particularly in temples, at the cemetery, in the home of the deceased or the descendants, and even in funerary centers.
9 www.stats-sh.gov.cn.
10 http://finance.sina.com.cn/china/20140404/060918709389.shtml.
11 Article 16 of the Regulations for the Management of Shanghai Cemeteries (*Shanghai Shi Gongmu guanli banfa*) forbids the sale of individual graves with surface areas over 1.5 m^2 and double graves larger than 3 m^2. www.shanghai.gov.cn/shanghai/node2314/node2319/n31973/n32004/n32016/n32018/u21ai858089.shtml.
12 The cemetery can even constitute a margin in the very heart of the city because of its surrounding walls and the beliefs that are linked to it. It should be noted that today in Europe cemeteries have been absorbed by towns and as the suburbs seek to melt

Cemeteries in Shanghai: beyond the margins   95

into the urban landscape, the primary function of cemeteries is no longer discernible (Urbain: 168, 262). On this topic, see also the summary report into cemeteries that belong to the SIFUREP: www.sifurep.com/fileadmin/user_upload/internet/pdf/ bibliotheque/comptes_rendus/Document_APUR_SIFUREP.pdf
   This trend is to be found in the landscaped cemeteries of Shanghai.

13 This is the case, for example, in the cemeteries of Bao'an and Ming Yuan.

14 These agencies can be found almost everywhere in the city and particularly in the central districts notably close to or even inside the enclosure of the funerary centers.

15 Article 3 of the regulation for the management of cemeteries in Shanghai, www. shanghai.gov.cn/shanghai/node2314/node2319/n31973/n32004/n32016/ n32018/u21ai858089.shtml.

16 A figure put forward in an article, "The Economy of cemeteries means that the population cannot afford to die" (Mudi jingji, rang ren sibuqi), published in the review *Global People* (*Huanqiu Renwu*), http://paper.people.com.cn/hqrw/html/2011-12/16/content_981513.htm?div=-1.

17 See the article published in *The People's Daily*, 4 April 2014 "Only 133 Hectares Available for Graves. Shanghai Cemeteries are Facing a Land Availability Crisis" (*Shanghai ke yong mudi jin sheng 2000 mu, bufen gongmu xianru « wudi weiji »*). www.chinanews.com/gn/2014/04-04/6031104.shtml

18 I did not manage to obtain any clear information about what became of the displaced remains. Regarding cemeteries that have been displaced to rural zones, see the work of Béatrice David (1996, 2016).

19 Milan Kundera *Laughable Loves.*

20 Wang Wei is the deputy head of the Civil Affairs Bureau in Shanghai.

21 On the Chinese Communist Party's website an article has been published about the thoughts of Zhou Enlai on the topic of cremation and the non-conservation of remains. "The location and the significance of the scattering of ashes by Zhou Enlai". (Zhou Enlai guhui sanluo didian yu hanyi). http://dangshi.people.com. cn/n/2015/0921/c85037-27611288.html

22 The generalization over a fairly short space of the practice of cremating the dead time can in effect be considered as a revolution insofar as cremation constitutes an infringement of a Confucian precept that maintaining the integrity of the body of the deceased is as an act of filial piety for the descendants.

23 Funeral Interment Service establishment under the authority of the Civil Affairs Bureau. See Aveline (2012: 85–86).

24 See the articles *in The Paper* and *China News* on the issue: "In Shanghai it is only possible to scatter the ashes of the dead at sea during a three-month period and waiting time is about six months, on average" (*Shanghai mei nian jin san ge yue ke haizang pingjun dengdai shijian wei bannian zouyou*), http://sh.sina.com.cn/ news/m/2018-03-24/detail-ifysnevm6710224.shtml; "In Shanghai the ashes of more than 37,000 bodies were scattered at sea, a number that is rising every year" (Shanghai yu 3.7 wan ming shizhe « guhui sanhai » haizang zhanbi zhunian pansheng), www.sh.chinanews.com/spxw/2017-03-26/20494.shtml.

25 See the article by *Dongfan Zaobao* available online since December 2012 on the website of the Civil Affairs Bureau of Shanghai, "Shanghai increases its subsidies in response to difficulties encountered with sea graves", Shencheng tisheng butie huanjie haizang nanti » www.shmzj.gov.cn/gb/shmzj/node4/node13/node1562/u1ai34623.html; see also "In Shanghai it is only possible to scatter the ashes of the dead at sea during a three month period and waiting time is about six months, on average." (*Shanghai mei nian jin san ge yue ke haizang pingjun dengdai shijian wei bannian zouyou*), http:// sh.sina.com.cn/news/m/2018-03-24/detail-ifysnevm6710224.shtml.

26 At the end of a funeral ceremony which I had attended as an observer when I was accompanying one of my privileged interviewees, specialized in funeral organization,

96 *Maylis Bellocq*

the son of the deceased gave him a gratuity. To my great surprise he then turned to me in order to give me a banknote which, as a reflex, I tried to refuse. Then seeing my puzzlement, my interviewee explained that it was important that I accept because I had "given face" to the deceased's family.

27 See for example:

> We cannot afford to die! In Shanghai the price of a grave is 11 times higher than the price of real estate and ten years after death you have to keep paying' (2018) (si bu qi! Shanghai mudi bi fangjia gui 11 bei si hou shi nian yao xufei »), www.sohu. com/a/226821750_383591; "The dilemma of the funeral sector: how to resolve the problem of the lack of means for dying (2017) (*Binzangye "chuwang" kunju: ruhe jiejue "sibuqi"?*)

http://tech.ifeng.com/a/20170531/44628138_0.shtml; "Can the Chinese not Afford to Die?" (*Zhongguo ren si bu qi?*), www.cankaoxiaoxi.com/rui/sbq/

28 The costs for funeral services vary from one funeral home to another, from one cemetery to another.

29 These informers have a small shop selling funerary items and they offer a parallel funeral service ranging from help with declaring the death up to the purchase of the grave. They organize the rituals which take place in the home as well as the ceremony at the funeral parlor and that at the cemetery. They also supply all the articles necessary for the smooth running of the funeral, except for the coffin itself which is sold exclusively by the funeral centers.

30 *Face* is an extremely important concept in China. On this topic, David Yau-Fai Ho (1976: 867) wrote:

> While it is not a necessity for one to strive to gain face, losing face is a serious matter which will, in varying degrees, affect one's ability to function effectively in society. Face is lost when the individual, either through his action or that of people closely related to him, fails to meet essential requirements placed upon him by virtue of the social position he occupies.

31 "'virtual cemeteries'" and "online cemeteries" (2009) ("*Shangwan gongmu*" yu "*gongmu shangwang*"), www.wangzang.cn/Newsindex.asp?id=418.

32 www.law-lib.com/fzdt/newshtml/20/20180908094518.htm

33 The funerary shops in Shanghai will be the subject of a future article.

Works Cited

Ahern, E. M. (1973). *The Cult of the Dead in a Chinese Village*. Stanford: Stanford University Press.

Ariès, P. (1975). *Essais sur l'histoire de la mort en Occident du Moyen Âge à nos jours* (p. XX). Paris: Points Seuil.

Aveline-Dubach, N. (2012). The revival of the funeral industry in Shanghai: A model for China. In N. Aveline-Dubach (Ed.), *Invisible Population. The Place of the Dead in East Asian Megacities* (pp. 74–97). Lanham: Lexington Books.

Bourdeloie, H. (2015). Usages des dispositifs socionumériques et communication avec les morts. D'une reconfiguration des rites funéraires. *Question de communication*, 28, 101–126.

Brossat, A. (2011). Habiter sans vivre: Le cimetière comme hétérotopie. *Le sujet dans la cité*, 2(1), 121–129.

Cohen, M. L. (1988). Souls and salvation: Conflicting themes in Chinese popular religion. In J. L. Watson & E. S. Rawski (Eds.), *Death Ritual in Late Imperial and Modern China* (pp. 180–202). Berkeley: University of California Press.

David, B. (1996). L'évacuation des sites funéraires villageois. *Perspectives Chinoises*, 34, 30–37.

Douglas, M. (1992). *De la souillure. Études sur la notion de pollution et de tabou.1967.* Paris: La Découverte.

Fang, L., & Goossaert, V. (2008). Les réformes funéraires et la politique religieuse de l'État chinois, 1900–2008. *Archives de Sciences Sociales des Religions*, 144, 51–73.

Foucault, M. (2004). Des espaces autres. *Empan*, 54(2), 12–19.

Gamba, F. (2016). *Mémoire et immortalité au temps du numérique. L'enjeu de nouveaux rituels de commémoration.* Paris: L'Harmattan.

Georges, F. (2014). *Identité post mortem et nouvelles pratiques mémoriales en ligne. L'identité du créateur de la page mémoriale sur Facebook* (pp. 501–519). Quebec, Les Cahiers du Gerse.

Golberg, C. A. (2012). Robert Park's marginal man: The carrer of a concept in American sociology. *Laboratorium*, 4(2), 199–217.

Gu, J. (2004). Binzang Xisu Gaige Yao Yushi-Jujin. In J. Zhu (ed.), *Binzang Gaige he Wenhua jianshe Chutan* (pp. 308–313). Shanghai: Shanghai Daxue Chubanshe.

Gu, J., Qiao, K., & Zhou, S. (2003). *Gongmu Guanli Yanjiu Xin Lun*. Shanghai: Shanghai Daxue Chubanshe.

Hallam, E., Hockey, J., & Howarth, G. (1999). *Beyond the Body. Death and Social Identity*. London, New York: Routledge.

Henriot, C. (2009). 'Invisible Deaths, Silent Deaths': 'Bodies without Masters' in Republican China. *Journal of Social History*, 43(2), 407–437.

Henriot, C. (2016). *Scythe and the City. A Social History of Death in Shanghai*. Stanford: Stanford University Press.

Ho, D. Y. F. (1976). On the concept of face. *American Journal of Sociology*, 81(4), 867–884.

Huang, X. (2015). Wangluo jisi fazhan qushi yanjiu. In B. Li & C. Xiao (Eds.), *Zhonguo Binzang Shiye. Fazhan Baogao (2014–2015)* (pp. 269–279). Beijing, China: Social Sciences Academic Press.

Ma, L., Liu, Q., & Yan, T. (2017). 'Hulianwang + Binzang' de Shijian yu Shiyong. In B. Li & C. Xiao (Eds.), *ZhonguoBinzang Shiye. Fazhan Baogao (2016–2017)* (pp. 231–248). Beijing, China: Social Sciences Academic Press.

Qi, Y., & Zhu, J. (2017). Tuixing Wenming Jisao, Shijian Lüse Binzang. In B. Li & C. Xiao (Eds.), *Zhonguo Binzang Shiye. Fazhan Baogao (2016–2017)* (pp. 99–109). Beijing, China: Social Sciences Academic Press.

Shanghai Binzang Wenhua Yanjiusuo. (nd). *Ha'erbin Huangshan Gongmu*. Conference proceedings, Strategies for the Development of Cemeteries in the 21st century, recueil de contributions. Internal document.

Sierra, A., & Tadié, J. (2008). Introduction. *Autrepart*, 45(1), 3–13.

Thomas, L. V. (1991). *La mort en question. Traces de mort, mort des traces.* Paris: L'Harmattan.

Thomas, L. V. (1994). *Anthropologie de la mort.* Paris: Payot.

Thoraval, J. (2014). La mort en Chine. In M. Godelier (Ed.), *La mort et ses au-delà* (pp. 203–240). Paris: CNRS Éditions.

Urbain, J. D. (2005). *L'archipel des morts. Cimetières et mémoire en Occident.* Paris: Payot.

Wang, W. (2004). Zhanshi Gongzuo, Jiji Tuijin Binzang Xisu de 'Di-er Ci Geming'. In J. Zhu (Ed.), *Binzang Gaige he Wenhua jianshe Chutan* (pp. 352–355). Shanghai: Shanghai Daxue Chubanshe.

Watson, J. L. (1988). The structure of Chinese funerary rites: Elementary forms, ritual sequences, and the primacy of performance. In J. L. Watson & E. S. Rawski (Eds.),

Death Ritual in Late Imperial and Modern China (pp. 3–19). Berkeley: University of California Press.

Whyte, M. K. (1988). Death in the People's Republic of China. In J. L. Watson & E. S. Rawski (Eds.), *Death Ritual in Late Imperial and Modern China* (pp. 289–316). Berkeley: University of California Press.

Zhou, J., & Gao, J. (2017). Dali Tuixing Jiedi Shengtai Zang Shixian 'Yuantou' Jiedi. Laizi Shanghai de Baogao. In B. Li & C. Xiao (Eds.), *Zhongguo Binzang Shiye. Fazhan Baogao (2016–2017)* (pp. 27–40).Beijing, China: Social Sciences Academic Press.

Ziller, R. C., Stark, B. J., & Pruden, H. O. (1969). Marginality and integrative management positions. *The Academy of Management Journal*, 12(4), 487–495.

Part III
Margins in Hong Kong

5 "My community doesn't belong to me anymore!"

Tourism-driven spatial change and radicalized identity politics in Hong Kong

Alex Siu Kin Chan and Wing Chung Ho

When the British government handed over sovereignty of Hong Kong to China in 1997, it was thought that many mainlanders would naturally come to China's first SAR (Special Administrative Region) either through traveling or emigration. This had prompted the implementation of certain regulations which would ensure that post-handover Hong Kong maintained certain autonomous status in both letter and spirit (Mok & Dewald 1999: 36). In 1997, partly due to the Asian financial crisis, only 2.2 million mainlanders visited Hong Kong (compared to around 35 million in 2014). Inbound tourism suffered another serious blow in 2003 with the number of tourists dropping to 427,254 in May, which was equivalent to a 68% drop compared with that in May 2002. In that year, Hong Kong faced the outbreak of severe acute respiratory syndrome (SARS) that killed nearly 300 people.[1] Helping Hong Kong to emerge from the post-SARS economic downturn, Beijing enacted the Closer Economic Partnership Arrangement (CEPA) in late 2003, which was accompanied by multiple entry and individual visit schemes that allowed mainlanders to more easily visit Hong Kong. Such liberalization of visas for mainlanders to visit Hong Kong resulted in a quick rebound in tourism. In 2017, Hong Kong received more than 58.5 million visitors from all over the world (76.1% of whom were from the mainland), which was more than eight times that of Hong Kong's population.[2] During 2010–2014, more than 173 million mainland tourists visited the SAR (CEDB 2013; Tourism Commission 2017), with mainlanders accounting on average for more than three fourth of all tourists.

Hongkongers have long complained that Chinese tourists are *atypical* tourists who visit the metropolis not merely for sightseeing or souvenir shopping. Rather, they also come to give birth[3] and/or to buy luxurious real estate properties.[4] Another major source of complaints is that mainland tourists often make bulk purchases of certain products; hence, they compete with locals for daily necessities such as milk powder, diapers or food (Time 2013). The huge demand for everyday staples by mainlanders has seen the rapid growth of local and mainland parallel traders who flood communities near the border. They purchase goods in big batches and carry them across the border and sell them with markups (SCMP 2013). Both the tourists and parallel traders have caused

102 *Alex Siu Kin Chan and Wing Chung Ho*

congestion, and, on occasion, shortage of supplies for locals; more importantly, they have turned many local neighborhoods, which were used to support diverse daily living needs of dwellers, into business-oriented arenas that cater mainly to the shopping needs of the outsiders.

In early 2012, the problems related to Chinese tourism culminated in an open confrontation between Hongkongers and mainlanders. In January, there were demonstrations against the luxury chain Dolce & Gabbana due to the retailer's discrimination against local Hongkongers. The retailer was criticized for prohibiting locals from taking photographs in front of the outlet but allowing mainlander customers to do so (Garrett & Ho 2014: 351). During the same period, public anger against competition from mainlanders for hospital resources reached an extremely high level.[5] In fact, during 2011–2012, mainland mothers and also those married to Hong Kong men were said to have led to "the shortage of hospital beds and of pre- and post-natal medical care available for Hong Kong citizens" (Constable 2014: 179). Under these circumstances, a group of Hongkongers placed a full-page advertisement in *Apple Daily* on 1 February with the title "Hongkongers have had enough!" The advertisement depicted mainlanders as locusts hovering over Lion Rock – a cultural symbol of Hong Kong identity – and stated that the Hong Kong SAR government should revise the Basic Law – the mini-constitution of the SAR – to prevent more mainlanders from giving birth in Hong Kong. In mid-February, rallies and drivers' processions were launched against the Hong Kong SAR government's plan to permit mainland tourists from Guangdong province driving their cars into Hong Kong under an *ad hoc* quota. On 19 February, about 1,600 people joined a protest demanding the government to abolish the scheme (Oriental Daily 2012). Recently, the overloading of medical in-patient service in Hong Kong hospitals has spurred another round of localist public discontent against mainlanders with a slightly different focus on new Chinese immigrants. On 17 February 2019, hundreds of people, including local medical practitioners, rallied to call for the scrapping of the "one way permit scheme" under which 150 mainlanders are allowed to relocate to Hong King daily. Protesters believed that the surge in mainland migrants contributed to the overloaded Hong Kong medical system (SCMP 2019).

One should note that such "local first" sentiment had already bred an even more parochial strain of "my community first" protests back to the early 2010s. Specifically, in response to the cross-border parallel trade that had resulted in shortages of daily necessities in certain areas, a protest initiated by Facebook users was held in the MTR (rail) station of Sheung Shui – a near-border community – on 15 September 2012. The protest wanted to get rid of cross-border traders with the slogan "Reclaim Sheung Shui! Protect our homes!" (SCMP 2012b). Even though new restrictions on the export of milk powder have been imposed since 2013, half of pharmacies in many areas of northern Hong Kong in 2015 still faced a serious shortage of the product.[6] The increasingly intense conflicts between Hong Kong and China reached a head in 2015. From February to March 2015, protests against mainlanders with the initiative of "my community first" spread from Sheung Shui to other shopping destinations for mainland visitors: Tuen Mun, Sha Tin, Yuen Long and Tsuen Wan. Protesters surrounded mainland-*looking* shoppers, "verbally insulted them and even kicked their luggage" (Kwong 2016: 430). In these incidents, a number of protesters who attacked shoppers and/or clashed with police were arrested and charged with disorderly conduct in a public place. In response, supporters of the regime and the establishment sought to frame the protests against mainlander tourism as criminal, fascist, xenophobic and contradictory to the "one country" concept stated in the Basic Law (Garrett 2017).

Recent scholarly studies have suggested that the post-2012 localist protests against mainlanders have spawned a particular kind of identity politics due to the fear among Hongkongers that integration with China would jeopardize Hong Kong's unique identity and way of life (Kwong 2016; Garrett 2017; Ho & Tran 2019). Statistics also indicate that more and more Hong Kong people tend to identify themselves more as "Hongkongers" than as "Chinese" since 2010 (Figure 5.1). The identity politics that involve the "Hongkonger vs. mainlander" and "Hongkonger vs. Chinese" oppositions had also been constituted and fueled by the political struggles during the same period concerning demands that Beijing let Hong Kong have universal suffrage. These pro-democratic struggles culminated in the civil disobedience movement of Occupy Central (also known as the Umbrella Movement), which took place in Hong Kong between September 26 and December 15, 2014. The movement failed to achieve its goal as Beijing, and its associated political and business elites still hold firm control over Hong Kong's political development (Chan 2015; Ortmann 2015).

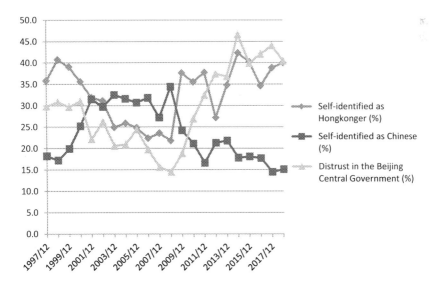

Figure 5.1 Hong Kong identity, 1997–2018.
Source: Public Opinion Programme, University of Hong Kong.

104 *Alex Siu Kin Chan and Wing Chung Ho*

As suggested, while some studies have examined the identity politics that emerged with the Hong Kong-China conflict since the early 2010s, no attention has been paid in understanding how the "local first" or "my community first" localist movement was related to the spatial change in the community, and in which way this change has fueled the formation of radicalized identity politics between "Hongkonger" and "Chinese" among Hong Kong residents, especially the younger generation. This study aims to fill this knowledge gap. Specifically, this study aims to examine the tourism-driven changes between 2011 and 2017 in three communities heavily affected by the presence of mainland tourists and parallel traders, namely, Sheung Shui, Tuen Mun and Yuen Long. These community changes are captured and measured through the systematic visual tracing of changing street views in the community with the innovative use of Google Maps. To supplement this visual analysis, 26 young residents (aged 18–34) in the three communities are interviewed to express their own views on the changing community landscape. Emphasis will be placed on how their perceived local changes are associated with the emergence of radicalized identity politics in wider society.

Methodology

Google mapping Google Maps currently provides a free web-based mapping service which allows users to enjoy panoramic, photographic street views of specific sites. The convenience of capturing urban landscapes at the street level at a specific time point contribute to specific sets of visual data that can be subject to systematic analysis. In this study, in order to capture and even measure the community changes due to the influence of tourism and parallel trading, we collected street view images of selected streets in three Hong Kong communities – namely, Sheung Shui, Tuen Mun and Yuen Long – which reported suffering from the presence of large numbers of mainland tourists and parallel traders. In 2017, the street view images from Google Maps were said to be those captured in 2011. We sent our assistants to go the same selected streets in 2017 and took photographs of shops. We then compared the photographs captured from Google Maps (2011) and taken from our onsite visits so we could identify and analyze the differences in longitudinal community landscape in terms of how street conditions and shop layouts have changed between 2011 and 2017. We call this innovative methodology "Google mapping".

Interview

The testimonies of young residents living in the three communities were solicited through in-depth interview in October 2018 and March 2019. Their narratives feature their experiences of the changes of their community in the past decade or so, and also their comments on the street view changes between 2011 and 2017 derived from the Google mapping analysis mentioned above. Interviews were conducted in a semi-structured manner and usually began with the question: "What changes in your community can you identify during the past decade or so?" The informants' replies were then followed up by questions which could be grouped into two broad categories: (i) What kind of personal experiences/stories do you have connected with these changes? Are they positive or negative? and (ii) How have these experiences/stories shaped/influenced your view of community life (e.g., views on mainland tourism and parallel trading), and toward the more macro political-economic-social environments (e.g., views on the intensifying Hong Kong-China conflict and emerging localism)? Interviews were mainly conducted in cafés, restaurants or social service centers in the community. Only two interviews were conducted via telephone. The duration of interviews ranged from 30 minutes to 1.5 hours. All interviews were audio-recorded with the consent of the informants.

Community

As mentioned before, three border communities – Sheung Shui, Tuen Mun and Yuen Long –were studied. The reasons that these communities were chosen included: (i) there were reports of residents' complaints about the massive influx of mainland tourists and parallel traders; (ii) there were localist protests reported during 2012–2015; and (iii) these three communities retain to a large extent the outlook of Hong Kong's traditional market-based communities such that street-level shops, rather than high-rise shopping malls, are still highly vibrant and popular among consumers. The vibrancy and popularity of street-level shops was the key point for adopting the methodology of Google mapping which only captures changes at the ground level.

Specifically, two or three street sections in each community were chosen for Google mapping analysis. These street sections were chosen because they were commonly considered by locals as "old", or "used-to-be" vibrant" shopping streets for local residents. The information of the chosen street sections are summarized in Table 5.1; their maps are indicated in Figures 5.2–5.5.

Table 5.1 Community, street sections and number of shops involved in Google mapping

Community	Street section	Number of shops (year)
Sheung Shui	San Hong Street & Lung Sum Avenue (Figure 5.3)	153 (2011) 143 (2017)
Tuen Mun	Yan Ching Street & Tak Ching Court (Figure 5.4)	77 (2011) 74 (2017)
Yuen Long	Tong Lok Street, Sau Fu Street, & Castle Peak Road (Figure 5.5)	228 (2011) 217 (2017)

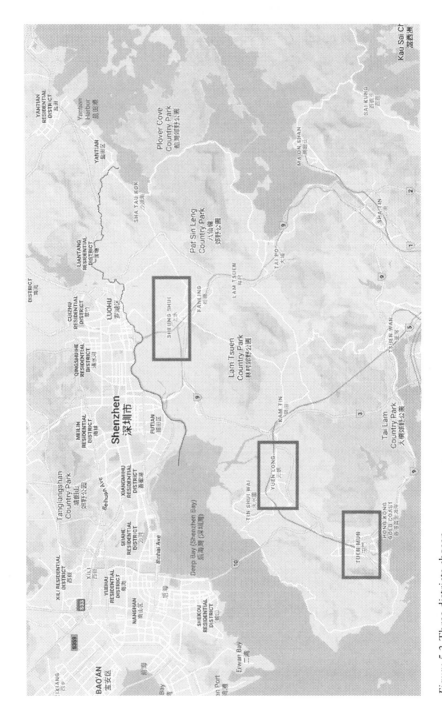

Figure 5.2 Three districts chosen.
Source: Author photo.

"My community doesn't belong to me" 107

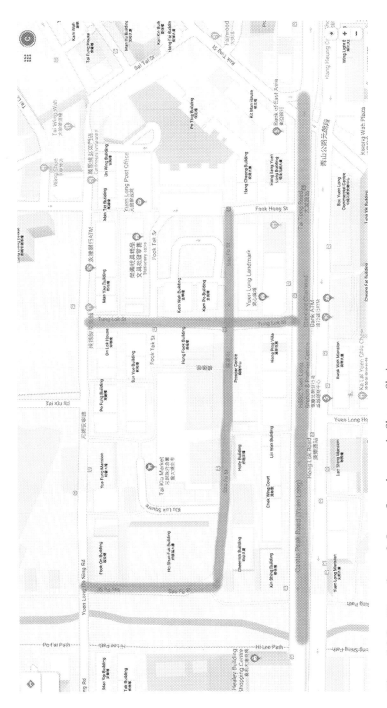

Figure 5.3 San Hong Street & Lung Sum Avenue, in Sheung Shui.
Source: Author photo.

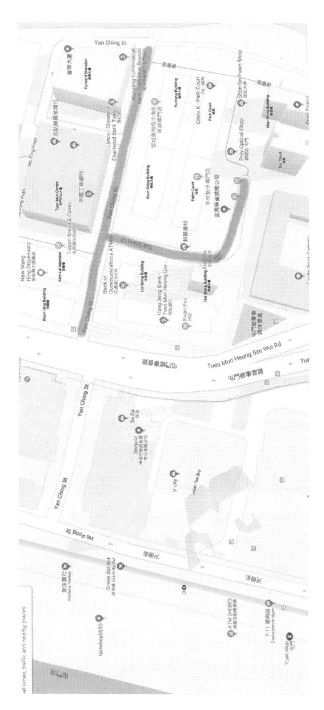

Figure 5.4 Yan Ching Street & Tak Ching Court, in Tuen Mun.
Source: Author photo.

"My community doesn't belong to me" 109

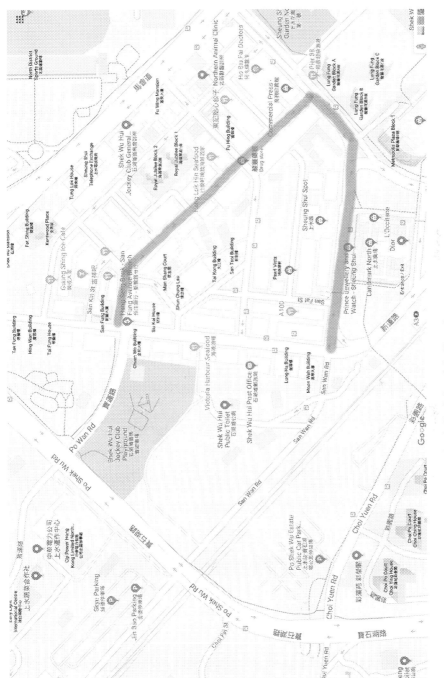

Figure 5.5 Tong Lok Street, Sau Fu Street & Castle Peak Road, in Yuen Long.
Source: Author photo.

Participants

Our original plan was to recruit local-born Hongkongers who have/had been living in the three communities for at least ten years. The localist movements mainly involved young people; therefore, one of the criteria for inclusion in the study was that informants must be aged between 18 and 34. Consequently, 25 residents with ages ranging from 20 to 34 were successfully interviewed. One informant from Sheung Shui (informant#6), who was aged 43, was also considered as a legitimate informant in subsequent analysis because he was an activist in organizing anti-parallel traders in the community. The narratives solicited from these 26 informants constitute the interview database that informs subsequent analyses.

The first few informants were recruited through the authors' personal and professional networks. Subsequent informants were recruited through personal referrals of the initial informants. The profile of the 26 informants are summarized in Table 5.2.

Analysis

The interview data requires a conceptual frame to attain intellectual and scientific rigor. In order to address the informants' narratives which necessarily touch

Table 5.2 Profile of informants

Informant	Age	Gender	Educational level	Community	Length of stay
Informant#1	31	Female	Associate degree	Sheung Shui	24 years
Informant#2	34	Male	High diploma	Sheung Shui	22 years
Informant#3	30	Male	Diploma	Sheung Shui	30 years
Informant#4	32	Male	High diploma	Sheung Shui	20 years
Informant#5	27	Male	Diploma	Sheung Shui	15 years
Informant#6[a]	43	Male	High diploma	Sheung Shui	14 years
Informant#7	20	Male	High diploma	Sheung Shui	20 years
Informant#8	33	Male	High diploma	Sheung Shui	33 years
Informant#9	31	Male	Bachelor	Sheung Shui	29 years
Informant#10	31	Female	Diploma	Tuen Mun	12 years (during 1991–2003)
Informant#11	28	Female	High diploma	Tuen Mun	28 years
Informant#12	30	Male	Master	Tuen Mun	30 years
Informant#13	25	Female	High diploma	Tuen Mun	15 years
Informant#14	29	Male	Diploma	Tuen Mun	14 years
Informant#15	22	Female	High diploma	Tuen Mun	16 years
Informant#16	33	Male	Master	Tuen Mun	33 years
Informant#17	26	Male	Bachelor	Tuen Mun	24 years
Informant#18	25	Male	Bachelor	Tuen Mun	16 years
Informant#19	31	Male	High diploma	Tuen Mun	31 years
Informant#20	24	Female	Secondary School Form 6	Yuen Long	19 years
Informant#21	20	Female	Associate degree	Yuen Long	20 years
Informant#22	23	Female	Secondary School Form 6	Yuen Long	11 years
Informant#23	24	Male	High diploma	Yuen Long	10 years
Informant#24	26	Male	Diploma	Yuen Long	14 years
Informant#25	30	Female	Bachelor	Yuen Long	30 years
Informant#26	30	Male	PhD candidate	Yuen Long	30 years

a Activist in localist movement since 2013.

upon their experiences of the changing social structures, we decided to adopt William Sewell Jr's well-known definition of social structures which is:

> composed simultaneously of cultural schemas, distributions of resources, and modes of power. Cultural schemas provides with meanings, motivations, and recipes for social action. Resources provide them (differentially) with the means and stakes of action. Modes of power regulate action – by specifying what schemas are legitimate, by determining which persons and groups have access to which resources, and by adjudicating conflicts that arise in the course of action. We can speak of structures when sets of cultural schemas, distributions of resources, and modes of power combine in an interlocking and mutually sustaining fashion to reproduce consistent streams of social practice. (Sewell 1996: 842)

Inherent in this definition is that social structures are composed of the interlocking dimensions of "distributions of resources", "cultural schemas" and "modes of power". We consider that Sewell's three-dimensional frame is of particular utility for us to make sense of the interview data as the informants' testimonies necessarily touch upon the reconfigurations of physical space and material structure (*resources*), their values and feelings attached to these reconfigurations (*cultural schemas*, or, simply, *values*), and how these feelings are related to the power structure of the society (*modes of power*, or, simply, *power*). We assume that the use of Sewell's frame better demonstrates how the actors' experiences in specific contexts represent the complex intertwining among these three elements.

Tourism-driven spatial change

As mentioned before, the degree of spatial change in the community is estimated and measured by the change of shops at the ground level of selected street sections. To facilitate estimation and measurement, shops are categorized into 11 basic types, namely: (1) medicines & cosmetics; (2) jewelry, watches, clocks & valuable gifts; (3) books, newspapers, stationery & gifts; (4) food, drinks & tobacco; (5) Chinese medicines & herbs; (6) furniture & fixtures; (7) electrical goods & photographic equipment; (8) clothing & footwear; (9) real estate agents; (10) shopping centers; (11) others, elsewhere specified. Types (1) to (9) can be further bifurcated into "chain store" or "independent" type of shop with the "chain-store" type having at least five branch shops anywhere else in Hong Kong. These 20 shop types thus constitute the basic categories for further analysis.

Based on the findings derived from Google mapping, Sheung Shui features the most substantial street view changes with nine types of shops entailing a major increase/decrease ($\geq$ or $\leq$45%); which was followed by Tuen Mun (six types) and Yuen Long (four types) (see Tables 5.3–5.5). In Sheung Shui, the community landscape is mainly shaped by the gigantic surge in the number of "medicines & cosmetics" shops from 13 to 43 (231%), the newly opened "shopping center" (from none to one) and the disappearance of three shop types, namely: "electrical goods & photographic equipment", "furniture & fixtures" and "real estate agents" – all drop from two shops to zero. In Tuen Mun, the community landscape is shaped by the surge in "medicines & cosmetics" shops from six to nine (50%), and newly introduced "real estate agent" shops from none to three (300%). The only shop which used to sell "Chinese medicines & herbs" in 2011 disappeared in 2017. In Yuen Long, like the other two communities, the number of "medicines & cosmetics" shops shows a major rise from 22 to 40 (82%). But, unlike other communities, Yuen Long's community landscape is also shaped by a major increase of "jewelry, watches, clocks & valuable gifts" shops from 9 to 14 (56%) which seem to be in demand to cater to the increasing number of high-end tourist customers.

While shop changes in the three communities possess certain unique patterns, "medicines & cosmetics" shops show a major increase in *all* three communities (Sheung Shui: 231%; Tuen Mun: 50%; Yuen Long: 82%). Independent "furniture & fixtures" shops show a common major drop in *all* three communities (Sheung Shui: 100%; Tuen Mun: 50%; Yuen Long: 50%). These common patterns generally confirm that mainland tourism and parallel trading are the key driving forces behind the community change as "medicines & cosmetics" shops are highly popular among mainland tourists and parallel traders for bulk purchases of milk powder, diapers and other personal hygiene products whereas "furniture & fixtures" shops mainly serve local residents.

One should note that the community landscape of Sheung Shui does not only show the most substantial change than that of the two communities, but also experienced the highest degree of *homogenization* between 2011 and 2017. This is because Sheung Shui features more of a major increase of shops of the

Table 5.3 Major change of shops types (≥ or ≤45%) in San Hong Street and Lung Sum Avenue, Sheung Shui

Types of shop	No. of shops in 2011	No. of shops in 2017	Difference	Change
Chinese medicines & herbs (chain store)	0	3	+3	+300%
Medicines & cosmetics (chain store)	3	10	+7	+233%
Medicines & cosmetics (independent)	10	33	+23	+230%
Food, drinks & tobacco (chain store)	1	3	+2	+200%
Shopping center	0	1	+1	+100%
Clothing & footwear (chain store)	0	1	+1	+100%
Electrical goods & photographic equipment (independent)	2	0	−2	−200%
Furniture & fixtures (independent)	2	0	−2	−100%
Real estate agent (independent)	2	0	−2	−100%

Note: Non-major change shop types include: "books, newspapers, stationery & gifts (independent)": 3 to 4 (−25%); "clothing & footwear (independent)": 21 to 16 (−24%); "food, drinks & tobacco (independent)": 26 to 22 (−15%); "Chinese medicines & herbs (independent)": 17 to 15 (−12%); "jewelry, watches, clocks & valuable gifts (independent)": 9 to 8 (−11%). For "others, elsewhere specified", shops change from 46 to 23 (−50%). Empty shops change from 4 to 2 (−50%).

"My community doesn't belong to me" 113

Table 5.4 Major change of shops types (≥ or ≤45%) in Yan Ching Street and Tak Ching Court, Tuen Mun

Types of shop	No. of shops in 2011	No. of shops in 2017	Difference	Change
Real estate agent (chain store)	0	3	+3	+300%
Food, drinks & tobacco (chain store)	0	2	+2	+200%
Medicines & cosmetics (independent)	6	9	+3	+50%
Clothing & footwear (independent)	2	3	+1	+50%
Chinese medicines & herbs (independent)	1	0	–1	–100%
Furniture & fixtures (independent)	14	7	–7	–50%

Note: Non-major change shop types include: "food, drinks & tobacco (independent)": 14 to 8 (–43%). For "others, elsewhere specified", shops change from 28 to 32 (+14.3%). Empty shops change from 0 to 1 (+100%).

Table 5.5 Major change of shops types (≥ or ≤45%) in Tong Lok Street, Sau Fu Street and Castle Peak Road; Yuen Long

Types of shop	No. of shops in 2011	No. of shops in 2017	Difference	Change
Medicines & cosmetics (independent)	22	40	+18	+82%
Jewelry, watches, clocks, & valuable gifts (independent)	9	14	+5	+56%
Furniture & fixtures (independent)	8	4	–4	–50%
Electrical goods & photographic equipment (independent)	11	6	–5	–45%

Note: Non-major change shop types include: "books, newspapers, stationery & gifts (independent)": 6 to 8 (+33%); "food, drinks & tobacco (chain store)": 5 to 6 (+20%); "Chinese medicines & herbs (independent)": 7 to 8 (+14%); "clothing & footwear (independent)": 60 to 40 (–33%); "food, drinks & tobacco (independent)": 25 to 18 (–28%). For "others, elsewhere specified", shops change from 8 to 10 (+25%). Empty shops change from 2 to 4 (+100%).

"chain-store" type and more of a major drop in "independent" shops than in Tuen Mun and Yuen Long. Specifically, in Sheung Shui, four "chain-store" types of shops feature a major increase (i.e., 300% in "Chinese medicines & herbs"; 233% in "medicines & cosmetics"; 200% in "food, drinks, & tobacco", and 100% in "clothing & footwear"); and three "independent" shop types feature a major drop (i.e., 200% in "electrical goods & photographic equipment"; 100% in "furniture & fixtures"; and 100% in "real estate agents"). In Tuen Mun, two "chain-store" types of shops feature a major increase (i.e., 300% in "real estate agents"; 200% in "food, drinks & tobacco") and two "independent" shop types feature a major reduction (100% in "Chinese medicines & herbs"; 50% in "furniture & fixtures") As in Yuen Long, no major increase in shop type belongs to chain stores; the two "independent" shop types which feature a major drop are "furniture & fixtures" (50%) and "electrical goods & photographic equipment" (45%).

114   *Alex Siu Kin Chan and Wing Chung Ho*

Narrating spatial experience

Interviews with the informants began with soliciting their views and feelings about the landscape changes in *their* community over the past decade. Since interviews always began with the topic of spatial change, their narratives inevitably were filled with stories associated with the resource dimension, which included the themes of "crowdedness", "product variety" and "cost of living".

Resource

Crowdedness seems to the most direct consequence of the presence of massive numbers of tourists and parallel traders in the communities. Informants generally conveyed negative sentiments toward the overloading of the already small street space; for example, what two informants said about Yuen Long were highly typical among informants on this theme:

> The streets are too crowded for walking, but they weren't in the years before. Now, people always bump into me. (Informant#23, Yuen Long)
>
> Because the streets in Yuen Long are very narrow, it was already difficult for one-way pedestrian flow, and now there are so many people on the streets. I think it's very inconvenient having to dodge right and left just to move forward. It's a major inconvenience caused by tourists. Yuen Long isn't large, but in recent years, there are more people and more stores, and you'd think that the road is getting narrower. (Informant#24, Yuen Long)

One should note that informants generally confirmed the results of our Google mapping analysis when we presented this to them such that they unanimously acknowledged the disproportionate increase in the number of "medicines & cosmetics" shops in their community, and in some cases, they lamented the disappearance of old shops with unique local flavor; for example, an informant from Sheung Shui complained:

> The giant pharmacy [i.e., the ubiquitous Lung Fung Group, which has a monopoly on pharmaceuticals in Sheung Shui] opened three years ago and its presence has changed the entire landscape of the street. A snake soup restaurant, which was once next to the shoe shop, was evicted to make way for a Lung Fung pharmacy. (Informant#1, Sheung Shui)

Two informants from Yuen Long reported inconvenience for locals in buying daily essentials due to the change in shop profile, and, by association, product variety in the community:

> I think that the gap is very large and unrealistic, because those stores don't meet our needs. I have to pass by two or three streets just to buy goods for everyday needs. In the past, I purchased those goods downstairs in my

"*My community doesn't belong to me*"   115

building. It was very close. Now, I think that my basic needs aren't so easily satisfied. Even if I want something as simple as fish balls, I can't easily eat them because I can't find any local street snack vendors. There are only pharmacies now. (Informant#21, Yuen Long)

As a resident of Yuen Long, the situation really affects me. For instance, it's now difficult just to buy snacks from somewhere nearby. (Informant#22, Yuen Long)

While many informants reported inconvenience in everyday purchases and homogenization of the community landscape, around one third of informants – mainly from Tuen Mun and Yuen Long – reported convenience in shopping, and even creativity in the community in juxtaposition with the tourism-driven changes; the testimonies of the following three informants explicitly pointed to these features:

When I need to take a rest without buying anything, I can sit at McDonald's. It's good that there are many shopping centres so that we can do shopping without getting wet when it's raining, since they are connected by bridges, as you can tell. (Informant#11, Tuen Mun)

Now, there are more chain shops, and the things sold in them have changed. There are shops like "Bestmart360" and stores with pirated Korean products. I think that they've brought some benefits to the local community, since the goods that they sell are relatively cheap, so I shop there too. Also, after the opening of the new stores, I don't have to travel a long way to other districts like Mong Kok or go to a large shopping mall like Tuen Mun Town Plaza to buy branded products like soccer boots. Now I can find a large variety of sporting goods and equipment on the streets of Yuen Long. (Informant#20, Yuen Long)

Empty shops are now being reopened with creative businesses. Far from taking the community backwards, the area is starting to emerge and flourish. The district is now being reborn all over again. It gives me more choice when I want to find restaurants that are not of local style. (Informant#13, Tuen Mun)

Another commonly mentioned theme was the cost of living. Many informants complained about the rising living costs in the community – especially in Sheung Shui and Tuen Mun – as the market seemed to be increasingly geared toward the wealthier mainland tourists and profit-seeking parallel traders rather than local inhabitants; for example, informants revealed:

A bowl of noodles that used to sell for slightly more than HK$10 now costs HK$20. I never eat out any more because the price of everything has skyrocketed. [...] Some new restaurants have emerged to fill the void created by the closure of existing eateries, although most are too expensive for local residents. Altogether, the communities have become much more tourist oriented. (Informant#1, Sheung Shui)

116 *Alex Siu Kin Chan and Wing Chung Ho*

The number of small independent shops and restaurants has declined perceptibly, while consumer prices and commercial rents have risen significantly, all of which has benefitted only large shopping malls and high-end shops. (Informant#2, Sheung Shui)

Ten plus years ago, Tuen Mun was in its heyday. There was a community, great affordable food, and everyone fit in. Now I have to get up at 8 am on a Saturday to avoid the stupid queues to get a bowl of congee at my local. (Informant#18, Tuen Mun)

However, a small number of informants – especially in Yuen Long – suggested that the goods sold in the new shops were inexpensive which could bring about a positive impact on the local economy; for example, an informant from Yuen Long said:

I think that they [i.e., tourists from mainland China] have brought some benefits to our communities, since the goods sold in the new shops are relatively cheap, and I go there to shop, too. They promote economic growth in Hong Kong. I think that it's very good. (Informant#24, Yuen Long)

While all informants began to narrate their experiences with their community in association with different themes along the resource dimension, they might proceed to other themes in relation to values or power dimension. The values dimension touches upon those themes related to the changing social norms in the community, including what were accepted as *normal* behavior, language use and community vibe, whereas the power dimension touches upon those themes related to the domination of the outsiders and the loss of autonomy on the part of locals in controlling present and future development of the community. We note that some informants might progress from the discourse of resources to that of values, and that some might progress from the discourse of resources to that of power. For example, an informant from Tuen Mun considered the tourism-driven spatial changes in the community had led to the impolite behavior – unacceptable behavioral norms – on the part of tourists which had lowered the quality of life of locals; he said:

Undeniably, they [i.e., mainland tourists] have given us many economic benefits, but normal residents like me haven't received any of that. On the contrary, their behaviour influences our quality of life. (Informant#14, Tuen Mun)

As for the shifting of discourse from that of resources to power with the implication that the outsiders seemed to be more catered to than the locals, the following two informants' testimonies offer two exemplar cases:

Stores that have survived, including pharmacies and jewelry stores, predominantly cater to mainlanders and parallel traders, who's growing numbers have transformed the structure of the market, which has resulted in higher prices for consumers. [...] I use the term "a shopping paradise for Chinese tourists" to describe Sheung Shui nowadays because there are many pharmacies and other types of shops catering to Chinese tourists. (Informant#1, Sheung Shui)

Half of the patients at my community family clinic are mainlanders. They are here for vaccinations and to see the doctors. So now the waiting time has become 1.5–2 hours. Last time when I was there, I also noticed that some of them are even from the Northern provinces of China. (Informant#30, Yuen Long)

Specifically, the informants' narratives along the dimension of values mainly touched upon two themes, namely, users' behavior and community vibe; and the their narratives along the dimension of power mainly touched upon the themes of alienation and Hong Kong-China conflict. These themes will be examined subsequently below.

Values

The "unusual" behavior of mainland tourists and parallel traders very often constituted part of the informants' experience of spatial change in their community. Complaints about the behavior of these outsiders were usually due to their "poor manners", "bad hygiene" and "bulk-buy-and-then-go" shopping pattern which were considered unusual to locals' understanding of what "good tourists" or normal shoppers should be. The following quotes captured well this sentiment:

Chinese tourists are not "good tourists" with good manners, and they have bad hygiene. I wouldn't say that I hate them, but I do have negative feelings toward them. I don't know why many of them misbehave: spitting and defecating on the street, talking loudly. (Informant#13, Tuen Mun)

They [i.e., the tourists and parallel traders] are always carrying their luggage when they walk around, and they often crash into me and that annoys me. (Informant#22, Yuen Long)

The self-proclaimed "tourists" are not genuine tourists. They come here for their job or business. They either smuggle or resell the goods they bought to make a profit and to make a living. They do not stay overnight or have expenses on food or accommodation. (Informant#8, Sheung Shui)

These outsiders' usual behavior did not only directly antagonize the residents, but – owing to the high purchasing power of tourists and parallel traders – indirectly caused local shops to become less willing to serve locals than before; for example,

In the past, when I entered stores, the staff would chat with me and greet me. Sometimes, I went with my grandma, and the shop owners would

118 *Alex Siu Kin Chan and Wing Chung Ho*

recognise her and say hello to us. However, something's changed now. Although the stores are the same, the owners no longer chat with me. All of the local customers feel the same. They [i.e., shop owners] only hope that we leave quickly after buying the goods we need because they don't want us to disturb their business with the mainland tourists who are buying in bulk. (Informant#11, Tuen Mun)

The shopkeepers don't treat me as friendly as they treat mainlanders at the stores that catered to them, as Hongkongers generally don't buy as much as mainlanders do. (Informant#25, Yuen Long)

In juxtaposition with the change in users' behavior are feelings of change of the original community environment and interpersonal relationships. For example, Informant#25 from Yuen Long noted that alongside the change in attitude of local shops to local residents came the shift of language use in the community; she said:

Many announcements are made in Cantonese [mother tongue of most Hong-kongers], Putonghua, and English nowadays to cater to the mainlanders, though the office language in Hong Kong are Chinese and English. It should now be Cantonese, English and Putonghua. Simplified Chinese and mainland terms are also widely used in my community. (Informant#25, Yuen Long)

The concerns of the change of community vibe such as the former warm hospitality among local residents and shop owners had been sharply reduced; for example, an informant said:

When you go for a meal in a small restaurant, you can chat with the staff. In chain restaurants, the staff won't chat with you. They serve you because they want your money. Also, when you enter a small shop, they might smile at you, whereas in chain shops, the workers just want to earn a living. The owners of small shops don't aim only at running a business, they want to make connections. Those kinds of stores have become fewer and fewer. (Informant#15, Tuen Mun)

Power

To many informants, the abovementioned changes in community vibe and original lifestyle were followed by the discourses of power such that they feel increasingly alienated (feeling estranged by the tourists and parallel traders) and marginalized (feeling subordinate to mainlanders) in *their* community. Testimonies of informants along this line utilized terms such as feeling "estranged from the community", lack of a "sense of community" or that the community does not "belong to me anymore":

Everything has changed. I'm mad as hell. The community has been ruined. I feel estranged from the community in which my family chose to live, and

"My community doesn't belong to me" 119

a bit scared that I'll never again find a place where I can feel comfortable. (Informant#1, Sheung Shui)

There is no sense of community about the experience of "going to the shops" where you might stop and chat to someone. I have to admit that it is a faceless, lonely experience. But I must emphasize that Hong Kong people never have had a sense of belonging. I don't think it's related to community change or Chinese tourists. (Informant#18, Tuen Mun)

I've started feeling like a stranger in Tuen Mun. Ten years ago, there weren't many mainlanders in my community. After 2003, with the liberalization of the individual visit scheme, conditions have changed a lot. I don't think that the community belongs to me anymore. (Informant#12, Tuen Mun)

Feeling alienated by what had changed apart, informants who tended to make sense of the community change in terms of the undercurrents of modes of power also expressed that Hongkongers had been relegated to "second class" and that the spatial change symbolized the consolidation of the mainland's authority over Hong Kong; for example:

I feel like Hongkongers have become a second-class group compared to mainlanders in Hong Kong. Even though Hongkongers work hard, they can't have the living environment they deserve. Now even the shops are catering to other people [mainlanders]. I'm quite disappointed. (Informant#25, Yuen Long)

Resentment of the growing number of tourists from mainland China could have partly stemmed from the idea that the increased mobility of tourists is designed to consolidate the authority of the mainland over Hong Kong. The simple issue of tourist inflows has assumed political overtones and resulted in protests and tension between Hong Kong and the mainland. (Informant#5, Sheung Shui)

Some informants – in particular those from Sheung Shui where the tourism-driven changes had been most conspicuous – even associated the spatial changes in the community to the wider political trends of Hong Kong-China integration, Hong Kong-China conflict and "mainlandization" such that the identity politics between "Hongkonger" and "Chinese" (or "mainlander") was played out in an oppositional manner; for example:

As the mainland relentlessly pursues integration with Hong Kong, locals worry about preserving the identity of their city, which they deem to differ starkly from that of the mainland, as well their personal identities as Hongkongers, which they believe stand in sharp contrast to those of mainlanders. (Informant#2, Sheung Shui)

In current China-Hong Kong relations, the mainland is clearly the big brother who makes decisions and formulates policies, and China's dominance has therefore become symbolised by streets swarming with visitors from the mainland. In a sense, resentment against the tourists is resentment against social and political integration with mainland China. (Informant#4, Sheung Shui)

It comes down to the number of people from mainland China and their distribution. For example, many parts of Hong Kong Island still maintain their unique characteristics, while the communities closer to the China border cannot handle the influx and have become mainlandized, which has severely affected the living quality of the local residents of those communities. (Informant#25, Yuen Long)

One particular resident from Sheung Shui cogently underscored the increasingly radicalized identity politics such that he felt stigmatized to be "Chinese"; he said:

Being Chinese is a stigma. We want to have our own unique identity separate from it. We need to put spotlight on our local [i.e., Hong Kong] identity to shadow this stigmatised identity. If China is a country its nationals can be proud of, I think more people in Hong Kong would be happy to have the Chinese identity in front of the Hong Kong identity. (Informant#7, Sheung Shui)

From estranged space to radicalized politics

Based on the themes explicitly mentioned in the informants' narratives, we identified a pattern that the more the community has changed due to mainland tourists and parallel traders, the more likely the informants touch upon the dimension of power – namely, the "alienation" and "Hong Kong-China relation" – *and* always endow a negative sentiment toward it. Table 5.6 suggests that informants from Sheung Shui – which has encountered more tourism-driven changes than the other two communities in the Google mapping analysis – are more likely to *politicize their spatial experiences* in the community than those from the other two communities.

Table 5.6 Informants and the dimensions their narratives touched upon during the interview

	Resource	*Values*	*Power*
Sheung Shui	#1, #2, #3, #4, #5, #6, #7, #8, #9	#1, #2, #3, #4, #5, #6, #7, #8, #9	#1, #2, #3, #4, #5, #6, #7, #9
Tuen Mun	#10, #11, #12, #13, #14, #15, #16, #17, #18, #19	#10, #11, #12, #13, #14, #15, #17, #18	#10, #12, #16, #17, #18
Yuen Long	#20, #21, #22, #23, #24, #25, #26	#22, #25	#25

It should be noted that the intellectual significance of the observed pattern between the degree of community change and residents' grievances toward external domination does not rest on its statistical thrust due to the lack of systematic sampling; instead, it offers a vehicle for one to glimpse into the actors' meanings of the emergent living space which involve both the nature of that space and how the very spatial experience is related to the emergent power relations.

Regarding the nature of the space, informants' narratives suggest that the tourism-driven changes in the community produce an *estranged space* in which residents experience nostalgia over their original way of life, and the feeling of unfamiliarity, on a few occasions, comes side by side with the feeling of more convenience and creativity. Such nostalgic sentiment of residents can be commonly spotted in the interview scripts. For example, when recalling the old good days of Sheung Shui decades ago, Informant#1 said the community was quiet and relaxing where most of the shops and restaurants closed at 7 pm. Now, she said: "I don't think that becoming more bustling is good for us. I would rather stay in the village during the holidays" (Informant#1, Sheung Shui). Another informant from Yuen Long said:

> Disappearing are the smiling, welcoming faces of local shop owners; appearing instead are the arrogant sneers of [mainland] tourists. I fear Yuen Long's uniqueness is being lost; soon, one could stand upon Castle Peak Road but not realise that it wasn't Nathan Road in Tsim Sha Tsui or Mong Kok. It used to be easy to ask shop owners to let us use their toilet, but now it is almost impossible. (Informant#25, Yuen Long)

Transforming his nostalgia over the original way of life into resistance against more recent developments, an informant from Tuen Mun said: "I won't shop in the new shops [to buy congee] because I view it as a way to show support for the old shop vendors" (Informant#18, Tuen Mun).

One should also note that production of the estranged space has prompted the actors to think of the political rationale behind which represents the central government's endeavor to control Hong Kong, "infiltrate" into Hong Kong society with an ultimate objective to make Hong Kong "another province of China". These political associations have aroused – understandably – the actors' antagonistic sentiment; for example,

> Resentment of the growing number of tourists from mainland China could have partly stemmed from the idea that the increased mobility of tourists is designed to consolidate the authority of the mainland over Hong Kong. The simple issue of tourist inflows has assumed political overtones and resulted in protests and tension between Hong Kong and the mainland. (Informant#5, Sheung Shui)
>
> Initially shop owners were Hongkongers in Sheung Shui, but later on more mainland investors participated in the business. Hence, (mainland investment) immersed and assimilated into the recurrent economic activities.

122 *Alex Siu Kin Chan and Wing Chung Ho*

> Now, the majority of shops are not owned by Hongkongers. Influence from China had infiltrated for many years, and it has become more obvious in recent years. (Informant#3, Sheung Shui)
>
> China will force Hong Kong to integrate with it through its economic influences, and eventually Hong Kong will become another province of China without its uniqueness. The living environment in which I was brought up is already a thing of the past, and I think it's getting worse for the next generation. (Informant#25, Yuen Long)

What has been observed in our interview data is that the political association of their spatial experience has further prompted the actors to increasingly oppose the "locals" against the "outsiders" and the "Hongkonger" against Chinese" or "mainlander". The radicalized identity politics has thus offered a rationale behind the rise of localist movement in the community. The way that the increasing estranged space in the community has spurred the radicalized identity politics, which in turn fuels the localist movement in Hong Kong, can be well summarized in the verbatim quote of an informant from Sheung Shui below:

> In current China-Hong Kong relations, the mainland is clearly the big brother who makes decisions and formulates policies, and China's dominance has therefore become symbolised by streets swarming with visitors from the mainland. In a sense, resentment against the tourists is resentment against social and political integration with mainland China. (Informant#4, Sheung Shui)

Discussion

Our foregoing discussion has sufficed to indicate that the influx of mainland tourists and parallel traders into Hong Kong has stunned many local residents in the border communities, who watch the streetscapes of their communities change before their eyes. Many locals feel themselves increasingly marginalized in such a way that they become strangers or even second-class citizens in their own neighborhoods, while the Hong Kong SAR government seems not to have adopted determined and effective measures to contain the situation.

In the present study, many informants resented the transformation of Hong Kong into what they conceive to be a giant shopping paradise for mainlanders and parallel traders. In Sheung Shui, the informants further observe that the number of small independent shops has shrunk significantly and the number of chains and franchised establishments has ballooned. Neighborhoods do not seem to be what they once were. Although a similar transformation continues to unfold in most urban areas worldwide, residents of Hong Kong can easily blame steep realty prices and frequent shortages of consumer essentials on the mainlanders who pour into their city day after day. One should note that the perception of spatial change at the community level has spurred the fear that both their neighborhoods specifically and Hong Kong in general will lose their uniqueness in the process of integration with the mainland. Such fear and discontent, as we have argued in the present study, have constituted the major force behind the emergence of the radicalized identity politics and the localist movement in society. We suggest that an "estranged space" has been produced at the community level which has fueled a nascent form of localism in wider society as Hongkongers yearn to preserve their local culture and characteristics and defend their political autonomy from the central Chinese government's influences. The resulting politics of identity has grown into both the sentiment against anti-China-driven development and nostalgia of Hongkongers' original way of life.

In Hong Kong, the increasing Hong Kong-China conflict remains an unresolved issue and has become more confrontational in recent years. The profoundly complex and legally enshrined ties between Hong Kong and mainland China could be dubbed as an unhappy arranged marriage. For many young Hongkongers, the palpable resentment against excessive tourist arrivals and parallel traders has seemingly given rise to concerns beyond the community level as to reach to those of ideological and geopolitical in nature. Thus far, protests and demonstrations against mainland tourism and parallel trading indicate broader struggles for the economic interests, identity and even jurisdiction of residents of Hong Kong. As the mainland relentlessly pursues integration with Hong Kong, locals worry about preserving the identity of "Hongkonger", which they believe stands in contrast to that of "mainlander".

Notes

1 From March to May 2003, Hong Kong had suffered an epidemic of atypical pneumonia called SARS (severe acute respiratory syndrome) which infected 1,755 people and killed 299. One should note that Hong Kong had suffered from six consecutive years of economic deflation from October 1998 to June 2004. A cumulative of 15% deflation rate was recorded during this period (Siu & Wong 2007). Median monthly employment earnings of employed persons had recorded a decline during 2002–2004, from HK$10,000 in 2002 to HK$9,500 in 2003 and 2004, while the unemployment stayed high at around 6.4–7.3%. The Hong Kong SAR government ran with fiscal deficits, first in the financial year of 1998–1999 and then in three consecutive financial years from 2000 to 2004. The tourism industry performed fairly well in 2002 with 16.5 million arrivals, but owing to the SARS outbreak in 2003, it was in the doldrums. The number of arrivals dropped sharply to 427,254 in May 2003 which was equivalent to a 68% drop compared with that in May 2002 (Information from the Census and Statistics Department and Information Services Department of Hong Kong SAR).
2 Information from the Census and Statistics Department of Hong Kong SAR.
3 According to Kwong & Yu (2013: 139), the number of births by mainland mothers in Hong Kong was 52 times more than in 2001. In late 2012, the Chief Executive, Leung Chun-ying, proposed preventing mainland mothers from giving birth in Hong Kong unless they had a husband who was a Hong Kong permanent resident. The number of mainlanders giving birth in Hong Kong plummeted after the policy was implemented (SCMP 2012a).
4 According to estimates, about one tenth of the first-hand property transactions were completed by mainland customers during 2007–2009, and in the relatively more expensive region of Kowloon district, over half of the property transactions were completed by them (Wong 2015).

5 On October 23, 2011, more than 1,000 local mothers held a protest when the Hong Kong Hospital Authority (HA) revealed that many mainland women were admitted to emergency units in local hospitals in order to give birth for free. According to HA's data, over 70% of mainland mothers who used Hong Kong public hospital services did not make an advance booking and would have been prohibited from giving birth in Hong Kong if it had not been an emergency (The China Post 2011).

6 From March 1, 2013 onward, travelers were banned from leaving Hong Kong with more than 1.8 kilograms of infant formula (BBC 2013; SCMP 2015).

Works Cited

BBC News. (2013). Ten arrested in Hong Kong over baby milk formula curbs, 1 March. Retrieved from: www.bbc.com/news/world-asia-china-21628147

Chan, K. M. (2015). Occupying Hong Kong: How deliberation, referendum and civil disobedience played out in the Umbrella Movement. *International Journal on Human Rights*, 21, 1–7.

Commerce and Economic Development Bureau. (2013). *Assessment report on Hong Kong's capacity to receive tourists*. Retrieved from: www.tourism.gov.hk/resources/ english/paperreport_doc/misc/20140117/Assessment_Report_eng.pdf

Constable, N. (2014). *Born out of Place: Migrant Mothers and the Politics of International Labor*. Berkeley: University of California Press.

Garrett, D. (2017). Contesting China's tourism wave: Identity politics, protest and the rise of the Hong Konger city state movement. In C. Colomb & J. Novy (Eds.), *Protest and Resistance in the Tourist City* (pp. 107–128). London and New York: Routledge.

Garrett, D., & Ho, W. C. (2014). Hong Kong at the brink: Emerging forms of political participation in the new social movement. In J. Y. S. Cheng (Ed.), *New Trends of Political Participation in Hong Kong* (pp. 347–384). Hong Kong: City University of Hong Kong Press.

Ho, W.-C., & Tran, E. (2019). Hong Kong-China relations over three decades of change: From apprehension to integration to clashes. *China: An International Journal*, 17(1), 173–193.

Kwong, K. M., & Yu, H. (2013). Hong Kong identity politics. In Y. N. Zheng & C. P. Yew (Eds.), *Hong Kong under Chinese Rule: Economic Integration and Political Gridlock* (p. 139). New Jersey: World Scientific.

Kwong, Y. H. (2016). State-society conflict radicalization in Hong Kong: The rise of "anti-China" sentiment and radical localism. *Asian Affairs*, 47(3), 428–442.

Mok, C., & Dewald, B. (1999). Tourism in Hong Kong: After the handover. *Asia Pacific Journal of Tourism Research*, 3(2), 32–40.

Oriental Daily. (2012). *'1600 ren you hang da dao 'zi sha you' (1600 People Protested against 'Suicide Travel')*, 20 February. Retrieved from: http://orientaldaily.on.cc/cnt/ news/20120220/00176_013.html

Ortmann, S. (2015). The Umbrella Movement and Hong Kong's protracted democratization process. *Asian Affairs*, 46(1), 32–50.

SCMP. (2012a). *Zero quota policy for mainland mothers has no legal basis*, 28 May. Retrieved from: www.scmp.com/article/1002221/zero-quota-policy-mainland-mothers-has-no-legal-basis-regina-ip

SCMP. (2012b). *Protesters rally in Sheung Shui against cross-border parallel traders*, 16 September. Retrieved from: www.scmp.com/news/hong-kong/article/1037962/ protesters-rally-sheung-shui-against-cross-border-parallel-traders

SCMP. (2013). *Border-town residents say traders cost them dear*, 17 April 2013. Retrieved from: www.scmp.com/news/hong-kong/article/1216247/border-town-residents-say-traders-cost-them-dear

SCMP. (2015). *Parts of Hong Kong suffering serious shortage of baby milk powder*, 11 February. Retrieved from: www.scmp.com/news/hong-kong/article/1709599/parts-hong-kong-suffering-serious-shortage-baby-milk-powder

SCMP. (2019). *Hundreds of Hong Kong protesters march to Kwong Wah hospital, claiming city's health care system overwhelmed by mainland Chinese migrants*, 4 February. Retrieved from: www.scmp.com/news/hong-kong/politics/article/2186540/hundreds-hong-kong-protesters-march-kwong-wah-hospital

Sewell, W. H. (1996). Historical events as transformations of structures: Inventing revolution at the bastille. *Theory and Society*, 25(6), 841–881.

Siu, K. F. A., & Wong, Y. C. R. (2007). The Asian Financial Crisis, deflation and structural change in Hong Kong. In Y. Shimizu (Ed.), *Economic Dynamism of Asia in the New Millennium: From the Asian Crisis to a New Stage of Growth. Advanced Research in Asian Economic Studies* (pp. 31–50). Singapore: World Scientific.

The China Post. (2011). *Mothers rally against mainland births in Hong Kong*, 24 October. Retrieved from: www.chinapost.com.tw/china/local-news/hong-kong/2011/10/24/320733/Mothers-rally.htm

Time. (2013). *Mainland Chinese traders milking Hong Kong for all its worth*, 4 February. Retrieved from: http://world.time.com/2013/02/04/mainland-chinese-traders-milking-hong-kong-for-all-its-worth

Tourism Commission, Commerce and Economic Development Bureau, Government of the Hong Kong Special Administrative District. (2017). *Tourism performance in 2016*. Retrieved from: www.tourism.gov.hk/english/statistics/statistics_perform.html

Wong, W. W. (2015). "Nei di ren lai gang zhi ye bu zai liu hang?" (Is Mainlander's House Buying in Hong Kong Not Popular Anymore?). *Hong Kong Economic Journal*. Retrieved from: www2.hkej.com/instantnews/property/article/1164567/

6 Surviving the collective subjectivity of Choy Yuen Village

From multiple marginalizations to irreversible resistance

Linda Yin-nor Tjia

Introduction

The social movement in Hong Kong against the demolition and forced eviction of Choy Yuen Village for the construction of the Express Railway Link (XRL) between 2009 and 2010 has received widespread attention locally and internationally (Chang 2010). The XRL project affected approximately 150 households living with a population of 450 and around two million 800 m² in size of agricultural land. With the aid of a group of youth activists, 47 households refused the forced demolishment and eviction at the beginning, and demanded collective resettlement from the Hong Kong Special Administrative Government (HKSAR Government 2010a) after failing to stop the statutory approval of the project's funding. The government offered a total of up to HK\$95 million compensation to the affected households, and another HK\$160 million to landowners in terms of land compensation (The Hong Kong Institute of Land Administration 2002).

The elites' discourse of development-led transportation planning, the activists' demand of justice-based democracy advancement and the villagers' collective subjectivity of agriculture-focused community rehabilitation became part of the *force majeure* provisions included in a series of irreversible conflicts between the multiple stakeholders and the marginalized villagers. The resulting two-year movement, from anti-eviction to anti-government, has become the focus of many scholarly studies in search for a better explanation for the emergence of an unusual cluster of activists, a new wave of a dramatic social movement, as well as an unexpected political space for democratic advancement (Ma 2011; Hung & Ip 2012; Chen 2015; Xia 2016; Lam-Knott 2018). Such empowering discourse, however, has missed out an equally critical discourse of marginalization and irreversibility, in which 47 non-indigenous households had settled in new Choy Yuen Village with much sorrow and emotion.

Resonated with the discussion of the worldwide sentimental populism and the discourses of victimhood throughout this volume, this chapter takes a victim-centered approach to investigating the various narratives that emerged from different stakeholders and how they have affected the immediate resettlement of the villagers, in particular for the 47 households which insisted on collective

Surviving the collective subjectivity 127

rehousing and weathered all the extreme hardships in their long-term process of re-habitation. The development-for-all and democracy-for-all discourse reinforced the impact of marginality in a way theorized by the concept of marginal man put forward by Park (1928) almost a decade ago. The affected households were literally torn apart "on the margin of two cultures and two societies, which never completely interpenetrated and fused" (Park 1928: 892).

Based on a thorough search on secondary sources such as relevant news articles, government, think tank reports, as well as scholarly research and journal publications between 2008 and 2019, supplemented by a series of fieldwork observation in new Choy Yuen Village, and a total of 13 in-depth interviews with villagers and activists between 2016 and 2019 (the profile of the interviewees are in Table 6.1), a mixed method of discourse analysis was conducted to explain the villagers' changing sense of being and to put Park's concept of marginal man into test. Specifically, this chapter interprets and explains the making of the

Table 6.1 Profile of interviewees

Names of informants	Gender	Age	Role[a]	Source
Ah Chuk	Female	58	Non-indigenous villager of the old Choy Yuen Village	Author's interview in March 2019
Mrs. Chan	Female	50s	Non-indigenous villager of the old Choy Yuen Village	Author's interview in January 2017
Mrs. Lee	Female	50s	Non-indigenous villager of the old Choy Yuen Village	Author's interview in January 2016
Ms. Cheung	Female	40s	Activist, member of the Choy Yuen Villager Support Group	Author's interview in March 2019
Ah Fong	Female	40s	Member of the Choy Yuen Villager Support Group	Author's interview in February 2019
Mr. Wong	Male	50s	Member of the Choy Yuen Villager Support Group	Author's interview in June 2018
Mr. Ho	Male	40s	Member of the Choy Yuen Villager Support Group	Author's interview in February 2018
Mr. So	Male	50s	Non-indigenous villager of the old Choy Yuen Village	Author's interview in March 2019
Ms. Lau	Female	50s	Non-indigenous villager of the old Choy Yuen Village	Author's interview in April 2017
Mr. Wong	Male	50s	Non-indigenous villager of the old Choy Yuen Village	Author's interview in March 2019
Mrs. Chong	Female	50s	Non-indigenous villager of the old Choy Yuen Village	Author's interview in April 2019
Mrs. Yuen	Female	50s	Non-indigenous villager of the old Choy Yuen Village	Author's interview in March 2019
Ms. Pang	Female	30s	Student activist	Author's interview in May 2018

a The interviewees are given pseudonyms to protect their identity. Detailed family background of the villagers has been thoroughly examined by the authority to verify their eligibility for compensation; such information of the informants is therefore not disclosed in order to prevent their identity from being traced.

128   *Linda Yin-nor Tjia*

nuances of the joyful and sorrowful emotions found among the villagers. The textual analysis and fieldwork investigation have resulted in three dominant narrations of development-for-all, democracy-for-all and community-for-all account the joys and sadness of resettlement and rehabilitation.

These discourses were ambivalent or contradictory, but all contributed to the fashioning of the villagers from victims to activists, and leading to an irreversible course of action and reaction. The survey of such diversified discourses is not aimed at making a moral judgment of right or wrong, good or bad, nor evaluating the results of the social movement. Instead, this systematic representation of various narratives is to shed light on the complexities of surviving among multiple processes of social exclusion and inclusion, as well as the challenges of living with the nuances between empowerment and impediment.

Conceptualization of victimhood

The studies of victims mostly focus on the process of victimization for crime- or disaster-related cases such as prostitution with violence, kidnap and mass killing. These researches enrich our understanding of the impact of victimization which revolves around multiple processes of social exclusion and inclusion as well as empowerment and impediment. For example, Roces (2009) argues that the transformation of former prostitutes into women activists in the Philippines empowers the victims of violent sex by reclaiming their dignity and restoring their cultural capital and community support. Van Dijk (2009) also investigates the testimonies of 11 high-profile victims. He discovers that despite having unexpected inner strengths to cope with the traumatic experience and altruistic motivation to engage in social activities for other victims of the same misfortune, the crime victims are bounded by a set of moral expectations to "accept a status limiting their freedom of behavior or actively engage in re-negotiating their identity" (Van Dijk 2009: 24). This research suggests that the process of victimization usually combines and complicates various discursive outcomes which eventually shape the victims' behavior in an irreversible way. In the case of the Choy Yuen Village resettlement, the affected households survived and recovered, but they were not totally liberated from the designated discourse of development and social movement.

Ruiz-Junco's (2013: 45–54) theorization of emotion suggests a new vantage point of view to explain the mechanism through which the process of victimization shapes the lives and experiences of the victims involved. He investigates the dynamics of a social movement from the framing of a victim's emotion to the manifestation of emotion culture, as well as the manipulation of emotional opportunity structures. Emotions in movements can be experienced spontaneously (Gould 2009) and cultivated strategically (Jasper 1997; Flam 2000). The framing of and integration of both in a way to justify and sustain a social movement have proved to be a powerful mobilization force. Yet, this kind of sentimental populist approach also intensifies the feelings and anger of being victimized.

Surviving the collective subjectivity   129

Social movements adopting a dramaturgy frame are also instrumental in further exaggerating the sentimental impact and attracting wider public attention. They also fashion an emotional culture through reciprocity, contagion and synchronization (Barsade 2002: 644–675), and leave the victims/activists with a limited choice of opportunity structure and an irreversible course of action. As a result, empowerment and impediment are two sides of a coin.

Based on the textual analysis of the process of victimization of the Choy Yuen Village, this chapter focuses on the villagers' emotional feeling, unpacks the process of victimization of the Choy Yuen Villager and explains how the villagers' emotion was framed by multiple narratives of social exclusion and social inclusion. The anti-XRL movement has resulted in an emotional culture and structure under which the villagers have not much choice but entered into an irreversible course of action. In an interview with one of the villagers, Mrs. Chan, about her life in the new Choy Yuen Village after resettlement, I was invited to visit her home. In the beginning, the informant was very contented with her new home and delighted to show me around her newly refurbished two-story small white house with a cozy garden. She kept saying in a smiling face, "Yes we finally made it after all the hassles. This is our home sweet home now" (Author's interview 2017). I sat down, looked around and asked specifically what the difficulties she encountered were; she replied saying that it was a very long and complicated story. I urged her to share with me one of the most challenging issues. She tried to recall and was about to tell me something. But soon her eyes were filled with tears. She could not speak for as long as 10 minutes. Finally, she managed to say just a few words with a sorrowful sigh, "I don't know how to begin. It was a hard time for us!" Chan then became very emotional and could not continue with the conversation.

Chan was with one of the 47 households which were resettled in the new Choy Yuen Village. She was one of the victims in this infrastructure-led forced eviction. Her sorrow was backed up by her neighbor, Ah Chuk, who used to be one of the most outspoken and optimistic villagers in the anti-XRL movement, and who ran for District Council election in the Pat Heung South Constituency Area in Hong Kong in 2011. She told a local news reporter that it was naive for many people to think that the new Choy Yuen Village represents a favorable outcome of the social movement against forced eviction, and can be copied elsewhere. On the one hand, Ah Chuk was proud of learning to be brave, strategic and optimistic after participating in the movement; on the other, she admitted that it was a painful process:

> If you have to go through all the hardship, you may not be able to endure this painstaking resilience strategy. People saw the result, but not the process. (Pang 2019 and author's interview in March 2019)

Another active representative of the villagers in Choy Yuen Village was Ko Chun Heung, who has been the chairperson of the Choy Yuen Village Concern Group (菜園村關注組) since 2008. Playing a leading role at the forefront of the

130 *Linda Yin-nor Tjia*

battleground against the forced eviction, Ko was involved in most of the public hearings and protests. She said that new Choy Yuen Village has finally become a new living space for the villagers after eight years' effort.

"Seeing our new homes begin to take shape, I should be happy. But frankly, I am not", Ko explained that it was complicated, especially when she thought of the passing away of her father and a good friend during the social movement:

> In the eight years of pro-longed resilience and re-settlement, conflicts emerged and ruined some of the relations among the villagers ... If I had known that we would have to go through all these hurdles for collective resettlement, I would have hesitated (to initiate the movement). (Law 2017)

I have visited the new Choy Yuen village for fieldwork three times between 2016 and 2019. After a one-hour train and bus ride, I had to walk pass another indigenous village, Yuen Kong Village, before arriving at a small circular public space resembling the entrance of the new Choy Yuen Village. Despite the remote location, it has always been a pleasant surprise to find this little wonderland taking shape especially in view of the skyrocketed property prices in Hong Kong. In contrast to such a peaceful and charming appearance, the consistent shifts between contented and sorrowful, optimistic and painful, as well as happy and regretful emotions embedded throughout the conversations with the new settlers shocked me and drove me to search for a systematic explanation for such nuances of feelings.

Based on a thorough textual analysis and in-depth interviews, three dominant thematic discourses of development-for-all, democracy-for-all and community-for-all were identified. These social exclusive and inclusive narratives together produce a combined effect on the irreversible course of action for the villagers and resulted in complicated nuances of emotions among them.

Development-for-all at the cost of the villagers

The first discourse of victimization was obviously the government's infrastructure-led development discourse. In view of the economic benefits to the entire population in Hong Kong brought by the construction of an express rail link connecting to the main trunk line of the Mainland, the demolishment and eviction of an en route village were justified at all costs (of the affected villagers). The development-for-all discourse gradually took shape after May 2000, when the Hong Kong SAR Government unveiled the "Railway Development Strategy 2000" to cater for the continuous population growth and increasing cross-boundary social and economic activities. Besides the six railway schemes which were identified as the shortlisted options to be combined with the existing rail lines to form the basic railway network, three more stand-alone railway projects were put forward to serve particular transport demands in Hong Kong: the West Hong Kong Island Line, the Regional Express Line and the Port Rail Line. This was the first time that the Hong Kong government proposed building

Surviving the collective subjectivity 131

what would later be named as the Express Rail Link (XRL) between Hong Kong and Shenzhen.

The initial idea of the Regional Express Line was to link Hung Hom station, the terminal of the existing East Rail line, and the boundary through Shek Kip Mei station with two optional routings: one via Fanling South in the New Territories and connect to Lo Wu at the boundary (See alignment 2 in Figure 6.1), and the other via Kam Sheung Road in the New Territories and connect to Lok Ma Chau, another site at the boundary (see alignment 1 in Figure 6.1). It was believed that this new express link would resolve the growth in annual cross-boundary passengers since 1996 at 19%–20% (HKSAR Government 2000).

In September 2002, Donald Tsang Yam Kuen, the then Hong Kong Chief Secretary, and his delegates attended the "Coordinating meeting of the Major Infrastructure Projects between the Mainland and Hong Kong" (內地與香港大型基礎設施協作會議) in Shanghai. He confirmed the construction of the

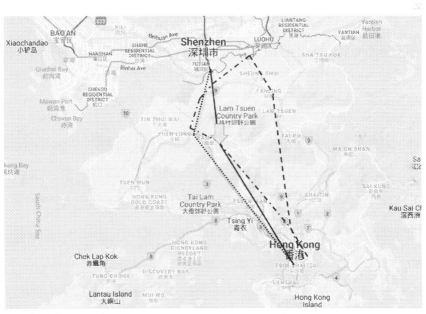

Map of XRL alignment and location of the affected area

- Proposed XRL alignment 1 suggested in 2000 ‒ · ‒ · ‒ · ‒
- Proposed XRL alignment 2 suggested in 2000 ‒ ‒ ‒ ‒ ‒
- Proposed XRL alignment 3 (shared corridor option) suggested in 2005. ················
- Final XRL alignment (dedicated corridor option) confirmed in 2007 ───────
- Affected area

Figure 6.1 Map of XRL alignment and location of the affected area.

132   *Linda Yin-nor Tjia*

Regional Express Line which was aimed at connecting Hong Kong to the mainland high-speed rail network and shortening the transport time between Guangzhou and Hong Kong from 100 to 60 minutes (HKSAR Government 2002).

Tsang later became the HKSAR Chief Executive in 2005. With the advice from the Executive Council, he ordered the adoption of a new routing which was named the "share corridor option" (see alignment 3 in Figure 6.1) in which the Regional Express Line would share tracks with the existing West Rail with a terminus at West Kowloon (Environment, Transport and Works Bureau 2006). The Executive Council ruled out the earlier option of connecting Fanling South and Lo Wu, as well as another proposed alignment which was a dedicated corridor involving the building of a long tunnel of about 30 km, the longest railway tunnels in the world. Despite the fact that the dedicated alignment would have saved 12 minutes on a trip between Hong Kong and the boundary, it was not accepted because of the prohibitive construction cost.

In January 2007, the Environment, Transport and Works Bureau Administration provided a supplementary brief to Legislative Council members about the Regional Express Line and reported that a number of new updates would affect the decision on the choice of the alignment. These included the possibility that 10–15 Mainland cities would wish to operate long-haul through trains to Hong Kong by 2020 and 2030, the addition of a new high-speed rail station at Futian in the Mainland, the need to link up with the Rapid Transit System of the Pearl River Delta area and the requirement from the Ministry of Railways in the Mainland to deploy wider train cars for the high-speed rail. In view of the potential increase in the patronage for the Regional Express Line, the conflicting platform configurations at Nam Cheong, Mei Foo and Tsuen Wan West Stations along the West Rail line with a width of no more than 3.1 m, and the need to integrate with the Mainland section of the high speed rail, the then Kowloon Canon Railway Corporation was asked to complete a consultancy study about the patronage forecast, financial viability and economic implications of the Regional Express Line by mid-2007 (Environment, Transport, and Works Bureau 2007).

Soon after the submission of the consultancy report, Tsang announced in August of the same year that the SAR government had decided to opt for the "dedicated corridor" alignment (red alignment in 6.1) for the Regional Express Line at the Tenth Plenary of the Hong Kong-Guangdong Co-operation Joint Conference (HKSAR Government 2007). He also incorporated this dedicated alignment of the express railway project with ten other major infrastructure projects in his first Policy Address in 2007. The Regional Express Line was finally conceived as the Guangzhou-Shenzhen-Hong Kong Express Rail Link (XRL), a high-speed national rail network of some 12,000 kilometers linking Hong Kong with other major cities in the mainland with a maximum speed of 200–300 kilometers per hour. These ten infrastructure projects were expected to bring huge economic benefits in terms of creating 250,000 employment opportunities, enhancing wage levels, cross-boundary integration and living environment (HKSAR Government 2007).

In April 2008, it became obvious that the various government agents had arrived at a consensus to support the dedicated corridor option and justify the construction of the XRL and the related work from different perspectives. First, the Hong Kong Executive Council advised and Tsang ordered that the Central Alignment with a dedicated 26-kilometer underground connection between the West Kowloon terminus and the Huanggang at the boundary be adopted for the Hong Kong section of the XRL (HKSAR Government 2008). Second, the Transport and Housing Bureau sought approval from the Legislative Council Panel on Transport Subcommittee on Matters Relating to Railways to support the funding application for the design and site investigation for the proposed alignment. Among other concerns such as financial, environmental and heritage implications, the Bureau ascertained that "the proposed design and site investigation works do not require any land acquisition" (Transport & Housing Bureau 2008). Third, the Mass Transit Railway Corporation Ltd (MTRL) put forward the XRL project profile for an Environmental Impact Assessment, and, for the first time, mentioned that the construction of the XRL tunnel would involve an underground emergency rescue station and a stabling sidings at the east of Shek Kong for depot facilities, basic maintenance and emergency repairs (see the location in Figure 6.1). While the Profile had outlined various potential environmental impacts on air, water, noise, visual, heritage and ecology during the construction and operation period, it was reported that appropriate mitigation measures would be developed to minimize the adverse impacts. In addition, the XRL would provide a green alternative for public transport (Mass Transport Railways Limited 2008).

Following the approval from the Finance Committee of the Legislative Council for funding the MTRL to conduct design and site investigation of the XRL project on July 8, 2008, the Central Alignment Scheme of the XRL was quickly gazetted twice under the Railways Ordinance on November 28 and December 5, 2008, respectively (Highways Department 2008). This was the first time that the residents of Choy Yuen Village got to know about the plan to demolish their homes to make way for the construction of the emergency rescue station and a stabling siding. After the Railway Scheme was gazetted, the Highways Department received 120 cases of objection with 2000 similar submissions and 20 inquiries from the public in terms of its alignment (Transport and Housing Bureau 2009). However, between the Railway Development Strategy put forward in 2000 and the consensus among government agents about the construction of the XRL in 2008, this project was designated as a development-for-all infrastructure scheme. The Hong Kong-Mainland connectivity was seen as strategically important for Hong Kong to become part of the mainland transport hub in the future. Furthermore, the additional 5,500 and 10,000 job openings during construction and after completion, respectively, were considered by the Hong Kong SAR Government as vital to the domestic job market.

Choy Yuen Village has gradually been seen as the victim of the XRL project. When the secretary of transport and housing visited the village in January 2009 to inspect the site and better understand the concerns of the affected residents,

134   *Linda Yin-nor Tjia*

the official approach to the forced eviction was framed as such that the affected households were limited to a small number of villagers who should give way to the XRL project and accept resettlement arrangements,

> In designing the tunnel alignment, the guiding principles are the safety of train operation, minimizing the impact on the community and maximizing social benefits. Considerations include impact on the whole community and environment, topographical and geotechnical factors, connectivity with the Mainland section of XRL ... etc. After balancing all these factors, we consider that the current scheme has the least impact on the community and the best overall performance. (Transport and Housing Bureau 2009)

Under such a utilitarian discourse, the justification for the greater goal of development-for-all became a curse for the victims: they were the minority and could be sacrificed. In principle, the affected villagers were not falling into the trap of absolute poverty because of the forced eviction. They, however, felt that they were marginalized because they were not properly consulted and informed in the planning process, and were left out in the development-for-all discourse. They did not trust the mainstream development model and therefore placed their faith in the alternative democracy-for-all and community-for-all discourse.

Democracy-for-all and the designated role of the villagers

Since Choy Yuen Village was located on flat land in the middle of the confirmed XRL alignment where the MTRL in their XRL profile report considered as the best place to build the rescue station and stabling sidings, the HKSAR Government requested the affected villagers to relocate and make way for the construction of the project. The resumption of private land for such a purpose was carried out under the Railways Ordinance (Cap.519). The landowners would receive a zonal ex gratia compensation from the government. According to the existing policy, the government would also rehouse the affected occupants in public rental housing if they were living in squatter quarters which had been registered in the 1984/85 Squatter Occupancy Survey, met the eligibility criteria for public rental housing and passed the Comprehensive Means Test. These occupants would need to follow the prevailing policy, that is, to apply for the Green Form Certificates[1] from the Housing Department and join the respective queue for applications for public housing. They were also allowed to purchase Home Ownership Scheme[2] flats under the Secondary Market Scheme[3] or the Sale Programme of Surplus Home Ownership Scheme[4] flats if they met the eligibility criteria and if the Sale Programme was available for application (Transport and Housing Bureau 2009).

As a result of these restraints, the majority of Choy Yuen Villager were not eligible for public housing or Home Ownership Scheme[5] resettlement. They could only choose to live in Interim Housing for less than one year or receive a one-off ex gratia removal allowance unless they were seriously sick, disabled or proved

Surviving the collective subjectivity 135

to have other social problems which entitled them to apply for "Compassionate Rehousing" through the Social Welfare Department (Transport and Housing Bureau 2009).

Affected farmers in the region could apply for "agricultural resite" to continue their farming, but they had to acquire their own piece of suitable private land which had to be acceptable by the government. They also had to obtain a confirmation from the Director of Agriculture, Fisheries, and Conservation that they were genuine farmers in order to receive an ex gratia Rehabilitation Allowance for reinstallations of the related fixtures including farm structures, irrigation pipes and wells. No rehousing would be offered for agricultural resiting (Transport and Housing Bureau 2009).

With a view to ascertaining the scope of the affected households and preventing free riders Lands Department officials went to Choy Yuen village to conduct an unannounced but thorough household registration by marking a serial number on all fixed structures in Choy Yuen Village on November 11, 2008 before the Railway Scheme was gazetted (Chen 2015). One of my informants, Mrs. Lee, was upset by the ad hoc approach the government adopted in the process of household registration:

> With no advance notice, these officials came and registered everyone in the village. We were then told to vacate our homes by November 2010. Some of the villagers were planning for getting married and giving birth to newborn. The household size and combination in 2010 would naturally be different from what was like on the day of registration. We felt bad. It was like all of a sudden an official came to freeze our headcount. (Author's interview January 2016)

The villagers soon formed the Choi Yuen Village Concern Group. They called a press conference and demanded "no clearance and no removal" on December 21, 2008 (Apple Daily 2008a). Moved by the plight of the Choy Yuen Village Concern Group and the villagers, Chu Hoi-dick, an independent news reporter and editor of an online media, Inmediahk.net, reached out to the villagers with his friends to offer a helping hand. They later formed the Choy Yuen Village Support Group in February 2009. Chu was also asked by the villagers to speak for them in a meeting with Yau Shing-mu, the Undersecretary for the Transport and Housing Department, in March, requesting more consultations regarding the evacuation and rehousing arrangements (Chu 2009).

As a member of a loosely organized alliance, "Local Action" (本土行動), Chu had participated in a number of social movements in Hong Kong, such as the hunger strike and protest against the demolition of the Star Ferry Pier and Queen's Pier in 2006 and 2007 respectively. These new waves of social movements for environmental and heritage protection were seen as an "outpouring of nostalgic sentiment" gradually emerging out of the resuscitation of community identity and non-material value after the outbreak of the SARS (severe acute respiratory syndrome) epidemic in 2003. Ma (2011) argues that the post-materialism arising

136 Linda Yin-nor Tjia

from the emphasis on personal health and community hygiene has enhanced the values of non-materialist aspects of life and local identity, as well as the hatred toward the business-oriented materialistic regime. Against such a political context, Chu focused his resistance agenda on relentless development. The XRL-led eviction of Choy Yuen Village fitted well into his political agenda and became the battleground for him to once again contest Hong Kong's long-term instrumental and materialistic development model.

Making use of their media network, Chu and a few like-minded alliances of Local Action began to mobilize more supporters. They successfully drew significant public attention by a running series of reports about the inadequate public consultation and injustice of the land resumption arrangements (Chan 2009; Chu 2009; Ip 2009). One of the activists, Miss Cheung, admitted that it was not easy at the beginning because the public did not care about the resistance of a small village:

> Chu was graduated from the Chinese University of Hong Kong. He has very good connections there and was able to mobilize university students to join the Choy Yuen Village Support group or participate in our activities. We coordinated with the Choy Yuen Village Concern Group and tried to collect signatures from citizens in the affected districts other than Choy Yuen Village. Some of the villagers joined us. But it was laborious and tiring to do that. (Author's interview in March 2019)

To diversify the public engagement initiative, activists and villagers also arranged guided tours for outsiders to visit Choy Yuen Village. They emphasized the importance of a sustainable agricultural community and alternative lifestyle preservation. They also used social media such as Facebook to reach out to potential supporters. The combined efforts of the villagers and activists did pay off in the beginning as 84% of respondents in a poll conducted in June 2009 supported the XRL project (Xia 2016). With a view to gaining more public support, the Support Group reframed their social movement from one with marginal demands for justice to a mainstream concern for an over-budgeted XRL at HK$66.9 billion. The massive expenditure of the XRL was seen as a white elephant project: while the business elites believed that it was worthwhile public expenditure as it would create more jobs and attract more mainland tourists, the opponents argued that it was a waste of public money and it could cause social inequality.

Between December 2009 and January 2010, the activists further escalated their actions. They initiated a dramaturgical movement by walking slowly with rice and seeds in their hands and prostrating once every 26 steps to signify what they called a peaceful resilience against the 26-kilometer length of the XRL Hong Kong section. Such a "slow march" not only caught massive attention from local and international media but also reinforced the emotional connections among the protestors. According to Ma (2017: 15), the prostrating walks served as a "moral mediation" through which "the activists' desires and aspirations for embracing and restoring a humanistic lifestyle connected with the land were unmistakably and powerfully expressed". The activists' aspirations for anti-materialism and pro-democracy were thoroughly communicated in their support for Choy Yuen Village. Such political awakening and emotional support are reciprocal. On January 1, 2010, the Choi Yuen Village Concern Group joined the march for universal suffrage organized by the pan-democratic group (Li 2013). One of the villagers, Ah Chuk, also ran for District Council election in the Pat Heung South Constituency Area in Hong Kong later in 2011. Obviously the role of emotion in democratic advancement was appealing and powerful (Marcus 2002; Westen 2007; Krause 2008). Public support for the anti-XRL movement peaked on January 16, 2010 when around 10,000 protestors went to sit outside the Legislative Council building and moved to the Government House to express their demand for the Finance Committee to disapprove the budget. The activists also raised their concerns about the possible conflicts of interests for some of the Functional Constituency legislators to vote for the XRL project. Despite the final approval of the funding for the XRL by the Finance Committee on January 16, 2010, the small-scale "no clearance, no removal" movement initiated by the Choy Yuen Villagers has metamorphosed into a wider "anti-XRL, localism, and democracy-for-all" movement. This movement has successfully consolidated a common emotional attachment toward the "local community" as a sustainable alternative to global development. The growing public support as a result of the increasing sympathetic concern toward the appropriation of the villagers' homeland soil was tactfully extended to a wider political agenda on localism. With the same Chinese character, *tu* (土), in the Chinese phrase of soil, *nitu* (泥), and localism, *bentu* (本土), the symbolic connection of the two ideas justifies the social movement which extends from protecting the home soil to demanding local autonomy. As a result, when the government-deployed caterpillar marched on the soil and knocked down people's homes in Choy Yuen Village, it was visualized as the hegemonic force crushing local freedom and alternative choice of development. One of the post-1990s youth activists, Willis Ho (2016), explicitly connected the community-based movement to being anti-government. In her own words, "community resilience is a way to resist hegemony" (社區自救，是抵抗強權的出路。)

Chu Hoi-dick and other activists later formed the Land Justice League and put forward a manifesto in 2012, framing land and agricultural as an integral conception for sustainable future and justice (Huang 2018). In Chu's later landslide victory in the 2016 Legislative election, he also developed related political rhetoric as "deep plowing and intensive farming" (深耕細作) to signify his down-to-earth political campaign. The "no clearance, no removal" resistance developed into an irreversible democracy-for-all movement. Seeing young people fight for their home in the beginning simply because of their belief in justice and democracy emotionally resonated with the villagers and thus inevitably drawn to become involved in wider political resilience.

138 *Linda Yin-nor Tjia*

Community-for-all and the collective subjectivity

The escalation of the contentious political movement facilitated the explosive growth of public attention toward the Choy Yuen Village protest. The recurrent demonstrations by thousands of people have built an inseparable bonding between the villagers and the activists. The democracy-for-all discourse has integrated their collective concerns about the destruction of community environment and sustainable life, their unified dissents into the clarification of the vested interests for the astronomical costs of XRL construction, as well as the eventual quest for full democratization of the Legislative Council in Hong Kong. Throughout the two years' time of movement, Chu Hoi-dick and other members of the Choy Yuen Village Support Group met regularly with the Choy Yuen Village Concern Group and other villagers. These activists were so involved in the movement that some of them considered the Choy Yuen Village as their second home and fought in full swing as if it was to protect their homeland. Some of the most involved activists literally moved to live in the neighborhood of Choy Yuen Village and became part of the community. Ah Fong and her husband traveled to the village many times a week to meet with the villagers. Her husband eventually suggested that they should move to live in the Village:

> We were all very involved in the social movement. One day, my husband asked me if I want a community. He said that we actually have one: the Choy Yuen Village! Many other activists also moved to live in the neighbourhood of the village. We became neighbours. (Author's interview in February 2019)

The social movement took on a life of its own to gradually associate farming with the aspiration for democracy. Both the activists and the villagers were drawn to an irreversible course of action in the name of a community-for-all movement. Mr. Wong was one of the Choy Yuen villagers who received Chu and explained to him the situation. He admitted that this was not something that they would have expected in the beginning:

> When the first time Chu came to visit us as a journalist, we were surprised to see him wearing a white sleeveless undershirt. We were not sure what he wanted and what he could do for us. But he and his friends kept coming back and eventually formed a Support Group to help us to resist the forced eviction. We did not know what to do and how to deal with the government officials but they were all multi-talented youth and brought in many innovative ideas for resistance. Some of them were university students who had skipped classes to make time for us. We were all very touched. Some of the villagers have developed exceptionally closed relations with these kids. There were like our grandchildren. (Author's interview in June 2018)

Surviving the collective subjectivity 139

My interview was resonated by the sentimental reflections made by the student activists. For example, Lala Lau, a student activist, sees both the Choy Yuen Village and the emerging political alliance as two of her new homes:

> Some people dislike the "carnivalisation" of the social movement, but it was through this process that I uncovered my sense of body aesthetic and cultural self-confidence…We were awakened, mobilised and touched … We gathered at this vaguely constructed new home. (Lau 2018)

Lala's fantasy of Choy Yuen Village as her new home grew out of the family-like care and reception provided by the villagers during the time when these young activists were forging alliance at the village against the government's forced eviction. The villagers expressed their gratitude for the support and involvement in the movement by treating these young activists with meals and homemade Chinese pudding. In return, the activists played music and sang songs during breaks to entertain the villagers and enhance the morale of the group. The reciprocity reinforced their relations and created a sense of belonging much like an extended family. At the end of the entire movement when Lala learned from the LED screen in front of the Legislative Council building in 2001 that the funding for the XRL construction had been approved, she collapsed and became pessimistic as if her newly emerged political aspiration was gone at the same time when the government decided to destroy her "new home" of Choy Yuen Village.

Ms. Pang was another post-1980s youth activist who had participated in the Choy Yuen Village movement. She was in her 20s in 2009 and was laughed by her university peers as "majoring in the social movement". She said it was harsh and tiring, but the warmth she felt in the village played a critical role in healing. Choy Yuen Village became the center of her life, and her relations with the villagers was as close as with her own family,

> I saw the dark side of the world, but I also saw the real virtue. This experience was profound. It was as if you would risk your life to protect for something you value. (Author's interview in May 2018)

The social movement leveraged on this community-for-all discourse and incorporated the demand for pro-local community in the original anti-XRL protest. Two months after the approval of the XRL budget, the Choy Yuen Village Livelihood Place was established to frame the importance of sustainable community lifestyle and/or organic farming as an alternative development model to the infrastructure-led capitalistic development. Mr. Ho rented a place to live in the close neighborhood of the Choy Yuen Village. He knew nothing about farming before but has become increasingly devoted to organic farming after participating in the movement. He was happy with his "half-farmer, half-X" mode of living now. According to Ho, this model was developed during the course of the

140 *Linda Yin-nor Tjia*

movement which showcased the possibility of living as a half-time farmer and taking a half-time role of any other profession:

> When we met at the village to discuss various resistance strategy, we stayed there for a long time because it was too far away to travel in and out all the times. As a result, there was plenty of idle time in between meetings. In addition to playing music and eating together, some of us began to learn about farming from the villagers. We decided to live the farmers' lives, and later incorporated it in our political agenda. Half-farmer-half-X could be an optimal mode of living for the entire community. (Author's interview in February 2018)

In a documentary video about the building of the Livelihood Place from its construction to its opening in March 2010, the activists were seen having a strong and affective bonding with the villagers. With such a strong community-based centrifugal force, many activists were committed to protecting the collective community of Choy Yuen Village until the last moment. For example, they formed the Choy Yuen Village Patrol Team to prevent the Lands Department from initiating land resumption in October 2010 (Ma 2017). The leading activist Chu Hoi-dick even named her daughter, being born in the middle of the movement, as "No removal" (不遷) – a symbolic meaning of not only a daughter to him but a daughter of the community.

Chu and his team described the community-for-all social movement as a happy resistance. The villagers also wanted to preserve such a collective identity. Mr. So was one of the villagers who has demanded collective resettlement:

> After the budget approval, we were well aware that we would have to give way to the XRL construction. We insisted on "no clearance, no removal" as a strategic way to bargain for a better resettlement arrangement. At the same time, we started to explore a suitable place for us together. We liked the collective life and we wanted to clone another Choy Yuen Village. (Author's interview in March 2019)

The quest for a community-for-all relocation, however, has resulted in a prolonged, irreversible and painstaking resilience. The villagers may not be regretful but were sorrowful after experiencing an unprecedented series of marginalization from the indigenous villagers as well as other community in the neighborhood.

Most of the villagers residing in the old Choy Yuen Village were non-indigenous villagers. In the process of forced eviction, they were first marginalized because of their non-indigenous identity. During the 1950s, a great number of mainlanders flooded to Hong Kong for political reasons. Many of these non-indigenous villagers arrived at the New Territories, built tin shacks and settled along rivers or around arable farmland; others swarmed into the sprawling squatter areas across the hills of the Kowloon peninsula and on Hong Kong Island.

Surviving the collective subjectivity   141

In 1982, a survey of different squatter areas in Hong Kong had been conducted to stocktaking all the structures, after which no major alterations were allowed. The government considered these structures as an unauthorized occupation of government land or leased agricultural land, "but they are tolerated to remain on a temporary basis ... until the Surveyed Squatter Structures has to be cleared for development, environmental improvement or safety reasons" (Lands Department 2016). Although such toleration does not imply any legal rights to the occupants, rehousing arrangement would be provided by the Housing Department to assist eligible occupants to resettle in a public or interim housing subject to the statutory income and asset test (Housing Department 2006).

Such a rehousing policy was also applicable to the initial rehousing arrangement for the Choy Yuen Village as depicted in the section on development-for-all discourse. However, after about half a century of habitation in the old Choy Yuen Village which was located at Shek Kong in the northwest of the New Territories, many households were not eligible for the original rehousing arrangement. This implied that although these villagers had been living on the soil for generations and their families and lives were severely affected by the construction of XRL, they were not eligible for the compensation. Ms. Lau was an active member of the Choy Yuen Village Concern Group. She and family were very shocked knowing about the eviction arrangement:

> The government had informed the indigenous households and landowners ahead of time before they announced the plan because the officials had to work out a way to fully compensate their loss in view of the XRL construction. They did not bother to inform us because they know we are non-indigenous villagers and were not entitled to many of the rehouse arrangements. Ironically, we were the residents physically residing in the village and had been affected most by the project. The landowners, for example, were not living in the village. They were either indigenous population or property developers. (Author's interview in April 2017)

Mr. Wong said that many villagers did not consider the rehousing arrangement as an adequate form of compensation. They demand collective resettlement and they wanted to continue their rural way of living:

> We were not consulted in advance and we were not given any preferential treatment as regards possible resettlement in the public or interim housing. In fact, we didn't want to be relocated to different high-rise apartments. Many of our villagers are in their 70s and 80s and they have been living in this village for 50 years. We had a collective community and these elderlies would not be able to adapt to such drastic change in the living environment. (Author's interview in March 2019)

Mr. Wong's comments were not an isolated case. Many villagers believed that the elderly would not survive long after being rehoused in a high-rise building

142 *Linda Yin-nor Tjia*

(Ho 2016; Apple Daily 2018b). There were about 500 non-indigenous villagers being directly affected by the XRL construction and they were the last to know about the eviction and received nominal compensation (Chang 2014). Kuan and Lau (1981) argued that the Hong Kong government has been relying on the leaders of rural indigenous villagers to play as middlemen for "indirect ruling" since colonial times. In the event of the land resumption for the XRL construction, indigenous villagers residing in the affected area would be assisted to rebuild their three-story permanent indigenous housing (*Ding Uk*) with 65 m² per floor. Mrs. Chong was a member of the Concern Group and she explained why there were a conflict of interest between the indigenous and non-indigenous residents:

> Those landlords and indigenous villagers, of course, did not want us to protest for collective resettlement. It was against their interests if the government eventually backed off because of our collective movement. They wanted the government to claim back their land and compensate them with money but we demanded to be able to resume our village community. (Author's interview in April 2019)

It was therefore widely reported that the non-indigenous villagers were greedy and wanted to take this rare opportunity to maximize their interest. For example, the Hong Kong Institute of Land Administration (2002), in an international conference of state land management in Hungary, reported that the government had eventually agreed not to follow strictly the original rehousing policy and adopted an unprecedented "humane approach" to offer a very generous rehousing package. With such a breaking of rules, they anticipated complicated implications for future land clearances and resumption.

The final cash allowance provided by the government comprised two parts. First, all the affected households residing in structures covered by the pre-clearance survey on November 11, 2008 (rather than the usual requirements of being registered in the 1982 Squatter Structure Survey) would be given the Domestic Removal Allowance, ranging from HK$3,000 to $10,000 according to the family size. Second, the eligible households will also be given an Ex-Gratia Cash Allowance (EGCA) of $600,000, or an EGCA of $500,000 plus an opportunity to purchase a Home Ownership Scheme (HOS) flat without being subject to/having to pass the Comprehensive Means Test.

Although the majority of the 500 affected non-indigenous villagers demanded collective relocation arrangement, some of them could not withstand the social pressure and therefore chose to arrange the relocation with the compensation on their own. Mrs. Yuen recalled that it was a stressful experience:

> The neighbouring communities regarded us as extremely greedy and materialistic. Many villagers were not emotionally prepared for being criticised by their neighbors. Some of them felt so stressful and depressed. It was very a hard time for many of them. (Author's interview in March 2019)

Surviving the collective subjectivity 143

Mrs. Yuen once took a taxi and asked the driver to drop her a few blocks away from the village as she was visiting a neighbor. The driver thought she was an outsider and started to chat with her, saying that the people residing in the Choy Yuen Village were troublemakers, "I was very upset. It was like we had done something bad to the community". In view of these emotional disturbances arising out of the process of resistance, some villagers gave up on collective relocation. As the chairperson of the Choy Yuen Village Concern Group, Ko felt sorry to have put some of the villagers through such a devastating experience (Law 2017).

The remaining 47 Choy Yuen Village households insisted on collective resettlement. In February 2010, the government relaxed the existing agricultural resite policy, allowing genuine Choy Yuen village farmers to find an appropriate piece of farmland, resume their agricultural activities, erect structures for domestic purposes in the vicinity of their farmland and live in a cluster community:

> in general an agricultural resite applicant needed to be verified as a genuine farmer and, at the same time, submitted a feasible farming plan providing information such as the location of the replacement agricultural site. The Administration understood that the affected villagers might not be able to find replacement sites in a short period of time to continue farming and submit their farming plans to the relevant department for examining their feasibility ... The applicant might locate a private agricultural site and submit a farming plan to the authorities concerned for approval after he or she was verified as a genuine farmer. (HKSAR Government 2010b)

Despite getting closer to their hope of collective resettlement, conflicts continued to mount. For example, some of the households in Choi Yuen Village began to register with the Lands Department for the verification process, and others wanted to resist longer for a better compensation package. The relations among the affected villagers became tense because different households had their own concerns and some of them started to calculate when they should give in so they would receive the best compensation. As the date of site clearance approached, there were also an increasing number of conflicts between the government officials and the villagers. The Choy Yuen Village Support Group mobilized more activists to form a patrol team to safeguard the structures and villagers. The battlefield-like environment had further intensified the depression and frustrating emotion among villagers. The irreversible resilience continued during a prolonged period of site clearance operation between November and December 2010 and May 2011 when the government finally resumed and cleared old Choy Yuen Village. As the XRL project affected approximately 150 households with a population of 450 and around two million 800 m^2 in size of agricultural land. The government has offered a total of up to HK$95 million compensation to about 230 affected households, and another HK$160 million to landowners in terms of land compensation (The Hong Kong Institute of Land Administration 2002).

144 *Linda Yin-nor Tjia*

Conclusion

Although the new Choy Yuen Village households were approved to continue their agriculture activities and erect a structure in the vicinity of their farmland under the Land Rehabilitation Scheme (Vegetable Marketing Organization 1998), they still have to prove that they were genuine farmers before the forced eviction. Mrs. Yuen told me that it took them almost six months to come up with the necessary evidence such as sales receipts. Besides proving their identity as genuine farmers, they also had to hunt for a suitable piece of farmland and a site for the new village. In August 2010, 59 farming licenses were approved out of 86 applications. These households managed to acquire a site of 13,570 m^2 with HK$18 million. Although a group of scholars and architects volunteered to assist in the design of a sustainable eco-village, countless hurdles followed. For example, they still had to resolve all the issues regarding a collective community, such as the right to use a private road connecting the new site to the main road. After the road rights were settled, they began to work on water and electricity provision. With a view to actualizing their collective lifestyle, these approved households have to seek common consensus before they can move forward. Collective resettlement was costing their time and effort, as well as emotional endurance.

In view of the development-for-all discourse of XRL construction, the democracy-for-all vision of the political movement and the community-for-all narrative of social resilience, the non-indigenous households in Choy Yuen Village eventually made it through to relocate collectively in a nearby cluster adjacent to Yuen Kong village. They have developed very close bonding among themselves as well as with the activists who had come to support them and involved in the process of resistance and social movement. Their resistance, driven by collective subjectivity, however, had become so strong that it paved the way for an irreversible evolvement of action that cost them enormous emotional disruption.

The case of Choy Yuen Village resistance against the construction of the XRL illustrates the emotional backlash against elites' discourse of globalization was powerful enough to initiate a social movement in Hong Kong. The quest for an autonomous community and an alternative way of living has given rise to populism in view of the visible project of globalization and capitalization. These democracy-for-all and community-for-all discourses complicate the nature of marginalization. The feeling of being left out in the process of the development-led economy traumatizes people in such a way that material compensation could hardly make up for the damage.

Notes

1 Green Form Certificate:
   Subject to detailed eligibility criteria on age, family composition, residence rule and so on to be announced by the Housing Authority (HA) prior to the launch of each sale exercise, the following categories of persons are eligible for Green Form status in buying Green Form Subsidised Home Ownership Scheme (GSH) flats:

   • Households of Public Rental Housing (PRH) units under the Hong Kong Housing Authority (HA) (with the exception of tenants under conditional tenancies, tenants allocated PRH units through the Express Flat Allocation Scheme within three years from the commencement of their tenancies or monthly licensees of HA Transitional Rental Housing Units) or the households of Hong Kong Housing Society (HS) of Group A rental estates (with the exception of households of Group B rental estates or monthly licensees of HS transitional Rental Housing units);

- Persons falling into one of the following categories who are holders of valid Green Form Certificates issued by the Housing Department (HD)/Urban Renewal Authority–

  i Successful PRH applicants whose eligibility for allocation of PRH has been established, and who are due for allocation of PRH in about a year's time;
  ii Junior civil servants under Civil Service Public Housing Quota, whose eligibility has been established;
  iii Clearees affected in clearance exercises initiated by the Government and victims of natural disasters whose PRH eligibility has been established;
  iv Clearees affected in urban renewal projects whose PRH eligibility has been established;
  v PRH residents whose eligibility for allocation of PRH flat has been established due to divorce/splitting; and
  vi Former PRH tenants holding a Letter of Assurance issued by the HD whose eligibility for allocation of the PRH flat has been established.

Staff of the Estate Assistant (EA)grade of the HD who is holding a valid Letter of Assurance (LA) issued by the HD; and Recipients of Rent Allowance for the Elderly Scheme (RAES) administered by the HA.

Source: Green Form Subsidised Home Ownership Scheme, Hong Kong Housing Authority, https://www.housingauthority.gov.hk/en/home-ownership/gsh-ownership/index.html (Accessed 28, 2019)

2 The Home Ownership Scheme.

(HOS) is a subsidized-sale program of public housing in Hong Kong managed by the Hong Kong Housing Authority. Source: Sale of Home Ownership Scheme flats, Hong Kong Housing Authority web page, www.housingauthority.gov.hk/en/home-ownership/hos-flats/index.html (Accessed August 28, 2019)

3 Secondary Market Scheme:

The Hong Kong Housing Authority (HA) formally established the HOS Secondary Market Scheme (HOSSMS) in June 1997. It enables public housing tenants and Green Form Certificate holders to purchase flats sold under Home Ownership Scheme (HOS)/Private Sector Participation Scheme (PSPS)/Tenants Purchase Scheme (TPS) (hereinafter collectively referred to as HOS flats) with the date of first assignment from the third years onward.

Source: White Form Secondary Market Scheme, Hong Kong Housing Authority, www.housingauthority.gov.hk/mini-site/wsm2019/en/general-info.html (28 August 2019).

4 Sale Programme of Surplus Home Ownership Scheme.

The government repositioned its subsidized housing policy and ceased the production and sale of HOS flats in November 2002. Since 2007 the Housing Authority has put up some 16,700 surplus HOS flats for sale by phases.

Source: Memorandum for the Subsidised Housing Committee of the Hong Kong Housing Authority: Revitalising the Home Ownership Scheme Secondary Market, Legco paperno, SHC32/2020. www.thb.gov.hk/eng/policy/housing/policy/consultation/2010/shc3210.pdf

5 Interim Housing.

Government's policy is to ensure that no one will become homeless as a result of natural disasters or clearance operations. To achieve this objective, the Housing Authority provides accommodation for households who are not immediately eligible for

146 *Linda Yin-nor Tjia*

public rental housing. These households are accommodated in Transit Centres and Interim Housing having regard to their individual circumstances. Interim Housing provides accommodation to: homeless households transferred from Transit Centres; squatter clearees not fulfilling the eligibility criteria for public rental housing; and unauthorized occupants of public housing estates.

Source: Legislative Council Panel on Housing
Policy on Interim Housing and Transit Centre, CB(1) 1192/0102(04)
www.legco.gov.hk/yr0102/english/panels/hg/papers/hg0304cbl-1192-4e.pdf

Works Cited

Apple Daily. (2008a). 'Shi gang cai yuan cun shou di ju min shi bao jia yuan' (Reclamation of the Shek Kong Choy Yuen Village: Inhabitants are Determined to Safeguard their Homeland), 22 December, A12.

Apple Daily. (2008b). 'Gao tie bi qian: cai yuan cun shi nian sheng si liang mang mang' (High Speed Rail and Forced Resettlement: Ten Years' Dim Life and Death of Choy Yuen Villagers), 19 September.

Barsade, S. G. (2002). The ripple effect: Emotional contagion and its influence on group behaviour. *Administrative Science Quarterly*, 47(4), 644–675.

Chan, J. H. (2009). 'Cong jiao xia liu zou de ben tu' (The Disappearance of Localism), 16 February, *Ming Pao*.

Chang, D. (2010). Inside Tsoi Yuen Village, the heart of the Hong Kong railway controversy, *CNN*, 11 January. http://travel.cnn.com/hong-kong/play/gallery-inside-tsoi-yuen-village-heart-express-rail controversy-474851/

Chang, N. (2014). *Development-based eviction becomes a grouping human rights issues in Hong Kong: UN's principles and guildlines, a new paradigm for SAR and NGOs to address the problem* (Master Thesis). City University of Hong Kong.

Chen, Y. C. (2015). Land Justice and the planning of democratization: Hong Kong experience. In K. Yeung (Ed.), *The Monstrosity of Development: Rethinking and Resisting the Illusion of Economic Growth* (pp. 153–169). Kuala Lumpur: Genta Media.

Chu, K. D. (2009). 'Zhong shuai guo jia zi xun' (Worse than Fake Consultation), 10 March, *Inmedia*. Retrieved from: www.inmediahk.net/node/1002532.

Environment, Transport and Works Bureau. (2006). Legislative Council brief: Northern link and Hong Kong section of Guangzhou-Shenzhen-Hong Kong express rail link, File Ref: ETWB(T)CR 1/16/581/99, www.thb.gov.hk/eng/archives/transport/legislative/others/LegCo%20Brief%20(E ng)%206-2-06.pdf.

Environment, Transport and Works Bureau. (2007). Legislative Council panel on transport subcommittee on matters relating to railways: Northern link and Hong Kong section of Guangzhou-Shenzhen-Hong Kong express rail link, January, CB(1)573/06–07(04), www.legco.gov.hk/yr0607/english/panels/tp/tp_rdp/papers/tp_rdp010 5cbl-573–4-e.pdf.

Flam, H. (2000). *The Emotional Man and the Problem of Collective Action*. Frankfurt am Main: Peter Lang.

Gould, D. B. (2009). *Moving Politics: Emotion and Act Up's Fight against AIDS*. Chicago: University of Chicago Press.

Highways Department. (2008). *Hong Kong Section of Guangzhou-Shenzhen-Hong Kong Express Rail Link*. www.hyd.gov.hk/en/road_and_railway/railway_projects/xrl/gazett al/scheme/index.html.

Ho, J. H. (2016). 'Hui wang cai yuan cun, wo kan jian tui tu ji qian de rou ren li liang' (Looking Back to Choy Yuen Village, I Witness the Resilience in front of Bulldozers), 9 June, *Initium Media*. Retrieved from: www.theinitium.com/article/20160609-hongkong-choiyuenvillage/

Hong Kong SAR Government. (2000). *Railway Development Strategy*. Hong Kong: Transport Bureau.

Hong Kong SAR Government. (2002). *Chief Secretary promotes the infrastructure cooperation between the Mainland and Hong Kong*, 20 September, www.info.gov.hk/gia/general/200209/20/0920159.htm

Hong Kong SAR Government. (2007). *Tenth plenary of the Hong Kong/Guangdong co-operation joint conference*, 2 August, www.info.gov.hk/gia/general/200708/02/P200708020266.htm

Hong Kong SAR Government. (2008). *Legislative Council brief: Northern link and Hong Kong section of Guangzhou-Shenzhen-Hong Kong express rail link*, File Ref.: THB(T) CR 1/16/581/99, www.legco.gov.hk/yr07-08/english/panels/tp/tp_rdp/papers/tp_rdp-thbtcr11658199-e.pdf

Hong Kong SAR government information. (2010a). *Government meets Choi Yuen Tsuen villagers to explain compensation package*, Press release, 18 January, www.info.gov.hk/gia/general/201001/18/P201001180266.htm

Hong Kong SAR government information. (2010b). *Agricultural resite policy allows farmers to live in clusters*, Press release, 22 February, www.info.gov.hk/gia/general/201002/22/P201002220287.htm

Hong Kong Housing Authority. (2019a). *Green form subsidised home ownership scheme*. www.housingauthority.gov.hk/en/home-ownership/gsh-ownership/index.html

Hong Kong Housing Authority. (2019). *Revitalising the home ownership scheme secondary market*. www.thb.gov.hk/eng/policy/housing/policy/consultation/2010/shc3210.pdf

Hong Kong Housing Authority. (2019b). *Sale of Home Ownership Scheme flats, Hong Kong Housing Authority web page*. www.housingauthority.gov.hk/en/home-ownership/hosflats/index.html

Hong Kong Housing Authority. (2019c). *White Form Secondary Market Scheme, Hong Kong Housing*. www.thb.gov.hk/eng/policy/housing/policy/consultation/2010/shc3210.pdf

Housing Department. (2006). *Rehousing of occupants upon clearance, Policies on Public Housing, Section A, Chapter 2*. www.housingauthority.gov.hk/en/common/pdf/about-us/policy-fo cus/policies on-public-housing/A02/A02.pdf

Huang, S. M. (2018). Urban farming as a transformative planning practice: The contested new territories in Hong Kong. *Journal of Planning Education and Research*, 1–16. doi: 10.1177/0739456X18772084.

Hung, H. F., & Ip, I. C. (2012). Hong Kong's democratic movement and the making of China's offshore civil society. *Asian Survey*, 52(3), 504–527.

Ip, Y. C. (2009). 'Liu dong ya dao di fang—guang shen gang gao tie de gong yi wen ti' (Space of Flow Becomes More Important than Space of Places: The Justice of Guangzhou-Shenzhen-Hong Kong Express Rail), 16 February, *Ming Pao*.

Jasper, J. M. (1997). *The Art of Moral Protest Culture, Biography, and Creativity in Social Movements*. Chicago: University of Chicago Press.

Krause, S. R. (2008). *Civil Passions: Moral Sentiment and Democratic Deliberation*. Princeton: Princeton University Press.

148 Linda Yin-nor Tjia

Kuan, H., & Lau, S. (1981). Planned development and political adaptability in rural area. In A. Y. C. King, & R. P. L. Lee (Eds.), *Social Life and Development in Hong Kong* (pp. 169–194). Hong Kong: Chinese University Press.

Lam-Knott, S. (2018). Anti-hierarchical activism in Hong Kong: The post-80s youth. *Social Movement Studies*, 17(4), 464–470.

Lands Department. (2016). *Squatter control policy on surveyed squatter structures.* www.landsd.gov.hk/en/images/doc/scpp_e.pdf

Lau, B. J. (2018). Hui gu fan gao tie: yu wang yu chuang shang de pin tu (Reflection on the Anti-High Speed Rail Campaign: A Combination of Desire and Tragedies), 8 October, *WeMedia01 (HK) Limited*, B19.

Law, Z. M. (2017). Cai yuan cun ba nian shi an dun 'xi sheng xiao wo, shi fou ke wan cheng da wo? (The Resettlement of Choy Yuen Village in Eight Years: Could The Sacrifice Benefit the Society at Large?'), *WeMedia01 (HK) Limited*.

Legislative Council Panel on Housing. (2019). *Policy on Interim Housing and Transit Centre.* www.legco.gov.hk/yr01-02/english/panels/hg/papers/hg0304cb1-1192-4e.pdf

Li, H. (2013). *Contentious politics in two villages: Comparative analysis of anti-high-speed-rail campaigns in Hong Kong and Taiwan* (PhD Thesis). The Chinese University of Hong Kong.

Ma, M. L. Y. (2017). Affective framing and dramaturgical actions in social movements. *Journal of Communication Inquiry*, 41(1), 5–21.

Ma, N. (2011). Value changes and legitimacy crisis in post-industrial Hong Kong. *Asian Survey*, 51(4), 683–712.

Marcus, G. E. (2002). *The Sentimental Citizen: Emotion in Democratic Politics.* University Park, Pennsylvania: The Pennsylvania State University Press.

Mass Transport Railways Limited. (2008). *Hong Kong section of Guangzhou-Shenzhen-Hong Kong express rail link project profile*, April, www.epd.gov.hk/eia/register/profile/latest/esb189/esb189.pdf

Park, R. E. (1928). Human migration and the marginal men. *American Journal of Sociology*, 33(6), 881–893.

Peng, L. F. (2019). 'Sheng huo da ren' (Life Expert), *Ming Pao*, 3 February, S01.

Roces, M. (2009). Prostitution, women's movements and the victim narrative in the Philippines. *Women's Studies International Forum*, 32(4), 270–280.

Ruiz-Junco, N. (2013). Feeling social movements: Theoretical contributions to social movement research on emotions. *Sociology Compass*, 7(1), 45–54.

The Hong Kong Institute of Land Administration. (2002). A review of the approach in land acquisition of Choi Yuen Tsuen (CYT) for the Guangzhou-Shenzhen-Hong Kong Express Rail Link (XRL) (Hong Kong Section) project, and recommendations for a possible and reasonable approach in land acquisition in future government projects, paper presented in State land management in transitional countries: Issues and ways forward, International seminar, Budapest, Hungary, 20–21 September, www.fig.net/resources/proceedings/2012/Hungary_2012_comm7/6.5_paper_fung.pdf

Transport and Housing Bureau. (2008). Legislative Council panel on transport subcommittee on matters relating to railways: Design and site investigation for the Hong Kong section of Guangzhou Shenzhen-Hong Kong express rail link, LC Paper No. CB(1)1376/07–08(01), www.legco.gov.hk/yr07-08/english/panels/tp/tp_rdp/papers/tp_rdp0502cb1-1376-1-e.pdf

Transport and Housing Bureau. (2009). Legislative Council panel on transport subcommittee on matters relating to railways progress of the Hong Kong section of

Guangzhou-Shenzhen-Hong Kong express rail link, 14 May, LC Paper No. CB(1) 1550/08–09(01), www.legco.gov.hk/yr0809/english/panels//tp/tp_rdp/papers/tp_rdp0514cb1-1550-1-e.pdf

Van Dijk, J. (2009). Free the victim: A critique of the western conception of victimhood. *International Review of Victimology*, 16(1), 1–33.

Vegetable Marketing Organization. (1998). *Land Rehabilitation Scheme*. www.vmo.org/en/index/page_support/item_plan/

Westen, D. (2007). *The Political Brain: The Role of Emotion in Deciding the Fate of the Nation*. New York: Public Affairs.

Xia, Y. (2016). Collective action frame and cultural context: A study of the anti-express-rail-link movement in Hong Kong. *Chinese Journal of Sociology*, 2(2), 300–323.

Part IV
Margins in India

7 Waste in the urban margins
The example of Delhi's waste pickers

Rémi de Bercegol and Shankare Gowda

With a global urban population of three billion, cities are currently generating around 1.3 billion tons of waste every year (Hoornweg, Bhad-Tata, 2012). By 2050, cities, most of them in the South, will account for two thirds of global demographic growth, producing even greater volumes of waste. Although widely neglected by urban policies, the question of urban waste has become a major issue in the context of global urbanization (Un-Habitat 2010). It is now commonly accepted that we need to better control the socio-environmental impacts of human emissions, a source of multiple pollutions and "environmental injustice" (Durand 2015), affecting in particular the margins of cities with the emergence of gigantic landfill sites and increasingly severe forms of pollution.

This chapter examines the marginalization of "waste workers" (Corteel & Le Lay 2011) who recover and recycle waste materials. "Waste pickers" are paradoxical figures: they are invisible and invisibilized, but remain eminently present and recognizable in public spaces; they usually live in the periphery, but have a very thorough knowledge of the city, its residents and their detritus (Bercegol et al. 2019). In a way, they are the perfect illustration of the "marginal man" (Park 1928) described in the introduction of this book. Of course, waste management has its own specific context, but it presents strong similarities with Park's concept: the persons who handle waste are stigmatized by society; they are seen as different, abnormal and as such relegated to the margins. Why and how does this marginalization manifest itself? Wouldn't it be legitimate to think that these workers should on the contrary be fully involved in the management of waste?

Our hypothesis is that it is worth supporting recovery and recycling activities happening in the margins, where the "people [of the informal recycling sector act] as infrastructure" (see Simone 2004). This could provide a highly efficient solution despite a number of drawbacks, which are partly due to this activity's relegation to informality by public authorities. To support this claim, we will examine empirical materials collected over the course of several field trips in Delhi, India: a city considered one of the most polluted metropolises in the world. The data comes from an ongoing ethnographic research project on waste recycling. The field work consists in tracking the "informal" actors of the waste recovery chain, from its collection through to its processing by industries. Because of its gigantic proportions, the case of India provides a concentrated image of the socio-environmental issues associated with the consumerist and productivist model, which generates a growing amount of urban waste while paradoxically marginalizing the people who contribute to reducing its volume. Waste recovery provides a particularly relevant point of observation to understand the sector's economic and environmental challenges, as well as the marginalization of waste workers. In India, waste recovery is heavily stigmatized due to its association with the impurity of waste. This phenomenon is reinforced culturally by caste exclusion. Most waste pickers come from hierarchically stigmatized castes. They are relegated to the very margins of society, marginalized both socially and geographically, and forced to live in dangerous areas. This relegation to informality creates situations of brutal exploitation, as well as diminishing the efficiency of the recovery and recycling process.

This chapter will first examine today's main waste management strategies and their translation in the context of India. Working from literature on this topic, we will see how the sector's modernization has worsened the marginalization of the poorest populations. Based on empirical observations, the second part describes the functioning of the reclaiming process. Despite its social and geographic marginality, this system reveals a rich and complex structure that challenges preconceptions. Finally, the last part discusses how the marginalization of waste recovery workers has also become a political object, with the emergence of discourses that legitimize this work, oppose the reforms or seek to adapt them. Beyond the case of India, this analysis sheds light on the process through which waste recovery is marginalized, while investigating potential courses of action that could help meet the challenges of sustainable urbanization.

From cast-off refuse into a valuable resource

The linear management paradigm

Beyond India, the very notion of "waste" remains a relatively recent invention in our societies, which followed the late nineteenth century's industrial revolution in the North (Barles 2014). Human settlements, and in particular cities, have always been a source of emissions, whether solid or liquid. For years, this residue was naturally reused or transformed (muckspreading, reusing wood, darning clothes, etc.). However, with the industrialization of European cities in the last century and the growth and transformation of these emissions, the "hygienist" movement (Berdier & Deleuil 2006) re-characterized this residue as being no longer a resource but a health hazard. Large-scale technical systems aimed at collecting and disposing of this residue were designed during this period, to transfer the risk into the peripheries in order to push out any harmful substances into marginalized spaces (Durand 2015).

Landfills symbolize the dead-end of this linear management model, also known as the "end of pipe". Burying waste is a doomed, unsustainable solution in the long run, with a growing need for increasingly large landfill sites, in India as in the north. Since the late twentieth century, this linear-engineering method has been gradually giving way to a circular understanding of flows, within which waste is increasingly perceived as a resource that can be reclaimed (Barles 2014) – although the paradigm of elimination remains predominant. In this perspective, waste incineration can appear as a circular technology, in the sense that it provides a potential source of electric power ("Waste-to-Energy" technology). However, the principle that presides over incineration with energy recovery is substantially similar to the "end of pipe" model with its landfill sites, since the final purpose remains the elimination of waste.

Waste recovery: a neglected alternative

On the contrary, this process can function as a circular metabolism where the reuse of secondary materials contributes to significantly reducing pressure on resources. In this context, southern cities appear as pathfinders: these are cities where "informal" waste recovery systems, considered more efficient than "modernized" formal services, have been established for years (Wilson et al. 2006, 2012), with rag pickers rummaging dumps and garbage cans in search of materials that can be resold, repaired, reused or recycled. Unlike in the north where this process forms part of an environment-centered approach, waste recycling in the south arises from need. This process provides a breeding ground for a vibrant economy that exists in close interaction with the formal sector.

In this respect, "Asian cities [that] have extensive 'waste economies'" (Furedy 1992) could indicate potential paths of action to tackle the challenge of sustainable urbanization. In Asia, reuse and recycling practices are deeply embedded in local culture and highly dynamic (Wu & Zhang 2016, 2019; Gill 2012). The retrieval of used materials contributes to reducing the pressure on resources while providing a livelihood for scores of laborers involved in the small-scale recycling industries. For Delhi's waste pickers and *kabariwalla*, who operate at the bottom of a vast and hierarchized recycling chain, waste materials are a valuable resource to be extensively exploited. The chain of reuse and recycling, which is only informal at its base (and then connects to formal traders and large industries), is an existing mechanism that reduces resource wastage and contributes to a more circular economy. According to such a de-centered perspective (Chakrabarty 2000), the urban margins of southern cities where these recovery industries have developed can be perceived, beyond their poverty, as a source of so far underexploited alternatives and as a model for a genuine circular economy.

Waste pickers earn an income through waste collection while complementing municipal services in cities where such services are insufficient. However, in spite of their contribution to the community, these activities are only rarely acknowledged. The waste pickers, who recover the goods that are discarded by other city dwellers, are pushed out to the margins of society. In addition to its lack of social recognition, this alternative is also marginalized by public policies. Recycling is still considered a degrading job, and waste pickers are frequently excluded from the restructuring programs delivered through public service reforms, although these programs have a major impact on their practices. Under the guise of "modernizing" the sector, rather than using existing local solutions, public authorities favor technical solutions that rely heavily on privatization, to the detriment of informal recovery agents (Cointreau-Levine 1994; Bartone 1995; Baud & Post 2003; Nas & Jaffe 2004; Coad 2005; Wilson et al. 2006). In Delhi, as in other cities, this status quo is symbolized by incinerators: while these are presented as "modern" facilities that can significantly reduce the volume of landfill waste, they can function correctly only if they are fed waste materials with a high heat generation potential such as plastics, paper and cardboard – the same materials that had traditionally been recycled by recovery workers.

Waste modernization in India: a pretext for the eviction of the poor

Delhi and its waste management issues

A major power on the international stage with a growth rate on par with European countries, India is struggling to control the impacts of fast economic development on its urban environment. While cities, which contribute 60%–65% of the country's GDP, act as a showcase for the country, they are literally drowning in their own waste. It is estimated that over 125,000 tons per day are disposed of every day (CPCB 2012). In Delhi for instance, the local authorities manage no less than 9,000 to 10,000 tons of waste per day. With a population of over 16 million (according to the 2011 Census),[1] India's capital sorely lacks space for the treatment of these gigantic volumes of waste. About 20 landfill sites have been shut down since 1975. By 2014, four large landfills remained active, three of which are overexploited and well beyond their life span (10–20 years), with meters-high mountains of detritus. In this context, waste incineration technologies appear as a panacea that could be all the more lifesaving that they could also provide a source of energy, produced from the incineration of materials. The government therefore contracted private operators to manage three new waste-to-energy facilities.

However, these Western-born technologies remain problematic in Delhi: first of all, for environmental reasons as their atmospheric emissions would worsen an already disastrous health situation, in a city where the concentration of fine particulate matter – under 2.5 μm – is already 15 times higher than the OMS standard. This option also poses technical issues due to the low calorific value of incoming waste materials: most of the materials that reach the plants are biodegradable since most of the best combustible materials have already been recovered by informal waste pickers, which reduces their energy recovery ratio. This strategy goes along with the modernization of waste collection, including the privatization of municipal collection points and carrier companies feeding combustible waste into the incinerators. This process thus competes directly with waste recycling, a marginalized alternative in Delhi as in other Indian cities.

The marginalization of "non-modern" practices

As in other developing cities around the world, the modernization of waste management in Delhi can be seen as an expression of the "sanitary ideal" (Melosi 2000) that seeks to replicate technical solutions developed in the north, leaving little or no place for the informality of poor neighborhoods and their "non-modern" waste recycling practices. On similar processes in Cairo, Bénédicte Florin notes that the "ideology" of modernization (Florin & Cirelli 2015) causes public sector decision-makers to consider informal sector actors as "ineligible" to be integrated into the new, planned system. Urban elites and funders (according to whom "the collection systems in India are primitive", The World Bank 2008: 19) see recycling workers as backward and incompatible with "modern" waste management (Wilson et al. 2006). On the pretext of sustainable development, this work must necessarily be placed in the hands of private organized companies and rely on mechanized equipment. In addition to being excluded from this process, many slum dwellers whose survival depends on waste recovery are "dispossessed" from their means of subsistence (Schindler et al. 2012). In this context, the privatization of the sector and the choice of incineration to solve the waste crisis and generate energy are not just innocuous socio-technical choices. They reflect a social choice that embodies the primacy of capitalist accumulation over the power of work:

> The process of [waste incineration] can be seen as an example of accumulation by dispossession, which means there is an inherent necessity of the owners of capital to separate, by force if necessary, labourers (waste workers) from the means of production (waste, transfer stations, etc). Once this process is complete, a small number of waste workers are offered the opportunity to sell their labour for a wage in waste-to-energy plants. (Schindler et al. 2012: 20)

When describing the informal recyclers of electronic waste in Bangalore who are experiencing a similar situation of dispossession, Reddy proposes the concept of "abjection", which describes not only the injustice of being excluded but also the humiliation of being expelled from a sector to which they have always belonged (Reddy 2015: 171). Reddy uses the metaphor of waste to describe "the humiliating experience of informal recyclers who become – to quote Wright (2006) – figures of waste" (ibid.: 171).

Thus the promotion of a so-called "modern" management system, based on Western models, reveals the desire to enhance control over an economy by relegating the informal actors involved in it. According to recent academic work about waste management transformations in Delhi, the infrastructural transformations taking place in the sector in Delhi can be read as a pretext using pollution to evict the city's proletarian categories (Gidwani & Reddy 2011; Gill 2012; Demaria & Schindler 2016), through the introduction of hegemonic environmental policies of neoliberal inspiration, which reveals the "violence of sustainable urbanity" (Swynguedouw 2014).

158 *Rémi de Bercegol and Shankare Gowda*

The stigmatization of poor populations

Ultimately, there appears to be an enduring association in public and political perceptions between "waste objects" and "social waste", that is, the waste pickers (Lhuilier 2005, cited by Florin 2016). These people do not fit the urban standards designed by the authorities. On a wider level, planning policies tend to deny the existence of populations relegated to informality and to produce "urban exclusion", pushing them away into the periphery (Kundu & Sarangi 2005). Political economy studies on the rise of the Indian civil society and its gentrification (Ghertner 2011) argue that the theme of environmental protection has made it possible to legitimize the relegation of poor populations, on the pretext of their adding to urban pollution. Since 1990–2000s, reforms encouraging civil participation have directly contributed to consolidating the growing influence of the powerful resident welfare associations (RWAs) in planned neighborhoods. Paradoxically, this has led to the marginalization of the poorest categories, by successfully imposing the interests of a sociologically dominant class in municipal councils, to the detriment of a poor and less organized population (Zérah 2007). The poor populations' lack of representation is particularly evident in the judicial sphere as legal procedures require financial and temporal means, which are not among these populations' prerogatives. Mobilized by the middle classes, the judicial institutions (Supreme Court of India, High Court of Delhi, Green Tribunal) have become important arbitrators whose decisions significantly impact urban governance, especially in conflicts concerning the environment – and waste in particular – promoting ecological considerations to the detriment of their social consequences. This results, for example, in the plastic recycling workshops in the city's north being shut down regularly after a ruling by the Green Tribunal: 30 units were shut down in June 2015 in Nangloi and Mundka, where the emblematic PVC market (where waste plastic is bought, segregated and resold in large volumes) has been relocated after being progressively pushed out from the city center to the periphery of Delhi (Gill 2012).

Baviskar's research on "bourgeois environmentalism" sheds light on how environmental discourses promoted by the Delhi middle class insidiously contribute to driving the poor out of the city: "For the bourgeois environmentalist, the ugliness of production must be removed from the city [...] urban spaces should be reserved for white-collar production and commerce, and consumption activities" (Baviskar 2002: 41). Legal decisions are made for local environmental reasons, with no consideration for more global environmental considerations (a reduction in the use of raw materials, for example), or for the voice of those in insecure employment. This bourgeois vision of the environment, reinforced by legal decisions in its favor, takes precedence over social considerations and amplifies the insecure situation of poor urban populations (Mawdsley 2004). The modernization of the waste sector also forms part of the "urban renewal" policies implemented in Delhi, which are in reality a euphemism for the demolition of insalubrious areas. Rehabilitation occurs in the periphery, on less expensive land: poorer inhabitants are evacuated toward the outer fringes, which sometimes worsens their living conditions (Dupont & Vaquier 2014). The "modernization" of infrastructures thus clearly forms part of a process of exclusion that relegates the poor to run-down peripheries outside the cities. Vinay Gidwani and Rajyashree N. Reddy put forward the concept of "eviscerating urbanism" (Gidwani & Reddy 2011: 1640) which is particularly relevant in the light of the last Delhi Master Plan with its "vision" of a "global city and a world-class metropolis" that has got rid of its pollution and its slums (DDA 2010: 2). Ghertner (2011) underscores the cultural importance of this aestheticization in the construction of the contemporary city, where the environmental ideal is based on the ideal model of a "world-class city". The city is created by the middle-class, to replicate model cities such as Paris, New York or Singapore, within which the poor have no place. This is actually a process that involves remodeling urban space to conform to the aesthetic models of the upper classes.

Working within the margins of Delhi's waste

From collection to recycling

This sector, despite not being formally integrated to the municipal service, is very well organized in India as it relies on dynamic caste networks from the collection of materials to their segregation and transformation. The waste generated by inhabitants is recovered informally. Waste pickers ride their rickshaws across the capital every morning to collect recyclable materials in large bags and carry them back to the slums. They also visit individual residents directly to collect all their garbage, hold on to recyclable materials and take the rest to the neighborhood's municipal collection point (the *dhalao*). Because of the garbage's impure nature and the status of the person who handles it, inhabitants usually leave their garbage bin outside their door. Nevertheless, this service is often remunerated by residents (usually around €1–1.50 per household, per month) as it spares them having to carry their garbage to the local collection point themselves. This door-to-door service, although informal, is highly structured and integrated to people's everyday lives. While this collection significantly contributes to the waste disposal process, it is not acknowledged by the municipal authorities.

Waste pickers work across the same areas daily and always visit the same houses, based on a schedule set by their *tekedar* (foreman). Each residential neighborhood (a "mine of waste", to quote Cavé 2015) is split between several buyers/wholesalers (the *kabaadiwala*) from the slum who then task their employees with collecting the materials, granting them informal rights on a residential plot. Deprived of any legal existence and particularly vulnerable, waste pickers can be chased by the police, sometimes subjected to racketeering, and often abused by residents. In order to avoid any damaging conflict, the waste pickers secure the agreement of municipal street cleaners (*safai karamchari*) before accessing an area. They also barter with private security guards to gain access to gated buildings, and negotiate their collection with resident associations in each neighborhood where they work. In some cases, the *tekedar* and the *kabaadiwala* pay out

160 *Rémi de Bercegol and Shankare Gowda*

a financial contribution to facilitate access to the materials, under the condition that the materials are exclusively sold to them by the waste pickers. Concretely, this means that each group of waste pickers is assigned a set number of buildings (ranging from 50 to over 100, depending on local arrangements) from which they are allowed collect waste. This system of informal rights is not systematic: there are also independent collectors who gradually manage to "secure" a territory without the support of a buyer/wholesaler.

This collection process forms the basis of the recycling system, which feeds secondary materials to the formal industry. The best materials collected from the residents are then selected and sold to a buyer, the *kabaadiwala*, who sells them to a wholesaler, who, after processing the materials, then sells them on as industrial inputs. By this stage, these resources have definitively lost their status of waste materials: they are sorted by type, color and quality, and are then ready to be dismantled, taken to pieces, cleaned, washed and compacted in order to be either transformed on the spot or resold to the formal sector's recycling workshops that buy this secondary material. The prices are strongly correlated to the evolutions of the international market of raw materials (Cavé 2015), which the wholesalers look up on a daily basis in specialized journals. The profit margin per kilo of recovered materials is low – 1 to 2 rupees between each intermediary – and the only way of securing an income of sorts is to process large amounts of materials. The tools and technologies can vary between places, but the workers' skills are evident throughout the process: dexterity, speed and the knowledge of the various components are all crucial to the recovery process. For example in Delhi, the *Khatik* workers of the PVC market are able to distinguish between all the various types of plastics. This does not take away from the harshness of their working conditions – repetitive and sometime dangerous tasks, uncomfortable positions and heavy loads.

Delhi, India, January 2016, photo by Rémi de Bercegol
    Caption: These four workers (Figure 7.1) are employed at a car bumper saw-mill in Tikri Kalan within the PVC Market, a market dedicated to the resell-ing of wholesale plastics where tons of materials are delivered everyday before being sorted, processed and sold on. Their job consists in sawing and grinding the car bumpers that appear in the background – a physically demanding, harsh and dangerous task. Their foreman authorized them to take a quick break so that we could chat for a few moments. Like most workers at the PVC Market, these men belong to the Khatik caste: a community traditionally as-sociated with the impure work of tanneries and relegated to the very bottom of Hindu society. For several decades however, this community has developed new skills and become able to tell apart all the different types of plastics (polypropyl-ene, polyethylene, polyvinyl chloride, polyurethane, etc.). Some Khatik became rich by marketing this knowledge (Gill 2012). Nevertheless, the four men only earn a meagre wage, in the region of 10,000 rupees (the equivalent of under €200 per month), although they do not dare to complain in front of their em-ployer. The bell rings for the end of the break and soon the workers return to the rumble of the sawmill.

Waste in the urban margins 161

Figure 7.1 At the Car Bumper Sawmill.
Source: Author photo.

Living in the margins

In Delhi, a significant share of the population (11% in 2011 according to the official census, and almost half according to other non-governmental bodies) lives in areas considered as illegal or in slums. The economy of waste plays a crucial part in these areas, as it provides the main source of subsistence for a number of households. There is a political micro-economy of waste pre-collection, with clearly structured hierarchies and collection rights. This feeds into a vast material recovery system which, although mostly informal, interacts with the formal and formalized economy as a supplier.

Every residential neighborhood is thus informally connected to a "marginal" neighborhood – including slums in the periphery or more central wholesalers' warehouses "established on vacant land or wasteland" (Bercegol et al. 2019). As noted by Bénédicte Florin (about Istanbul), these facilities generate "significant health and environmental externalities on the recovery workers' living and working environment, because by clearing the city centres and wealthy areas from their waste, recovery workers make their own areas and population more vulnerable" (Cirelli & Florin 2016: 11). In addition, the sites where the sorting and processing activities take place, including the waste workers' homes, generally lack basic facilities with no access to drinking water and basic sanitation systems. These people live and work in Delhi's most marginal neighborhoods, which suffer from their negative association with impurity, waste and poverty. Some wholesalers illegally grab a piece of land in the slum to accommodate their pickers. Some of the pickers/employees can sometime be hosted in exchange of the waste they collect for their owner. But most of the time, they must pay a rent that ranges from 1,000 to 3,000 rupees (€15–45 depending on the house's surface area and on the slum's location within the city).

Marginality is thus materialized by under-equipment and geographic relegation. In Delhi, waste workers have always been pushed out to the margin and into the city's "gaps": the waste is sorted in landfill sites and in the confines of Delhi, in very dilapidated central areas or in the far periphery. Sorting, weighing, packaging and recycling activities take place in almost undetectable in-between spaces: in this sense, waste-related work combines spatial and social marginalization. These living and working places are being gradually pushed away from the city center and relegated first into the margins and later into the city's remote peripheries.

The spatial marginalization of casteless populations has always existed in India. However, this relegation has been exacerbated by the deepening of inequalities brought about by urban capitalism. While the neoliberal system transforms some spaces to turn them into a showcase for India's economy, it marginalizes others to hide or eradicate them. Recovery workers complain about regular raids by the police who confiscate their rickshaws, a crucial tool for their morning collection. This occurred, for instance, in February 2019 in Hanuman Mandir, a neighborhood of waste pickers in the center of the rich municipality of South Delhi. In more peripheral neighborhoods, police brutality goes along with physical attacks or even murder attempts: for instance, in June 2018 in Mandanpur Khadar, a nationalist group voluntarily set fire to a camp of Muslim waste workers of likely Bangladeshi origin.

The workers and entrepreneurs of the recycling chain

Who are the waste workers?

In India, an individual's decision to join this marginalized line of work is strongly correlated to their caste of origin. Waste pickers have a similar sociological profile: they are either casteless or belong to a lower caste, some of them Muslims. Family and professional genealogies show that waste pickers are often in this profession from father to son, and sorters from mother to daughter. Similarly, belonging to the Dalit caste is inherited from one's parents. However, with the boom of waste caused by urbanization in the 1980–1990s, the sector also had to recruit beyond the communities of *Scheduled Caste*. Depending on opportunities, those can include, for instance, members of *Other Backward Class* like trader castes, farm workers or members of religious minorities, and in particular Muslims, an already stigmatized group relegated to marginalized jobs.

In general, pickers are recruited within the wider network of a *tekedar*, who often comes from the same region. These are usually poor families from the rural regions of Uttar Pradesh, Bihar or Rajasthan. Traditionally discriminated or relegated to menial tasks and field labor, they see this work as an opportunity to significantly improve their living standards and acquire relative financial stability. In recent years, undocumented Bangladeshi migrants have found work opportunities in waste recovery. However, they are relegated to the very bottom of the social ladder of waste recovery: for instance, many of them can be found at landfill sites, rummaging through incinerator residue for pieces of metal.

Although stigmatized by society and unrecognized by the government, the category of "waste workers" remains a collection of individuals with diverse statuses according to their role and profession. As noted by Florin (2017), recovery workers do not form a homogeneous group: the further down the chain of waste they work, the more relegated and excluded is their position. These degrees in the profession are connected to the status of waste: those who do the dirtiest of the "dirty job" (Hughes 1962, cited by Florin 2016) are those who work in landfills, where recovery work is particularly tough and dangerous. Fermentation produces methane, forming pockets of highly flammable and explosive gas that can create ground collapses burying the workers and causing fires. Landslides and collapses of hills of waste are frequent, like the deadly incident of September 2017 that was due to a partial collapse in the of Ghazipur landfill site in Delhi. The juice generated by the waste (lixiviate) is loaded with organic and chemical pollutants and heavy metals. These hazards are combined with the high incidence of health risks due to diseases and wounds (Chokhandre et al. 2017). At the Bhalswa landfill site, at about 4 am when the garbage trucks start to pour off their load from the top of the dump, about 50 persons are already present and over 300 gather there throughout the day: these people live at the margins of the margin, collecting the worst of the detritus. Amongst them are Bangladeshi workers: the most invisible of the invisible, the undocumented who leave in fear of being deported from the country.

An increasingly professional sector

At the very top of the social ladder, large entrepreneurs can run one or more sorting and processing factories. Thanks to their ability to adapt to the needs of the formal industry and to their access to lineage-based networks of mutual support, these waste pickers have turned into real entrepreneurs. The most fascinating example is certainly provided by the plastics sector, a material whose volumes continue to grow: recycling materials often include products that have already been recycled. All the activities of the recycling chain are present in Delhi's industrial estates, including the compression of materials into bales, the packaging of semi-finished products bound for the formal sector, the grinding of plastics (bottles, film, etc.) and the production of granulate that is then sold on to national companies. Upward mobility is not accessible to all, but it is a possibility. The increase in the quantity of waste generated from the 1980–1990s has significantly contributed to the progression of some of these workers toward entrepreneurship: some were able to save money, develop their skills, hire workers and buy equipment and vehicles. By gaining access to real estate and investment, some individuals are able to develop their waste recycling activities. Some waste workers acquired workshops that transform materials into semi-finished or finished products before they are commercialized (see Box 7.1).

164 Rémi de Bercegol and Shankare Gowda

Box 7.1 Excerpt from interview with Harinder Kumar, the owner of a plastics recycling factory in the Narela industrial estate.

When I moved to the city, I had nothing. 100 rupees in his pocket. He worked for the local Kabariwala. That was one of the only contacts he had. He would pick through the local garbage bins for him and collect whatever he could, bottles, newspapers, metals, etc., and he would bring those back to him before sorting it by type and being paid depending on what he brought. He worked hard and lived off almost nothing, and he started slowly saving a few rupees. Little by little, with his meagre savings, he began to buy materials directly from other intermediaries and selling larger amounts. That was the beginning of plastics, the volume of waste started to increase steadily and so did his profit; he was able to invest in a small hangar, at the border, to help with storage and sorting; he even brought a few people over from his village to help him manage the collection, transportation, sorting and sale of recovered materials. A few years later, he specialized in plastics and he rented out a much larger space in Bhopura, on the other side of the border, in Uttar Pradesh, and he hired some workers there. He bought a grinder and a tank to wash the plastics, which he then sold on to Delhi's industrial estates. In 2012 we were allocated a space in Narela and we invested in an extruder to produce plastic granulates to supply to the local factories. Today, I am the one managing the factory. We employ 28 people. Your garbage is gold for my family.

(C-125, Narela, Delhi February 2019)

A wide range of professions sit between these two extremes: some workers are in charge of collecting waste from homes; others of sorting, washing, grinding and selling; etc. The complex social ladder of "waste workers" mirrors the diverse segments of a "continuum" of activities that connect the informal and the formal sector (Scheinberg et al. 2011; Cirelli & Florin 2016; Scheinberg et al. 2016). The circulation of materials, money and people thus relies on a "socio-technical continuum" (Jaglin & Zérah 2010, on basic services in developing countries), rather than on an opposition between "formal" and "informal" (Florin 2017): waste pickers collect waste on behalf of intermediary buyers (formal or informal), who are in turn connected to entrepreneurs whose business develops through the transformation of garbage into industrial inputs. In many instances, the wholesaler acts as an intermediary who manages the transaction of materials between the waste pickers and the industry of recycling. These players play a crucial role in the functioning of the recycling chain: they provide the interface between, on the one hand, the waste pickers who operate outside the so-called official waste management system, and, on the other, the so-called formal economy, by transforming a material – recovered waste – into an industrial input. The hybridization and interconnection of practices and the mixed management models blur the boundaries, while distinct stakeholders can have interconnected and complementary strategies. For instance, the recycling process ties together the garbage pickers, the buyers, the owners of warehouses where the materials can be stored and the manufacturers. Waste is collected in precarious working conditions, generating a modest income for waste pickers; the materials are then moved on to warehouses, where they are processed; they eventually reach retail circuits managed by formal firms at a significant profit (as also noticed in non-Indian contexts by Cirelli & Florin 2016: 7–8).

"Leaving the margin":[2] legitimizing waste recovery

Resistance movements and counter-discourses: when competition reveals the value of waste

Over the past decades in India, this resource has been made increasingly inaccessible by a string of reforms: privatization entered in direct competition with the already existing but informal collection of reusable waste, which forms the basis of the informal recycling economy. The public authorities are reluctant to recognize these unofficial but existing collection practices, as they raise "conflicts over appropriation" with private formal firms (Cavé 2014). For instance, Cavé (2014) shows that this "conflictual dichotomy" between the organized private sector and the informal economy can be explained by the new sense of value attached to waste, now considered a commodity and as such the object of a competition that manifests itself through appropriation conflicts.

After the privatization of the *dhalaos*, the organized private sector now plans to contract some of the waste pickers, for example with IL&FS taking over private door-to-door collection in the blocks of South Delhi under its new subsidiary Dakshin Dilli Swachh Initiatives Limited (DDSIL – South Delhi Clean Initiatives Limited), in order to access waste with a high calorific value before it gets picked up by the informal recycling chain. This shift shows the implicit recognition by the private sector of the positive role played by traditional informal actors in segregating waste at its source. In particular, a former employee of Ramky created Pompom, a small start-up company that takes its inspiration from the work of garbage pickers. It offers an innovative mobile phone application that enables its users to sell their waste to a company that comes directly to their home to collect it and eventually resell it to the informal chain of recycling industries: "Don't throw it away, give it to me, waste is a valuable resource" (Interview with Pompom Manager in December 2014). This modern replication of the traditional *kabaadiwala* waste collection system through ICT evidences this system's legitimacy and efficiency, which clearly demonstrates the essential role that decentralized collection needs to play in the recovery of waste.

166 *Rémi de Bercegol and Shankare Gowda*

However, the competition of private companies contributes to further marginalizing the workers, who were already carrying out this collection work. The competition for waste and the sector's privatization are making this resource increasingly hard to access. Only few of the waste pickers will be regularized by the formal privatization. In most of the environments where they work, pickers of recyclable waste have devised strategies to work their way around these reform policies that tend to exclude them by negotiating with the employees of privatized collection points, for example by doing their rounds before the trucks. In some cases, these people also speak out through the voice of their leaders or through collective action to demand the recognition of their work and their integration to the system, or oppose waste management policies that favor privatization and incineration.

The claims of recovery workers

Waste workers often internalize their marginalization, which refrains most of them from speaking out against this widespread oppression. However, in the face of stigmatization, waste pickers also seek to remind people that they are first and foremost humans. During a conversation, Ratwaya, a prominent wholesaler from the PVC market, commented that "for them [the government], we are just *kabaadiwala*; for you [researcher] we are just *Khatik*; but for me, I'm an entrepreneur!" They stress the positive effects of their work through discourses that legitimize their contribution to the environment. Ratwaya often repeats:

> They're all talking about "Cleaning up India" [the title of a central government programme] but that is just what we do: we are cleaning up India! And we are not asking the government for anything, except that they let us work in peace!

Workers from diverse waste sorting, trading and recycling facilities, from formal industrial estates to informal recycling sites, often mention their environmental contribution to the community. Some of them seek to acquire collective legitimacy by forming groups of waste workers to defend their work and their access to the resources. These groups range from community-based associations (for instance the association of the *Khatik* workers of the PVC market), to more unionized organizations such as the *Safai Sena*, or literally the army (*sena*) of street sweepers (*safai*). These movements focus on the notion of injustice on every level. They often mention the waste workers' professional skills and knowledge: "We are capable of telling apart a hundred different types of plastics, and to recycle each one of them. Rather than burying or incinerating them, we are able to reclaim these materials", says Jai Prakash Chadhury (former Secretary of Safai Sena).

The sector's workers demand first and foremost to be allowed to work. However, while workers demand the right to work, entrepreneurs do not necessarily ask for their activity to be formalized as this would involve more controls and taxes. For instance, the wholesalers of the PVC market are fighting for the cancellation of the Goods and Services Tax: a tax they have been subjected to since 2017 after being previously exempted from it, and which they perceive as profoundly unfair. According to them, they should not be paying tax on materials that are considered as waste but should on the contrary be supported by the public authorities. Thanks to their lobbying, they succeeded in reducing the rate from 18% to 5%, but they are still fighting to have the tax canceled entirely. In addition to these fiscal constraints, they are also subjected to sometimes unfair environmental standards regulating polluting activities. Plastic wholesalers protested against the closure of the PVC market for two weeks in November 2018, due to the fact that the sector was said to contribute to New Delhi's air pollution peaks – although the market was only a sorting and trading facility with no discharges or emissions. Since 2018–2019, processing plants in industrial estates – which are on the contrary highly polluting facilities – must now be equipped with water filters to sanitize the liquid waste resulting from the rinsing of shredded materials. However, in the absence of any subsidies helping them to comply, the cost of these changes forces some entrepreneurs to relocate some of their activities to other neighboring states around Delhi (Haryana, Rajasthan and Uttar Pradesh) where the regulations are less stringent.

De-marginalizing a legitimate activity

An environmental contribution

Waste workers are relieving the city from large volumes of waste, all for free. Recognizing the existence of local recycling initiatives would improve the efficiency of the waste management system and contribute to reducing the volume of waste. Despite the competition with formal private operators, the sector continues to recover and process vast quantities of materials, including paper, plastics, glass and metals (Chaturvedi & Gidwani 2011; Gidwani & Reddy 2011; Cavé 2014). Nevertheless, given its informal nature, this sector remains extremely difficult to quantify. Our empirical data provides a rough assessment based on a sample of 15 families or groups of workers in Hanuman Mandir, a slum in South Delhi that is mainly inhabited by rag pickers who collect waste from neighboring middle-class areas. We followed these groups for two weeks in December 2016 around Safdarjung Enclave, an upper-middle-class area located next to the slum. We found that an average of 40–50 kilograms of waste materials (excluding glass bottles) were collected per family and sold daily to a local wholesaler. For a municipality of this size, this could mean that around 2,000–2,500 tons of waste per day are informally diverted for recycling, based on a conservative estimate of 50,000 waste picking families working in Delhi (Interview with Chintan manager in January 2016). This would amount to 20% of the waste generated daily in Delhi, which concurs with the figure commonly advanced by NGOs and waste pickers' advocates. Waste pickers appear altogether more skilled and efficient than the formal system in terms of gathering and segregating the waste (Chaturvedi & Gidwani 2011: 59) – a fact also observed by researchers in other developing countries (Gunsilius et al. 2011).

Chintan (www.chintan-india.org), a non-governmental organization working to support informal waste pickers in Delhi, estimates that, as well as reducing the amount of waste sent to landfill sites, the informal workers help to reduce emissions by 900,000 tons of CO_2 per year by recycling materials free of cost for the public authorities, saving the municipality 15 million rupees per day (307,000 USD/day) if the waste pickers were getting paid a minimum wage like the 60,000 municipal sweepers. Calls for tenders for an organized door-to-door collection service were issued in December 2014 to the large-scale private organized sector, for the expansion of this collection to the entire city. Advocacy groups working on behalf of the waste pickers such as the NGO Chintan in Delhi, or unions like All India Kabari Mazdoor Mahasangh and Safai Sena,[3] are fighting for the informal sector to be recognized and fairly included: "Collection has to be formally given to those who have been doing it for ever and are already helping to reduce the waste crisis" (Interview with Chintan Manager in January 2016). Similar points are made by the Alliance of Indian Wastepickers, who asked the Indian Ministry of Environment for the new regulations on solid waste to factor in the part played by waste pickers in waste management and their integration to the system. Thanks to these organizations' lobbying, waste pickers are now explicitly mentioned in the Solid Waste and Management Rules, for the first time in an official document on municipal waste management. However, this integration process continues to face challenges: the public authorities often tend to eradicate some links in the chain, and in particular the most precarious waste pickers.

An economic need

In a city characterized by major inequalities, waste retrieval is one of the main means of subsistence for a large number of poor households, and their sole employment: "We make our living out of waste", says a rag picker (Interview with Hanuman Mandir in January 2016). If the sector was better integrated, the workers' jobs would be guaranteed, from the lowest-level collectors to the manufacturers at the top of the pyramid – along with the countless professions specializing in the collection, sorting, reselling, cleaning, crushing and transformation of materials. It has been estimated that the total social value added from waste-marketing activities in Delhi could be around Rs 3,587 million per year (USD 56 million) (Hayami et al. 2006: 63–64). This waste recovery economy provides a basic income for hundreds of families and ultimately, at the end of the chain, sustains the formal industries that produce consumer goods. The regulation of the recycling sector and its inclusion into the waste management process would make it possible to gradually introduce social and environmental standards to avoid the sector's numerous socio-environment shortcomings. It is therefore necessary to move beyond the sordid image of a sector that is doubtless

Waste in the urban margins 169

imperfect in many respects, but whose abuses (in particular exploitation and child labor) are in fact facilitated by its very informality.

Without any recognition of the sector's legitimacy and any proper public support, the workers' precarious labor conditions will keep deteriorating. This can already be seen in the impact of the Okhla waste-to-energy plant for the rag pickers living in its vicinity. In this area, workers' earnings have decreased by 21% according to a survey based on a sample of 109 persons working there (Chintan 2012: 12). As stated by the Alliance of Indian Wastepickers,

> Informal workers are highly vulnerable, needing special and urgent attention. Strong measures like increased social security need to be undertaken to reduce the risk. In the coming years, we must commit ourselves to the campaign of social security for informal workers and fight for the 'Right to Social Security' to become a justiciable right. In addition, the questions of housing, education, skill-building, nutritious food and clean environment all need answers, preferably sooner than later. (Arora 2016)

Waste pickers' advocates would like to see the introduction of a management model inspired by the SWaCH (Solid Waste Collection, and Handling) cooperative in Pune, a large city in the state of Maharashtra. Regarded as a model of its kind in India, it consists of a partnership between a union of 6,000 workers (the Kagad Kach Patra Kashtakari Panchayat) and the municipality, which has led to the regularization of 2,300 workers in parts of the city. To a certain extent, this formalization has been reproduced in certain areas of Delhi by RWAs. One example in place since 2003 is Defence Colony, one of the upper-class wards of South Delhi, where the RWA for Block-A (around 1,000 households) has set up, in cooperation with the NGO Toxics Link, a decentralized management system that has led to the regularization of 17 workers. These were paid 100 rupees each per dwelling per month in 2016 for the in situ sorting of waste. Six pits were dug to receive part of the green waste and produce good quality compost, which can be sold easily to local residents and provides a source of income to finance the maintenance of the system (protective clothing for the workers, purchase of carts, digging of new pits). Although half of the waste still needs to be discarded in the *dhalao*, this decentralized system helps "to reduce significantly the amount of waste to be evacuated to the centralised treatment facilities by 50%, [and has] notably improved the social conditions of the workers" (representative of the Defence Colony Resident Welfare Association, January 2016). However, although this integration model is promising, it is not free from perverse effects: for instance, it can lead to more marginalization for the portion of the rag pickers who do not benefit from these initiatives (see for example Durand et al. 2019, in a Latin American context). As things stand, the integration of these workers does however attach a certain level of dignity to their activity, opening the way for a better social recognition of their work. Waste workers will otherwise remain relegated to their precarious working conditions, symbolized by their garbage bags (see Figure 7.2).

Figure 7.2 Bag seller.
Source: Author photo.

> *Lunch, Nangloi, Delhi, India, January 2016, photo by Rémi de Bercegol*
> *This man is having lunch in his small shop in Nangloi, a working-class neighbourhood in the West of Delhi, settled just opposite a slum of waste pickers. His job consists in collecting and repairing large plastic bags, which are piled up in rolls behind him, and which he then resells to the inhabitants of the slums. The waste pickers carry these large thick bags on their backs, filling them up with the waste they pick up around the city, until their bag is packed with large amounts of recyclable materials. Organisations for the protection of waste pickers demand the authorities to recognise their contribution to the cleaning of public spaces, which would include providing them with more adequate equipment. As long as these workers are not integrated, these basic bags remain an essential tool for the collection of waste and a symbol for the precariousness of waste recovery, a poorly recognised and protected job.*

Conclusion

Despite its utter banality, waste is a mirror of our society and of its paradoxical relation to its environment. In India, as elsewhere, waste is seen by some as

Waste in the urban margins 171

a source of pollution, a disgusting object that needs to be kept at a distance; but for others, it is considered as a resource whose value can be recovered. For the "Kabariwalla" of Delhi as well as the "dong nat" of Hanoi, or the "pengepul" in Surabaya, which are at the bottom of a vast waste recycling pyramidal chain, waste materials are still considered as a valuable resource to be extensively exploited. This echoes to Chinese cities where similar waste economies have already been documented (Wu & Zhang 2016, 2019). In many of those cities, it appears that the people whose work is dedicated to the recovery of waste are symbolically associated by others with the impurity of waste and are, just like waste itself, relegated to the margins of society. This marginalization is not only spatial and social but also political, and it detracts from the socio-environmental contribution that could be made by waste recovery and by the recycling it enables.

On the one hand, political stakeholders consider that these activities should be abolished because of their degrading nature. This forms part of a broader theory of under-development and modernization: waste recovery is seen as a marginal activity associated with the informal sector and bound to disappear when the country achieves a higher level of economic development. More generally, the informal activities that live on in spite of modernization are associated with the survival economy. On the other hand, waste collectors consider that they are being stripped of their source of income and excluded, although they consider that they are providing an important service for the city. This perspective concurs with the Marxist theory according to which the informal economy is a structural component of the capitalist economy, providing work for poorer populations while reproducing relations of domination.

Unacknowledged and stigmatized, waste workers are almost invisible, although they are paradoxically very present in public spaces. Although they work in the waste sector and contribute to the production of secondary raw materials, they are cut away from sector reforms and debates on the environment. Management policies based on the modernization paradigm and on the transfer of Western models materialize through new technologies, of which incineration is the most visible incarnation, and which affect the entire chain of recycling from the collection stage, which has now been privatized. Turning waste into a technical issue that should be handled by the private sector is also a way of de-politicizing the issues of urban margins and socio-spatial inequality. Nevertheless, the example of waste pickers shows that the "margins" are not just a geographic concept but also a discursive category – and, more importantly, a political one. The marginalization of these workers is first and foremost the product of dominant representations and stigmatization practices. Waste is superimposed on the people involved in its transformation. This stigmatization is more or less acute depending on a worker's geographic origin, caste, gender and profession. Although it is no panacea, the recovery sector's de-marginalization could contribute to increasing the volumes of recovered waste, thus reducing the volume of landfill waste while securing the activity of recycling sector workers. We must therefore move beyond the miserabilist image of this sector, which remains ambivalent in many respects but provides socio-environmental solutions to a major issue. Ultimately, this raises the question of the "right to the city" (Lefebvre 1968) understood here in its reformist sense of rights *in* the city (Zérah et al. 2011) – or, more broadly, that of the recognition of fundamental rights, including the right to a livelihood (theoretically guaranteed by the Indian Constitution). This right is being ignored by the current reform of the waste sector which could instead support the existing alternative, more inclusive, and full of ecological potential, which remains relegated to the margins. Beyond the Indian case, in the context of fast-growing Asian cities, the recognition of the importance of the informal recycling sector seems to be fundamental to achieve a better socio-environmental sustainability of any given infrastructural waste system.

Notes

1 This is a ten-year census. Full and detailed results of the last census, conducted in 2011, are at http://censusindia.gov.in/. Accessed September 1, 2019.
2 In French, *sortir de la marge*: see Cirelli & Florin (2016: 11).
3 "Safai Sena" (www.safaisena.net/).

Works Cited

Arora, K. (2016). "2016 A Benchmark Year for Wastepickers", posted by *Alliance of Indian Wastepickers* on *Global Alliance of Waste Pickers*' website, http://globalrec.org/2016/12/30/2016-abenchmark-year-for-wastepickers/ (Accessed 28 December 2016).

Barles, S. (2014). History of waste management and the social and cultural representations of waste. In M. Agnoletti and S. Neri Serneri (Eds.), *The Basic Environmental History* (pp. 199–226). Springer International Publishing.

Bartone, C. R. (1995). *The role of the private sector in municipal solid waste service delivery in developing countries. Keys to success.* A paper presented at ISWA Conference on Waste Management Role of the private sector, Singapore.

Baud, I., & Post, J. (2003). Between markets and partnerships: Urban Solid Waste Management and contributions to sustainable development. *Global Built Environment Review*, 3(1), 46–65.

Baviskar, A. (2002). *The politics of the City.* Seminar – Shades of green: A symposium on the changing contours of Indian environmentalism, 516 (August), 40–42.

Bercegol (de), R., Cirelli, C., & Florin, B. (2019). La mise en image du rebut. *EchoGéo*, 47, 1–31.

Berdier, C., & Deleuil, J. M. (2006). The system 'city-waste' put into perspective. In E. Dorier Apprill (Ed.), *City and Environment* (pp. 453–466). Paris: Sedes.

Cavé, J. (2014). Who owns urban waste? Appropriation conflicts in emerging countries. *Waste Management & Research*, 32(9), 813–821.

Cavé, J. (2015). *La ruée vers l'ordure: Conflits dans les mines urbaines de déchets.* Rennes: Presses Universitaires de Rennes.

Central Pollution Control Board Status report on municipal solid waste management. (2012). Ministry of Environment & Forests, www.cpcb.nic.in/divisionsofheadoffice/pcp/MSW_Report.pdf

Chakrabarty, D. (2000). *Provincializing Europe.* Princeton: Princeton University Press.

Chaturvedi, B., & Gidwani, V. (2011). The right to waste: Informal sector recyclers and struggles for social justice in post-reform urban India. In W. Ahmed, A. Kundu & R. Peet (Eds.), *India's New Economic Policy: A Critical Analysis* (pp. 125–153). New York: Routledge.

Chintan. (2012). *Give Back Our Waste! What the Okhla Waste-to-Energy Plant Has Done to Local Wastepickers.* www.chintan-india.org/documents/research.../chintan-report-give-back-our-waste.pdf

Chokhandre, P., Singh, S., & Kashyap, G. C. (2017). Prevalence, predictors and economic burden of morbidities among waste-pickers of Mumbai, India: A cross-sectional study. *Journal of Occupational Medicine and Toxicology,* 12(30): 1–8.

Cirelli, C., & Florin, B. (2016). Les récupérateurs de déchets: entre marginalisation et reconnaissance. Mouvements des idées et des luttes (ISSN: 1291-6412), Où va l'homo detritus?, http://mouvements.info/recuperateurs-de-dechets/nouvelles-concurrences-et-convoitises-autour-du-dechetacteur%c2%b7e%c2%b7s-enjeux-ettensions. <halshs-01718935>

Coad, A. (2005). *Private Sector Involvement in Solid Waste Management: Avoiding Problems and Building on Successes* (No. 2), St. Gallen: Collaborative Working Group on Solid Waste Management in Low and Middle-income Countries (CWG), 32.

Cointreau-Levine, S. (1994). *Private Sector Participation in Municipal Solid Waste Services in Developing Countries, Volume 1* (p. 68). Washington, DC: The Formal Sector, Urban Management Programme (The World Bank).

Corteel, D., & Le Lay, S. (2011). *Les travailleurs des déchets,* Toulouse, Érès, coll. « Clinique du travail ».

Delhi Development Authority. (2010). *Master Plan for Delhi – 2021.* New Delhi: Ministry of Urban Development, Government of India.

Demaria, F., & Schindler, S. (2016). Contesting urban metabolism: Struggles over waste-to-energy in Delhi, India. *Antipode,* 48(2), 293–313.

Dupont, V., & Vaquier, D. (2014). Slum demolition, impact on the affected families and coping strategies. In F. Landy & M. C. Saglio-Yatzimirsky(Eds.), *Megacity Slums. Social Exclusion, Urban Space and Policies in Brazil and India* (pp. 307–361). London: Imperial College Press.

Durand, M. (2015). *Gestion des déchets: Innovations sociales et territoriales.* Rennes: Presses Universitaires de Rennes.

Durand, M., & De Oliveira Neves, F. (2019). L'intégration des cueilleurs de déchets latino américains ou la création d'une nouvelle marge, *EchoGéo* [En ligne], 47 |, mis en ligne le 21 avril 2019, consulté le 10 mai 2019. http://journals.openedition.org/echogeo/16894; DOI: 10.4000/echogeo.16894

Florin, B. (2016). « Rien ne se perd! » : Récupérer les déchets au Caire, à Casablanca et à Istanbul », *Techniques & Culture [En ligne],* Suppléments au n°65–66, mis en ligne le 31 octobre 2016 http://tc.revues.org/8020

Florin, B. (2017). « De l'indignité à l'indignation : petites luttes, résistances quotidiennes et tentatives de mobilisation des récupérateurs de déchets à Istanbul », *Cultures & Conflits* [En ligne], 101 | printemps 2016, mis en ligne le 19 mai 2017, http://journals.openedition.org/conflits/19184; DOI : 10.4000/conflits.19184

Florin, B., & Cirelli, C. (2015). (Eds.). *Sociétés Urbaines et déchets,* Tours: Presses Universitaires François-Rabelais.

Furedy, C. (1992). Garbage: Exploring non-conventional options in Asian cities. *Environment Urban,* 4, 42–61.

Ghertner, D. A. (2011). Gentrifying the state, gentrifying participation: Elite governance programs in Delhi. *International Journal of Urban and Regional Research*, 35(3), 504–532.

Gidwani, V., & Reddy, R. N. (2011). The afterlives of "waste": Notes from India for a minor history of capitalist surplus. *Antipode*, 43(5), 1625–1658.

Gill, K. (2012). Of poverty and plastic: Scavenging and scrap trading entrepreneurs in India's urban informal economy, Oxford: Oxford Scholarship Online.

Gunsilius, E., Chaturvedi, B., & Scheinberg, A. (2011). The economics of the informal sector in solid waste management. *CWG-Collaborative Working Group on Solid Waste Management in Low-and Middle income Countries*, GIZ – Deutsche Gesellschaftfür InternationaleZusammenarbeit (GIZ) GmbH.

Hayami, Y., Dikshit, A. K., & Mishra, S. N. (2006). Waste pickers and collectors in Delhi: Poverty and environment in an urban informal sector. *The Journal of Development Studies*, 42(1), 41–69.

Hoornweg, D., & Bhada-Tata, P. (2012). *What a Waste: A Global Review of Solid Waste Management*. Urban Development Series; Knowledge Papers No. 15. Washington, DC: World Bank.

Hughes, E. C. (1962). Good people and dirty work. *Social Problems*, 10(1), Summer, 3–11.

Jaglin, S., & Zérah, M. H. (2010). Urban water in the South: Rethinking changing services. Introduction. *Revue Tiers Monde*, 3, 7–22.

Kundu, A., & Sarangi, N. (2005). Issue of urban exclusion. *Economic and Political Weekly*, 40(33), 13–19 August, 3642–3646.

Lefebvre, H. (1968). *Le droit à la ville*. Paris: édition Anthropos.

Lhuilier, D. (2005). Le "sale boulot". *Travailler*, 14, 73–98.

Mawdsley, E. (2004). India's middle classes and the environment. *Development and Change*, 35(1), 79–103.

Melosi, M. (2000). *The Sanitary City: Urban Infrastructure in America from Colonial Times to the Present*. Baltimore, MD: Johns Hopkins University Press.

Nas, P. J., & Jaffe, R. (2004). Informal waste management: Shifting the focus from problem to potential. *Environment, Development and Sustainability*, 6, 337–353.

Park, R. E. (1928). Human migration and the marginal men. *American Journal of Sociology*, 33(6), 881–893.

Reddy, R. N. (2015). Producing abjection: E-waste improvement schemes and informal recyclers of Bangalore. *Geoforum*, 62, 166–174.

Scheinberg, A., Nesic, J., Savain, R., Luppi, P., Sinnot, P., Petean, F., & Pop, F. (2016). From collision to collaboration: Integrating informal recyclers and re-use operators in Europe, a review. *Waste Management & Research*, 34(9), 820–839.

Scheinberg, A., Spies, S., Simpson, M. H., & Mol, A. P. (2011). Assessing urban recycling in low- and middle income countries: Building on modernized mixtures. *Habitat International*, 35(2), 188–198.

Schindler, S., Demaria, F., & Pandit, S. B. (2012). Delhi's waste conflict. *Economic and Political Weekly*, 47(42), 18–21.

Simone, A. (2004). People as infrastructure: Intersecting fragments in Johannesburg. *Public Culture*, 16(3), 407–429.

Swyngedouw, E. (2014). The violence of sustainable urbanity. *Metropolitics*, 10 November. Retrieved from: https://www.metropolitiques.eu/The-Violence-of-Sustainable-Urbanity.html

UN-Habitat. (2010). *Solid Waste Management in the World's Cities*. London: United Nations Human Settlements Programme, 228.

Wu, K.-M., & Zhang, J. (2016). Waste pickers in a Chinese megacity. *Anthropology News*, 57(10), 65–68.

Wu, K.-M., & Zhang, J. (2019). Living with waste: becoming 'free' as waste pickers in Chinese cities. *China Perspectives*, 2, 67–74.

Wilson, D. C., Rodic, L., Scheinberg, A., Velis, C. A., & Alabaster, G. (2012). Comparative analysis of solid waste management in 20 cities. *Waste Management & Research*, 30(3), 237–254.

Wilson, D. C., Velis, C., & Cheeseman, C. (2006). Role of informal sector recycling in waste management in developing countries. *Habitat International*, 30(4), 797–808.

Wright, M. W. (2006). *Disposable Women and other Myths of Global Capitalism*. New York: Routledge and Taylor & Francis.

Zérah, M. H. (2007). Middle-class neighbourhood associations as political players in Mumbai. *Economic and Political Weekly*, 42(47), 61–68.

Zérah, M. H., Dupont, V., & Tawa Lama-Rewal, S. (2011). *Urban Policies and the Right to the City in India, Rights, Responsabilities and Citizenship*. New Delhi: UNESCO.

8 Living on the margins of the legal city in the southern periphery of Chennai
A case of cumulative marginalities

Véronique Dupont and R. Dhanalakshmi

Introduction[1]

Since the turn of the century, the promotion of specialized economic corridors and large-scale infrastructure projects aimed at attracting national and international investments has impacted the urban and economic development of Chennai, one of the largest metropolitan cities in South India[2] and the regional capital of the state of Tamil Nadu. Among those, the Information Technology (IT) corridor, located in South Chennai along a major road, epitomizes the vision of transforming Chennai into a global city region (Kennedy et al. 2014). The development of this corridor has been associated with land speculation, the extension of the Mass Rapid Transport System (MRTS) and beautification operations, especially along the Buckingham Canal that flows parallel to the IT corridor – in short urban transformations that usually entail displacement of informal settlements. As summarized by Coelho and Raman (2010: 19), "Beautification, restoration [of water ways] and development serve as metonyms for slum clearance".

In this chapter, we examine the critical issues facing the people living in a precarious settlement located in the southern periphery of Chennai along the Buckingham Canal, in the zone affected by the development of the IT corridor. The specific location and characteristics of this settlement allow us to approach the meaning of "living on the margins of the city" from several angles, and to explore several dimensions of marginality.

We understand the "margins" as being necessarily a relational notion, and implying the idea of a limit, a border, more or less clearly defined, beyond which, or outside of which, the margins are located, in physical or abstract terms. We start from a spatial approach and identify the margins as spaces with specific location characteristics, which are correlated to other discrimination factors.

At the outset, we approach the margins *of the city* from their original geographical dimension, with reference to their peripheral location far away from the core of the city. The primary discriminating factor here is the spatial distance from the core. We then compound this mere geographical approach by introducing an environmental or geophysical dimension, namely, the location in a low-lying, flood-prone area. In an urban context, living in such a location means

Living on the margins of the legal city   177

living on the margins *of building land*, in other words beyond land meant for sustainable urbanization, with dire consequences for the inhabitants. Next, we consider the administrative boundaries: living on the margins of the *administrative* city signifies in our case study living beyond the boundaries of the Chennai Municipal Corporation area. The geographical and administrative margins often overlap, but not permanently as administrative boundaries may change, with tangible effects, as illustrated in our settlement study. Last but not least, we examine the legal dimension of the margins and the consequences of living on the margins of the *legal* city, to wit, of living in a squatter settlement, categorized as an "objectionable slum". Here the discriminating factor refers to town planning rules and regulations, and related categorizations, which intersect with geophysical factors, although not always in a consistent and rational way. In cities of the Global South, the margins of the legal city occupy a significant place in demographic terms (UN-Habitat 2013), especially in Indian cities (Dupont 2011). In sum, in Chennai, as in other contexts, urban margins prove to be "a spatial and social construct that helps us better understand urban development" (Sierra & Tadié 2008: 4 – our translation).

Our socio-spatial approach of the margins departs from the pioneer approach of the Chicago school of sociology. In our case study, a "marginal city dweller" does not correspond to the "marginal man", a migrant from a different culture whom Park (1928: 892) likened to the "stranger" of Simmel (1908). The "marginal" man or woman in our settlement case, mostly a migrant, is primarily someone living on the margins of the city, with regard to the various aspects outlined above. From this perspective, the overarching research question addressed in this chapter is: what are the effects of the various dimensions of marginality on the concerned dwellers? This leads us to examine the links between marginality, exclusion and deprivation. In the context of squatter settlements in Delhi, we showed how forced eviction without proper rehabilitation entailed a process of multi-fledged impoverishment for the displaced families, with "cumulative effects through losses of rights and chain deprivations [...], until it combine[d] to jeopardize the right to the city and the right to live with dignity" (Dupont & Vaquier 2014: 334). In other words, from living on the margins of the legal city, those slum families rendered homeless were pushed to the margins of the urban society. In the precarious settlement under study in Chennai, we also contend that one type of marginality goes hand in hand with other types of marginality, entailing cumulative deprivation. The different dimensions of marginality are indeed entangled.

In the course of our argumentation, we question the social marginalization of the urban poor whom the urban authorities and the judiciary consider encroachers. Although we analyze here marginality as the situation resulting from the process of being pushed to the spatial, geophysical and illegal margins of the city, we do not consider "marginal" urban dwellers as mere passive victims of an urban development associated with increasing inequality. Rather, we follow an actor-centered approach that recognizes "the exercise of agency by subaltern subjects" (Baviskar 2003: 97), even in the context of slum evictions. Thus, we examine both the effects of the various dimensions of marginality on the "marginal" urban dwellers, and the responses of the latter to face or mitigate the adverse effects of their situation. While doing so, we show how the residents of the urban margins create further discrimination among themselves and how the figure of the "marginal man" likened to the "stranger" of Simmel emerges.

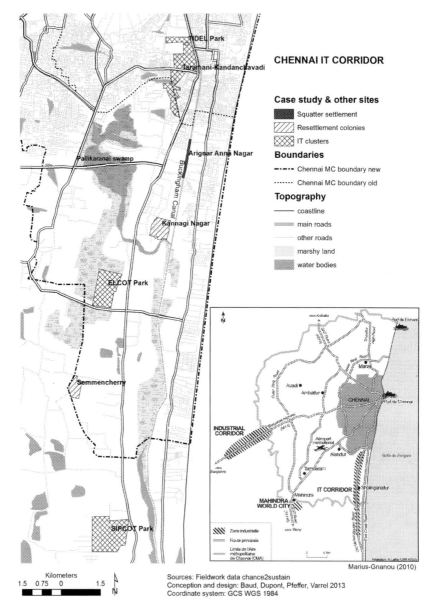

Figure 8.1 Chennai IT Corridor.
Source: Author photo.

Living on the margins of the legal city 179

Our case study focuses on a precarious settlement called Arignar Anna Nagar (AAN), one of the Canal Bank Road squatter settlements (Figure 8.1). We carried out field investigations in several rounds, mainly between October 2011 and March 2013, with a follow-up visit in July 2015, and spot updates in December 2015 and November 2018. We conducted a series of in-depth interviews with various stakeholders. This included first of all inhabitants of AAN, covering three different residential situations: current residents of the settlement, previous residents who were evicted and relocated in a resettlement colony in Kannagi Nagar, and returnees from this resettlement colony. We also interviewed activists involved in issues of slum evictions and relocation, government officials of the Tamil Nadu Slum Clearance Board (TNSCB) and the (then newly elected) Municipal Councillor of the area. We completed these interviews by a press review and the collection of secondary data, maps and reports.

Finding a place on the margins of the city

AAN is located on the southern periphery of the city, around 20 kilometers by road from the Municipal Corporation office. It is part of the Neelankarai area, which was outside the boundaries of the Chennai Municipal Corporation until November 2011 and had the status of a village. The first settlers in AAN arrived around 35–40 years ago, and today about 2,000 households are living in this settlement, which stretches along 1.5 kilometers on both sides of the Buckingham Canal.

Most of the settlers are Tamils, and, though some are Chennai natives, most are migrants coming from other districts of Tamil Nadu, who resided previously in other areas of the city. The most recent settlers include migrants from North India, bachelors working in the nearby industrial area, who are tenants. People belong mainly to backward classes or scheduled castes (the formerly untouchable castes), and are mostly Hindus, with nevertheless a notable Christian community as well as Muslims. The men are mostly construction workers, auto-rickshaw and car drivers, security guards and unskilled industrial workers employed in the nearby industrial area. The women work as domestics and local vendors. Some of the young generation work in the electronic industry and in the call centers provided by the development of the IT corridor. Overall, the AAN residents belong to low-income groups.

In the beginning, the dwellers built small huts, with thatched roofs and mud floors. These were improved and consolidated over time. Since most dwellers could not afford to hire labor, they built their houses using their own family labor. Nowadays, one can find many consolidated houses, mainly on the inner streets, including some with an additional floor. Most of the houses have a provision for tenant occupancy on the same premises with a common courtyard or alley. The land use in this settlement is essentially residential, apart from a few convenience shops concentrated around the main bridge. Over time, the area spread out and comprised two or three rows of houses along each side of the canal, linked by a concrete bridge built by the government, and a small pedestrian

180   *Véronique Dupont and R. Dhanalakshmi*

bridge built by the residents. This settlement process may be described as "the quiet encroachment of the ordinary", with reference to the phrase coined by Bayat (2010), and that "encapsulates the discreet and prolonged ways in which the poor struggle to survive and to better their lives by quietly impinging on the propertied and powerful, and on society at large" (ibid.: 15).[3]

From a rural to an urban settlement: administrative boundaries matter

During our first field visits, in 2011 and early 2012, this settlement was characterized by its acute deficit in basic urban services and physical infrastructure, as is the case in many informal settlements. Access to potable water was particularly critical. Although the *panchayat* (village authorities) had installed an overhead tank and public taps, the water supplied was not potable, and people had to buy bottled water for drinking and cooking. Furthermore, water from the public taps was supplied at best twice weekly for a couple of hours, and in some sections of the settlement once every ten days for two to three hours, a situation that required individual storage arrangements. There is still no drainage and no sewage system in the settlement, and no public conveniences. Some houses are equipped with sceptic tanks, but the houses located just along the canal have connected their individual toilets (when applicable) with a pipe and outlet directly into the canal. Since not all houses are equipped with individual toilets, defecation also occurs in open spaces.

The lack of a drainage and sewage system, and until very recently of garbage collection, contributed in making the locality highly unsanitary. The canal has become an open drain filled with polluted water and garbage – a breeding place for mosquitoes (Figure 8.2). In addition to individual toilet outlets, industrial effluents and untreated or poorly treated sewage water are also released into the canal. Those living closer to the canal suffer from the constant stink in the air, mosquito menace, and have health problems, especially skin diseases. The present situation contrasts sharply with the memory of the early settlers of a time when the canal water was salty but clean and how they used the water for purposes other than cooking and drinking, and could play and swim in the canal.

The situation in the settlement is better in terms of electricity supply. The houses have electricity connections that the Tamil Nadu Electricity Board regularized in 2004–2005, providing a deposit by the dwellers.

The bad connectivity of the settlement with the rest of the city was another major issue that exemplifies the negative impact of living on the outskirts of the city. Not only is AAN far from the city center, but until very recently public transport was not easily accessible. In order to access public transport, the residents needed to walk a minimum of 20 minutes from their houses to the main roads – East Coast Road or Old Mahabalipuram Road – to find buses and at least one hour to reach the nearest MRTS rail station. Before recent improvements, auto-rickshaw drivers were also reluctant to go inside the settlement because of the bad state of the roads. Apart from a couple of concrete streets, the rest were earthen roads or lanes, which became extremely muddy during the rainy season.

Living on the margins of the legal city 181

Figure 8.2 Pedestrian bridge built by the residents of Arignar Anna Nagar over the polluted Buckingham Canal in Chennai (March 2013).
Source: Author photo.

The settlement also lacked any social infrastructure such as schools, nurseries, an Integrated Child Development Service, a primary health center or a dispensary, and had to depend on the neighboring legal localities. Only a few private doctors operated in the settlement itself.

To sum up, the spatial location of this squatter settlement, on the margins of the city, compounded by its unauthorized status, has gone along with a lack of access to proper urban amenities. Nonetheless, in November 2011, the Chennai Municipal Corporation Area was extended and now includes the settlement of AAN, which has thus access to the municipal services. Our field visits in 2013 and 2015 did reveal notable improvements, especially in the water supply (installation of water tankers and more public taps), street lighting, garbage collection and upgrading of roads, including the consolidation of the old bridge. A mini-bus also services the area. This shows that being inside the city as per its administrative limits or outside, on its margins, affects the access of informal dwellers to urban amenities.

Other effects of remoteness and poverty

The remarkable feature about the socio-political organization in AAN is the lack of grass-root representatives and of community-based organizations. There is neither a recognized leader representing the entire locality, nor leaders

182   *Véronique Dupont and R. Dhanalakshmi*

representing smaller distinct communities. There is no resident welfare association and no church association in the settlement. Though non-governmental organizations (NGO) are commonly found working in poor urban areas, no NGO could be traced in this settlement. Small self-help women groups are present in the locality, but they are essentially involved in micro-credit activities, and not in collective action on a larger scale. Furthermore, volunteers and cadres from the two main political parties,[4] promoting both a regionalist and populist agenda, are not active in this settlement, although the inhabitants are part of their vote banks. Because of their geographical remoteness on the fringe of the city, the Canal Bank Road settlements have also remained out of reach of the major social movements for workers and slum dwellers in the city, which have a greater impact in the old industrial northern areas of Chennai. The Democratic Youth Federation of India (DYFI), affiliated with the Communist Party of India (Marxist) – CPI(M), is the only organization with active local members tackling some issues in the settlement.

However, this state of affairs, which may be described overall as weak organizational structuring, does not mean that the residents of AAN endure their living condition passively. Since the inception of this settlement, they have continuously struggled to obtain basic amenities (such as water, electricity and roads), through repeated representations to the local authorities (earlier the village panchayat and now the municipal councilors). The services obtained were not without counterpart, as the panchayat used to collect money for "roof taxes", a kind of pseudo property tax, although the land squatted upon belong to the Public Works Department. It is also only after repeated representations that the government built a bridge across the canal in AAN, which could be used by small vehicles. Such interactions with the lower level of state bureaucracy, as a way for the urban poor to access public services and safeguard their territorial claims, evoke the practice of "occupancy urbanism", analyzed by Benjamin (2008) in the context of other Indian cities.

The DYFI local members played an active role in addressing some of the settlement problems in AAN, although their popularity proved to be mainly limited to one street. Nevertheless, in the mid-2000s they collected financial contribution from people in the area in order to build a wooden pedestrian bridge over the canal (in addition to the government-built bridge), demonstrating that people could organize themselves when necessary and achieve results (Figure 8.2). In 2011, DYFI members further approached the TNSCB (located in Chennai city center) to put forward their demands for social services in the settlement such as government schools and an Integrated Child Development Service. Since at that time the area was not under the purview of the Chennai Municipal Corporation, but that of a neighboring district, they were redirected to the concerned district collector's office. This implied traveling a much longer distance, and, after a first trip and representation, they could not follow up and press their cause by going back to this distant office. They simply could not afford to lose a day's wage and in addition pay for transport. Their economic conditions thus barred the mobilization efforts of the residents. As also observed in Delhi (Kumar 2008; Dupont et al. 2013), economic precariousness proves to be a structural factor that limits the possibility of long-lasting engagement in collective actions.

The CPI(M) has supported the DYFI members in their endeavor to improve the living conditions in their settlement. The patronage of this political party is also a way for the DYFI members to scale up their demands: they participate in party activities and try to address their problems to the government during party meetings.

Living on the margins of building land: the environmental risk

The settlement of AAN is located in a low-lying marshy area, prone to flooding – in other words on the margins of the land meant for sustainable urbanization. When the first settlers came, the place had to be filled with heavy earthen materials to lay the foundation for houses with the residents shouldering the cost. Nevertheless, in case of heavy and continuous rains lasting several days, the settlement is still flooded, and the evacuation of houses is a common experience. When this happens, the residents can take refuge in the schools and other community buildings in nearby localities. In 2011–2012, the Public Works Department built a wall along the canal for flood control. However, it had no effect during the devastating floods that submerged the entire city of Chennai in November–December 2015, the settlements along the Buckingham Canal in the southern periphery being among the worst affected.

As underlined by Arabindoo in her article on the Chennai floods (2016: 810), for the urban poor living in "risky environment which includes unsanitary living conditions, polluted drinking water and a myriad set of health-related hazard, floods are one of the many risks that need to be balanced and overcome through a carefully constructed set of strategies against multiple others occurring often at the same time". Unsanitary living conditions are indeed a characteristic of AAN, and have been only partly mitigated by the integration of the settlement into the Municipal Corporation Area. Living by a canal that turned into an open drain aggravates the unhealthy living conditions of the residents while exposing them at the same time to the recurrent risk of flooding. This points to the cumulative effects of entangled urban and geophysical marginalities.

Living on the margins of the legal city: the risk of eviction

A survey conducted in 2003–2004 for the TNSCB identified 444 "undeveloped slums" (not upgraded) within the metropolitan area of Chennai; of those, 212 were categorized as "objectionable slums", comprising 144 squatter settlements located along waterways that housed 41,383 families, the rest being located along road margins, railways and the seashore (TNSCB & TNUIFS 2005 & 2006). Due to its location on the bank of the Buckingham Canal, AAN falls in the category of "objectionable slums". The land is the property of the Public

184 *Véronique Dupont and R. Dhanalakshmi*

Works Department, on which private constructions are not authorized. Consequently, the inhabitants are considered as squatters, encroachers; they have no security of tenure and are under recurrent threat of eviction.

Earlier settlers could occupy the land free of cost, but successive settlers had to "buy" it from politicians and local real estate dealers or landlords who controlled the area. They got a document called "B-memo notice" for this transaction. They also paid pseudo property taxes to the former panchayat. Whereas some dwellers believe that such documents will help them prove their ownership to the land, or even consider the "B-memo notice" to be a land title, this notice is in fact a "statement showing the details of unauthorised encroachments on Government lands, the use of which is regulated by [the] village *Panchayat*".[5]

Therefore, the most critical issue in the Canal Bank Road squatter settlements, as in all "objectionable slums", is the risk of eviction. Initially, several settlers were unaware of the illegality of their tenure. As mentioned above, some were under the impression that the "B memo notice" that they got when they purchased the land from private realtors and the taxes that they paid to the village panchayat were proof of ownership. Such illegal transactions and subsequent benefits for the panchayat suggest rather connivance between land grabbers and local politicians. Other settlers were informed of the risk of eviction when buying their plot, but did not take it seriously, as many others also were buying land at that time and, in any case, they could not afford to buy a plot in an authorized residential colony. Some of the early settlers said that officials warned them against occupying the land, and instructed them to vacate the lots. They used to leave for a while, but then returned to the same places. This was a regular happening at the time. Since there was no strict action taken by the public authorities to evict the settlers, the settlement extended gradually and most of the houses were at least partly consolidated. Nevertheless, for those living closer to the canal, and therefore the more exposed, the lack of secure tenure deterred them from spending money to improve their houses. In such cases, combined geophysical and legal marginalities contributed to a substandard habitat.

The situation had radically changed by the 2000s, when plans to restore the waterways of Chennai were in the pipeline. By that time, the width of the Buckingham Canal had shrunk considerably. To allow the de-silting of the canal as part of the flood alleviation program, the Ministry for Public Works declared in July 2002 that about 5,000 houses had to be removed along the Buckingham Canal. Subsequently, from the last week of July to the first week of August, about 2,300 families were evicted from the canal banks, in the IT corridor zone, including almost 500 from AAN.[6] The remaining families were to be evicted the following months. That large-scale operation mobilized officials of the Public Works Department, the Slum Clearance Board, the Revenue Department and the police. The evicted families were relocated in the Kannagi Nagar resettlement colony, although the flats were not ready for occupancy (as detailed below).

Living on the margins of the legal city 185

The eviction was described in the press as "a swift, low-resistance operation" (Ahmed 2002), which was confirmed by our interviews in AAN. Evicted residents explained that they cooperated with the government officers who came to survey them, took their photos and distributed tokens for allotment, because they feared losing their entitlement to a flat and becoming homeless if they did not do so. The large deployment of police was another deterrent factor. In fact, the displaced families were informed of the exact date of eviction at best one week beforehand, and some realized it only on the eve of the eviction when they got their allotment tokens. According to some residents, the lack of accurate information sufficiently in advance regarding the eviction was a deliberate government strategy to avoid the organization of protests.

Collective responses to the risk of eviction

Low resistance in the settlements at the time of eviction did not exclude prior collective protest actions. Although residents were informed at the last moment of the exact date of eviction, for the last five years there were oral warnings through the panchayat officers that the settlements in the area would be demolished for the "beautification" of the canal. Following each new threat, the residents reacted by meeting government officials or submitting petitions to the chief minister. For instance, a signature campaign conducted through the All India Democratic Women Association (affiliated with the CPI(M)) collected 5,000 signatures from the dwellers of the Canal Bank Road settlements. Before the 2002 eviction, a road blockade was organized on a big road junction, as well as a later rally to the Secretariat (seat of the State Government) to make representations to the chief minister (the demonstrators were however not allowed on the premises). Residents from all the settlements along the canal participated in this rally (around 750–1,000 people). The main demands included no eviction, provision of all civic amenities and ownership rights with proper land titles. However, this protest had no effect, and ironically, the actual demolition in AAN took place on the day when its inhabitants were demonstrating in the city. The rally was organized by the CPI(M), but all other political parties participated. The CPI(M) also helped the evicted families to get their allotment tokens (in case they missed the distribution, or for any other reason) and during their resettlement process in Kannagi Nagar.

Following this major demolition drive, no one could ignore the risk of further evictions. Faced with this threat, most residents in AAN seem to accept that being on government land, in an "objectionable" settlement, inevitably leads to their future relocation, although they remain very critical of the living conditions in the big resettlement complexes (an issue that we discuss later). There is indeed a discrepancy between the dwellers' resignation and pragmatic vision, and the more radical stance of the CPI(M) activists. The low resistance to eviction observed in the Canal Bank Road squatter settlements also reflects the "gradual weakening and eventual collapse of slum-based, struggle-oriented collective action against evictions" since the 1990s (Coelho & Raman 2010: 23; Coehlo & Venkat 2009).

New threats of eviction and cumulative marginalities

Plans for the IT corridor area and recent developments bear new threats of demolition for the squatter settlements along Buckingham Canal. The IT corridor project envisaged the beautification of the Buckingham Canal, including water quality management, beautification of MRTS pillars and landscaping and agriculture (Malmarugam & Narayan 2006) – proposals that are still at the blueprint stage. As part of the national waterways linking projects, further plans were publicized in 2008 to revive Buckingham Canal as a navigation channel for efficient and cost-effective transportation[7] (Karthikeyan 2008a, 2008b). After several years of stand-by, these revival plans made the news again in 2014 (Kumar 2014) and in 2017 (Venkateshwarl 2017). The construction of a wall along both sides of the canal in the IT corridor area also started in 2011, officially for flood control, with a possible hidden agenda to protect the banks from new encroachments. Furthermore, in March 2012, the removal of all "encroachments" along waterways, including Buckingham Canal, was announced (Lopez 2012a). The identification of the families to be relocated faced strong political opposition in some zones of the city at that time (Lopez 2012b; The Hindu 2012), and no mass eviction took place. Nonetheless, the call for removing encroachments along waterways to restore their water-holding and flood-carrying capacities has remained a leitmotiv of not only the government (Lopez 2019) but also the judiciary. Two ongoing court cases illustrate this last point.

The first case refers to a matter taken *suo motu* by the National Green Tribunal since 2013, in relation to the pollution of the Adyar and Cooum rivers and the Buckingham Canal in Chennai. This involved the removal of encroachments, viewed as an obstacle to implement de-silting and widening works, and as conflicting with "the interest of the environment and the people" (National Green Tribunal 2018: para. 9). In its order dated October 31, 2018, the tribunal expressed its disappointment in this regard, noting that: "out of a total of 26,300 encroachments [in the Chennai Metropolitan Area], only 408 have been evicted leaving the balance of 25,892 encroachments still to be dealt with" (ibid.: para. 6). Consequently, the Tribunal directed the Government of Tamil Nadu to take action for removing encroachments on the water bodies concerned and, "considering the inordinate delay", imposed a penalty of 20 million rupees (288,000 US dollars) to be deposited with the Central Pollution Control Board (ibid.: para. 10 & 12).

In the second case, the Madras High Court in September 2018 took serious note of encroachments of water bodies in Chennai against the backdrop of recurring floods in the city. With reference to the fundamental right to life (Article 21 of the Constitution), the court declared that:

> providing of water and protection of water bodies and water resources are to be construed as fundamental rights of citizen and infringement by few men to be construed as grave offence. The encroachers in water bodies are committing the grave offence of infringing the right of all other citizens at

large. Thus, those encroachers are not only [to] be evicted, but also to be prosecuted. (Madras High Court 2018: para. 34)

Large-scale encroachments of water bodies and water resources were further held responsible for preventing the state from dealing adequately with heavy rain and flood-related situations (ibid.: para. 39). Terming such encroachers as "grave offenders", the court proclaimed: "all these encroachers of water bodies and water resources are not entitled for any Flood Relief Funds from the taxpayers' money (Government Funds)" (ibid.: para. 41). In closing, the court issued a series of directions to various government officials to ensure the eviction of all encroachments of water bodies and that the government would not extend any Flood Relief Fund to these encroachers (ibid.: para. 43).

These various projects and judicial directives highlight the insecurity of the slum dwellers living on the banks of the Buckingham Canal. More generally, the court's observations and orders show how these dwellers, like thousands of families living on the edge of water bodies, on the margins of building land, are stigmatized as encroachers, polluters, grave offenders and as a threat to the environment. They are thus pitted against the "welfare of the people at large", or even the "rights of the citizens at large" (ibid.: para. 4, 25). Furthermore, the Madras High Court, by depriving them from entitlement to any government relief in case of natural disaster, turns them into second-class citizens. During the 2015 torrential rains, all the people affected by the floods received 5,000 rupees (around 70 US dollars) per family from the government as monetary relief, including those living in "objectionable slums". With the enforcement of the court order, with the advent of future floods, the latter would be discriminated against. Starting from a situation of urban and geophysical marginality resulting from their economic precariousness, the residents of unauthorized settlements such as AAN are exposed not only to environmental hazards and risk of eviction but also to social marginalization by the judiciary branch of the state.

Relocation in Kannagi Nagar resettlement colony: from one urban margin to the other

The situation of slum dwellers displaced to Kannagi Nagar draws our attention to another urban marginal space. Both this large complex and the Semmencherry resettlement colony were established in the 2000s in the southern periphery of Chennai, outside the limits of the Municipal Corporation at that time. They illustrate the policy shift of the TNSCB, from in situ reconstruction whereby multi-storied tenements were constructed on the same location for the slum dwellers, to resettlement in large-scale complexes on alternative sites at the outskirts of the city (Raman 2011).

Kannagi Nagar resettlement colony is located about 25 kilometers from the city center, and is included in the same municipal zone as AAN since November 2011 (Figure 8.1). This large housing complex of 15,650 one-room tenements in two- or three-storied buildings was developed by the TNSCB for slum dwellers evicted from different places in the city, to make way for infrastructure projects or due to their location on objectionable sites such as the banks of the Buckingham Canal; it also accommodated many victims of the December 2004 tsunami (Figure 8.3). The first relocated families arrived in 2000, followed by several waves of resettlement. Lack of adequate facilities in the colony and limited access to urban resources have been critical issues. Yet, without solving these infrastructural problems, in 2009 the TNSCB launched the construction of 8,000 additional flats (PUCL 2010).

The relative proximity between Kannagi Nagar and the Canal Bank Road squatter settlements makes relocation in Kannagi Nagar comparatively less disruptive to the dwellers of these settlements and more acceptable than to people from inner city slums. However, all of them suffered from acute infrastructure and service deficiencies in the resettlement colony.

When people were relocated in 2002 from the Canal Bank Road to Kannagi Nagar, they found a resettlement complex in a deplorable state. The tenements were soiled, the toilets clogged; there was no power or water supply, and no street lighting. There was also no bus facility to serve the area. In other words, Kannagi Nagar was a colony planned by a government agency to resettle people from slums, without addressing the most basic needs of the relocated families. The colony gained the reputation of being "a ghetto of poverty, crime, and squalor" (Coelho et al. 2012: 53). People from the demolished areas in AAN were also divided into different groups and were allotted flats in different blocks in the resettlement colony. This broke down older socio-spatial arrangements and made solidarity between neighbors more difficult to establish at a time when it was the most needed. The living conditions in big resettlement complexes on the city margins, such as Kannagi Nagar, were denounced by human rights

Figure 8.3 Kannagi Nagar resettlement colony in a floodplain of the southern periphery of Chennai (July 2015).
Source: Author photo.

Living on the margins of the legal city 189

organizations (PUCL 2010; HLRN 2014). Scholars also emphasized a process of degeneration into "spaces of advanced marginality" (Arabindoo 2011: 5) and of reproduction of urban poverty (Coelho et al. 2012).

Nonetheless, the residents themselves proved their capacity to mobilize for better amenities. They formed the Kannagi Nagar Welfare Association and, with the strategic support of a rights-focused NGO, they organized in 2008 a postcard campaign demanding adequate basic amenities and public services, which were still lacking eight years after the establishment of the colony (PUCL 2010). About 50,000 postcards were addressed to the then Minister for Slum Clearance and Accommodation Control. Importantly, the media were invited to follow this campaign and politicized the issue. Other modes of engagement of the residents with the state in order to improve their living conditions included protests such as blocking the nearby highway and, more frequently, addressing collective complains to government officers (mostly to the local TNSCB office) and local politicians. These mobilization endeavors resulted in notable steps forward. For instance, following the postcard campaign, a police station was established (Cummings 2012). However, improvements took a long time to be provided. In 2012, there was still no public health center for a colony housing around 70,000 people at that time (ibid.). In particular, water supply and drainage have remained unsatisfactory, and social infrastructure is grossly inadequate.

The many resettled families who eventually left Kannagi Nagar after selling or renting out their tenements further highlight a form of individual protest to unsustainable living conditions in the resettlement colony. Although such transfers of occupancy were irregular, they concerned as much as 44% of the tenements according to an official survey conducted in 2012.[8] These transactions also help understand the coping strategies and rationale of the affected families in the highly constrained context of removal of objectionable slums, such as those along the Buckingham Canal. If the eviction is seen as inevitable, efforts are better focused on getting some compensation in the form of a resettlement flat with secure tenure, under a highly subsidized hire-and-purchase scheme:[9] an asset and a prospective profitable good that they can rent out or resell for monetary returns. When people come back to their previous locality, as observed in AAN, it also shows the attachment to a place and community where they managed to make a living over the years, despite the precarious status of that settlement.

Another peculiar feature of Kannagi Nagar is its location in a floodplain (Figure 8.3): this questions the economic and ecological rationalities of "the state filling water bodies to house people, then removing people to restore water bodies and relocating them onto other water bodies" (Coelho and Raman 2013: 146). For the resettlement colony's residents, this entails additional vulnerability and hardship during the rains due to water logging. Overall, for residents of the squatter settlements along the Buckingham Canal, being relocated to Kannagi Nagar amounts to being displaced from one marginal urban space to another.

190 *Véronique Dupont and R. Dhanalakshmi*

Social marginalization within the margins: the tenants as "marginal men"

The resettlement process evidenced the social divide between house owners and tenants, whose presence is very significant in the Canal Bank Road settlements. On the one hand, the former suffered heavy losses with the demolition of their house and the wiping out of all the investments made to improve their habitat and local environment (in addition to the initial cost of the plot). On the other, the latter would be winners in a resettlement program as they had no loss of fixed asset and would gain a flat under an advantageous hire-and-purchase scheme. This was a unique opportunity for them to improve their residential status. Tenants are not excluded in the government resettlement programs for slum dwellers, providing they can submit proof of identity and residence. It is precisely this point that usually generated conflict between house owners and tenants, with owners trying to grab more allotments by barring the tenants from claiming their entitlements, or fierce negotiations between the two parties where the tenants eventually needed to pay compensation to their landlords to be able to claim their allotment. As a result, some tenants were de facto excluded from the resettlement program. Such behavior on the part of the house owners may be viewed as an attempt to marginalize the tenants, and to treat them as less legitimate residents in the settlement. This discriminatory treatment was more apparent when the tenants were male migrants from North India, clearly considered as aliens to the place, though the migrants themselves, especially the bachelors, were less interested in striving for an allotment in Chennai.

More generally, the integration of migrant workers in the settlement proves to be complicated, as shown by another study conducted in AAN (Venkat 2014). The relationship between the migrants from northern states and the Tamil people is marked by tensions and suspicion against the former. On the one hand, the local house owners benefit monetarily from the migrants to whom they rent out rooms, hence "the migrants appear to be welcome, as harbinger of better economic times, but [on the other hand] they are still outsiders who need to be viewed with caution and kept under control" (ibid.: 94). Against the backdrop of this working-class informal settlement in Chennai, the male migrant worker from North India, a tenant and bachelor, emerges as a figure of the "marginal man" (within Park's meaning), that of the "stranger" speaking a different language and with different cultural habits.

Conclusion

The case study of AAN, a precarious settlement along Buckingham Canal in the southern periphery of Chennai, shows how living on the urban margins can be understood as a condition that results primarily from economic deprivation and entails cumulative effects. The lack of economic resources pushes people to live in substandard settlements outside the legal sector. Vacant places to occupy are more likely to be available on the outskirts of the city, on non-building land such as the edge of water bodies in low-lying areas. The ensuing settlements are categorized as "objectionable slums", under the threat of eviction. Such a geophysical location

Living on the margins of the legal city 191

also exposes their dwellers to environmental risks, especially floods. These dwellers are furthermore stigmatized as encroachers, offenders and polluters, and, hence, are socially marginalized. After eviction, they are relocated to other marginal spaces in another substandard habitat. Lastly, among these multidimensional marginal urban dwellers, some prove to be more marginal than others, namely, the tenants, especially the migrants from the northern states of the country.

Slum eviction in the name of environment protection (in this case to protect waterways) has been a common occurrence in Chennai (Coehlo & Raman 2010, 2013), as well as in other Indian metropolises such as Delhi (Dupont 2008; Baviskar 2011) or Mumbai (Zérah 2007). This points to a broader context that Baviskar (2002) denounces as a "bourgeois environmentalism" characterized by "its hostility to the poor in pursuit of a 'clean and green' environment" (Baviskar 2011: 50). From this viewpoint, Baviskar argues that the presence of the poor becomes synonymous with pollution. Slums have been further portrayed as a nuisance, including in the courts of justice, and this legal "nuisance discourse" was used as "the primary mechanism by which slum demolition [took] place" in the 2000s, as demonstrated by Ghertner (2008: 57) in the case of Delhi. Returning to the tension between the "brown" and the "green agenda", we should recall that often the conflict between housing for the poor and the protection of the environment results from social injustice, as the poor, unable to afford housing in the legal city, squat in unclaimed urban spaces, on the margins of the city, including ecologically vulnerable and fragile zones.

The significance of the issues addressed throughout this case study extends beyond the context of Chennai and other Indian cities. For instance, the relationship between environmental risks and the displacement of the urban poor from precarious settlements is a question that arises in many cities of the Global South. This is likely to become increasingly important with the challenges of climate change, especially in the densely populated coastal areas of Asian countries.

Regarding examples of cumulative marginalities in other cities, a case in point in Asia would be the hardships of migrant workers during the preparation and staging of mega-events in Chinese cities (Shin 2012). As shown in several studies, migrant workers, already made vulnerable by their administrative status, emerged as stigmatized city dwellers, "strangers in the city" (Broudehoux 2007: 389). They were further discriminated against at the time of the 2008 Olympic Games in Beijing, and were victims of the "physical" as well as "social beautification" of the city (ibid.: 390). Thus, they were often displaced from their habitat by environmental improvement projects (Shin & Li 2013), and then expelled from the city during the games (Broudehoux 2007; Li 2012; Shin & Li 2013). More generally, from a heuristic perspective, the lens of cumulative marginalities provides a relevant analytical tool to better understand the condition of discriminated sections of the society in various national contexts, including in the Global North.

Notes

1 This chapter is based on the findings of a study conducted as part of an international program, "Urban Chances – City growth and the sustainability challenge", funded by the European Commission Framework Programme (FP7), from 2010 to 2014.

192 *Véronique Dupont and R. Dhanalakshmi*

Further financial support from IRD (French national Research Institute for sustainable Development) is acknowledged. This chapter draws on an abridged account (Dupont & Dhanalakshmi 2016), which has been revised, expanded and updated.

2 The urban agglomeration of Chennai (formerly Madras) had 8.7 million inhabitants as per the 2011 Census, and 10.5 million in 2018 as per the estimates of the United Nations – Population Division.

3 Bayat's analysis pertains to the context of Middle Eastern cities before the Arab Spring.

4 The Dravida Munnetra Kazhagam or DMK, and the All India Anna Dravida Munnetra Kazhagam or AIADMK.

5 Source: The Tamil Nadu Panchayat (Restriction and Control to Regulate the use of Porambokes in Ryotwari Tracts) Rules, 2000. [*Poramboke* land means village or government land set apart as common land for the whole community, and on which private construction is not authorized.]

6 The exact number of evicted families from AAN is not known; 500 is a rough estimate taking into account the information provided by different respondents.

7 The British constructed the Buckingham Canal in 1806 as a salt-water navigation canal aimed at connecting the natural backwaters along the coast between Tamil Nadu and Andhra Pradesh. With a total length of 420 kilometers, it was once a major channel for trade and industry between these two regions.

8 Source: Tamil Nadu Slum Clearance Board

9 The instalments over 20 years were initially 150 rupees (2 US dollars) per month, afterward revised to 250 rupees (3.6 US dollars).

Works Cited

Ahmed, F. (2002). Evicted slum dwellers shifted to Okkiyam Thoraipakkam, Chennai. *The Hindu*, 30 July.

Arabindoo, P. (2011). The spatial (il)logic of slum resettlement sites in Chennai. Paper presented to the conference. *The City in Urban Poverty*. London: University College London.

Arabindoo, P. (2016). Unprecedented natures? An anatomy of the Chennai floods. *City*, 20(6), 800–821.

Baviskar, A. (2002). *The politics of the city.* Seminar – Shades of green: A symposium on the changing contours of Indian environmentalism. 516, 40–42.

Baviskar, A. (2003). Between violence and desire: space, power, and identity in the making metropolitan Delhi. *International Social Science Journal*, 55(175), 89–98.

Baviskar, A. (2011). What the eye does not see: The Yamuna in the imagination of Delhi. *Economic and Political Weekly*, 46(50), 45–53.

Bayat, A. (2010). *Life as politics. How ordinary people changed the Middle East.* ISIM Series on life in contemporary Muslim societies. Amsterdam: University of Amsterdam Press and Stanford, CA: Stanford University Press.

Benjamin, S. (2008). Occupancy urbanism: Radicalizing politics and economics beyond policy and programs. *International Journal of Urban and Regional Research*, 32(3), 719–729.

Broudelhoux, A.-M. (2007). Spectacular Beijing: the conspicuous construction of an Olympic metropolis. *Journal of Urban Affairs*, 29(4), 383–399.

Coelho, K., & Raman, N. (2010). Salvaging and scapegoating: slum evictions on Chennai's waterways. *Economic and Political Weekly*, 45(21), 19–23.

Coelho, K., & Raman, N. (2013). From the frying pan to the floodplain: negotiating land, water, and fire in Chennai's development. In A. Rademacher & K. Sivaramakrishnan (Eds.), *Ecology of Urbanism in India* (pp. 145–168). Hong Kong: Hong Kong University Press.

Living on the margins of the legal city   193

Coelho, K., & Venkat, T. (2009). The politics of civil society: neighbourhood associationism in Chennai. *Economic and Political Weekly*, 44(26 & 27), 358–367.

Coelho, K., Venkat, T., & Chandrika, R. (2012). The spatial reproduction of urban poverty. Labour and livelihoods in a slum resettlement colony. *Economic and Political Weekly*, 47(47 & 48), 53–63.

Cummings, C. (2012). *Contesting the Governance of slum resettlement. Power, interests and relations in the resettlement and rehabilitation of slum dwellers in Chennai, South India* (Master Thesis in International Development Studies). Amsterdam: Graduate School of Social Sciences, University of Amsterdam.

Dupont, V. (2008). Slum demolition in Delhi since the 1990s. An appraisal. *Economic and Political Weekly*, 43(28), 79–87.

Dupont, V. (2011). The challenge of slums and forced evictions. In M.-H. Zérah, V. Dupont, and St. Tawa Lama-Rewal (Eds.), *Urban Policies and the Right to the City in India. Rights, Responsibilities and Citizenship* (pp. 76–97). New Delhi: UNESCO & Centre de Sciences Humaines.

Dupont, V., & Dhanalakshmi, R. (2016). Evictions in the Chennai IT corridor and new threats: low resistance in squatter settlements along the Buckingham Canal. In V. Dupont, D. Jordhus-Lier, C. Sutherland, & E. Braathen (Eds.), *The Politics of Slums in the Global South. Urban Informality in Brazil, India, South Africa and Peru* (pp. 174–179). Abingdon: Routledge.

Dupont, V., Saharan, T., & Gowda, M. M. S. (2013). Delhi, India. In E. Braathen (Ed.), *Addressing Sub-Standard Settlements. WP3 Settlement Fieldwork Report*. Chance2Sustain Fieldwork Report No 2, Bonn: EADI, February 2013, 4–37. www.chance2sustain. eu/index.php?id=48 (Accessed 20 December 2019).

Dupont, V., & Vaquier, D. (2014). Slum demolition, impact on the affected families and coping strategies. In F. Landy & M. C. Saglio-Yatzimirsky (Eds.), *Megacity Slums. Social Exclusion, Urban Space and Policies in Brazil and India* (pp. 307–361). London: Imperial College Press.

Ghertner, D. A. (2008). Analysis of new legal discourses behind Delhi's slum demolitions. *Economic and Political Weekly*, 43(20), 57–66.

HLRN. (2014). *Forced to the Fringes. Disasters of Resettlement in India. Report Two: Kananagi Nagar, Chennai*. New Delhi: Housing and Land Rights Network.

Karthikeyan, A. (2008a). Buckingham Canal to be revived with waterway plan. *Chennai: The Times of India*, 11 June.

Karthikeyan, A. (2008b). Buckingham Canal to be made navigable again. *Chennai: The Times of India*, 10 December.

Kennedy, L., Varrel, A., Denis, E., Dupont, V., Dhanalakshmi, R., Roumeau, S., Baud, I., Pfeffer, K., Sridharan, N., Vijayabaskar, M., Babu, M. S., Seifelislam, A., Rouanet H., & Saharan, T. (2014). *Engaging with Sustainability Issues in Metropolitan Chennai*. Chance2Sustain City Report Series. Bonn: European Association of Development Research and Training Institutes. www.chance2sustain.eu/66.0.html (Accessed 20 December 2019).

Kumar, A. (2014). Soon, a boat trip down the canal. *Chennai: The Hindu*, 1 September.

Kumar, R. (2008). Globalization and changing patterns of social mobilization in urban India. *Social Movement Studies*, 7(1), 77–96.

Lopez, A. X. (2012a). Eviction along the canals, on roads to begin in April. *Chennai: The Hindu*, 7 March.

Lopez, A. X. (2012b). Identification of slum residents suspended. *Chennai: The Hindu*, 30 April.

Lopez, A. X. (2019). 66 slums along Buckingham Canal to be demolished. *Chennai: The Hindu*, 29 May.

194 *Véronique Dupont and R. Dhanalakshmi*

Madras High Court. (2018). *In the High Court of Judicature at Madras, Orders pronounced on 06.09.2018*, W.P. Nos 2511 to 2519 and 2735 of 2014, Chennai.

Malmarugan, K., & Narayan, S. (2006). *Evolution of an integrated urban facility. The IT Corridor Story*. Chennai.

Marius-Gnanou, K. (2010). Nouvelles activités économiques et dynamiques métropolitaines : le cas de la périphérie Sud de Chennai. *Annales de Géographie*, 671–672: 28–51.

National Green Tribunal. (2018). *Original Application No 556/2018, Tribunal on its own motion vs The Principal Secretary, Environment & Forest, Govt of Tamil Nadu & others, Order of the Tribunal*, 31 October 2018, New Delhi. www.indiaenvironmentportal.org. in/files/file/Cooum_River_pollution_NGT_order.pdf (Accessed 20 December 2019).

Park, R. E. (1928). Human migration and the marginal man. *American Journal of Sociology*, 33(6), 881–893.

PUCL. (2010). *Report of PUCL Fact Finding Team on Forced Eviction and Rehabilitation of Slum Dwellers in Chennai. Fact Finding Report*. Chennai: People's Union for Civil Liberties.

Raman, N. (2011). The board and the bank: changing policies towards slums in Chennai. *Economic and Political Weekly*, 46(31), 74–80.

Shin, H. B. (2012). Unequal cities of spectacle and mega-events in China. *City: Analysis of Urban Trends, Culture, Theory, Policy, Action*, 16(6), 728–744.

Shin, H. B., & Li, B. (2013). Whose games? The cost of being "Olympic citizens" in Beijing. *Environment & Urbanization*, 25(2): 550–576.

Sierra, A., & Tadié, J. (2008). Introduction. In A. Sierra & J. Tadié (Eds.), *La ville face à ses marges. autrepart*, 45, 3–13.

Simmel, G. (1908). The stranger. In N. L. Donáld (Eds.), *On Individuality and Social Forms*. Chicago: University of Chicago Press.

The Hindu. (2012). Smart cards work now suspended in city's north. *Chennai: The Hindu*, 4 July.

TNSCB & TNUIFS. (2005). *Pre-feasibility study for identification of environmental infrastructure in slums in Chennai Metropolitan Area. Final Report – Chennai Corporation Area*. [Indian Resources Information & Management Technologies, Ltd, Hyderabad in association with Community Consulting Indian Pvt Ltd (TGC India), Chennai], Chennai: Tamil Nadu Slum Clearance Board and Tamil Nadu Urban Infrastructure Financial Services limited.

TNSCB & TNUIFS. (2006). *Pre-feasibility study for identification of environmental infrastructure in slums in Chennai Metropolitan Area. Final Report – Chennai Metropolitan Area (excluding CMC)*. [Indian Resources Information & Management Technologies, Ltd, Hyderabad in association with Community Consulting Indian Pvt Ltd (TGC India), Chennai], Chennai: Tamil Nadu Slum Clearance Board and Tamil Nadu Urban Infrastructure Financial Services limited.

UN-Habitat. (2013). Planning and design for sustainable urban mobility. *Global Report on Human Settlements 2013*. Abingdon: Earthscan–Routledge.

Venkat, T. (2014). Hustling for property: emergence of an entrepreneurial community in Neelnakarai. In K. Coehlo (Ed.), *Settlement and Struggle on Chennai's Buckingham Canal: Working Class Histories of the City* (pp. 83–96). Chennai: Madras Institute of Development Studies.

Venkateshwarl, K. (2017). An ambitious plan to revive the Buckingham Canal. *Chennai: The Hindu*, 5 August.

Zérah, M. H. (2007). Conflict between green space preservation and housing needs: The case of the Sanjay Gandhi National Park in Mumbai. *Cities*, 24(2), 122–132.

Index

Note: **Bold** page numbers refer to tables; *italic* page numbers refer to figures and page numbers followed by "n" denote endnotes.

Adriaanse, M. L. 2, 7
age: impact on residents *28*
agricultural resite 135, 143
Alexis, Sierra 77
All India Democratic Women Association 185
Alvaderdo, F. 3, 4
American urban society 1
ANR FunérAsie program 78
anti-XRL movement 129, 137
anxiety 2, 6, 7, 50
Apple Daily 102
Arabindoo, P. 183
Arignar Anna Nagar (AAN) 179–185, 187, 189, 190
Article 36 of Regulation for Management of Funerary Affairs 91
Ashworth, G. J. 59
Asian economic crisis (1997) 62–63
Asian financial crisis of 1997 *see* Asian economic crisis (1997)

Baviskar, A. 158, 191
Bayat, A. 180
Beijing 60; self-employed in 23–25; switching jobs in 25–26; unemployed in 26; vendors leaving 26
Benjamin, S. 182
Bestmart360 115
Binhai Guyuan cemetery *76*, 83, 88, 89
B-memo notice 184
bourgeois environmentalism 158, 191
Brexit 2
British colonialism 9
Brossat, Alain 94n3

capitalism, power 6
carnivalisation 139
Carroll, T. 3, 5
cast-off refuse 154–156
Cavé, J. 165
cemeteries: dematerialization of 87–92; edges of city 82–87; marginalization 11; in Shanghai 75–96; social and spatial margins 82–87
Chadhury, Jai Prakash 166
charity cemeteries 87
Chennai: administrative boundaries 180–181; building land, living on margins 183; collective responses, eviction risk 185; cumulative marginalities 176–192; discriminating factor 177; environmental risk 183; eviction risk, living on margins 183–185; Kannagi Nagar resettlement colony 187–189; living on margins of 176–192; margins of city 179–180; new threats of eviction 186–187; remoteness and poverty 181–183; rural to urban settlement 180–181; social marginalization 190; tenants, marginal men 190
Chennai floods 183
Chennai Municipal Corporation 181, 182
Chen Yingfang 72n9
China-Hong Kong relations 122
China's urbanization: family manager 44–46; information about interviewees **39–40**; rural *dama* in 36–50; theoretical perspectives 37–38; unattractive and unproductive labor 42–44; urban strangers 47–49

196   *Index*

China Today Is Remaking Its Urban Form 60

Chinese nationalism 2, 5

Chintan 168

Choy Yuen Village: collective subjectivity of 126–146; community-for-all 138–143; democracy-for-all 134–137; development-for-all 130–134; Support Group 143; victimhood conceptualization 128–130

Chu Hoi-dick 137, 138, 140

civic engagement 12

civil disobedience movement 103

Closer Economic Partnership Arrangement (CEPA) 101

Coelho, K. 176

Communist Party of India (Marxist) CPI(M) 182, 183, 185

community-for-all: collective subjectivity and 138–143; relocation 140; social movement 140

Comprehensive Means Test 134, 142

conflictual dichotomy 165

conspicuous consumption 6

Contractor, F. J. 4

cosmopolitanism 3

crowdedness 114

Cultural Revolution 81

cultural schemas 111

Dabla-Norris, M. E. 4

Dakshin Dilli Swachh Initiatives Limited (DDSIL) 165

Day of the Dead festival 92

Deke-Erh 66, 67

Delhi: waste management issues 156; waste pickers 153–172

Demgenski, P. 56, 61

democracy-for-all 128, 138; and role of villagers 134–137

Democratic Youth Federation of India (DYFI) 182

democratization 138

denial of death 76

development-for-all 128; cost of villagers 130–134

Dhanalakshmi, R. 6

displacing graves *86*

Donald Tsang Yam Kuen 131

Douglas, M. 79

Dupont, V. 6

economic contribution 37

economic migrants 61

electoral-democratic systems 7

emotion culture 128

emotions 128

entrepreneurs 162–165

estranged space 123; radicalized politics 120–122

ethno-nationalism 2, 8

Evenett, S. J. 4

Ex-Gratia Cash Allowance (EGCA) 142

Express Rail Link (XRL) 126, 131, 133, 134, 136, 137, 139, 141–144

face concept 96n30

family manager 44–46

farmers' market: policy reflections 32–33; residents' demand for 31, *31*

farmers' market demolition 17–33; data and methodology 19–21; food market, emergence 21–23; vendors' responses, demolishment 23–26

fecundity 86

fengshui principles 85

financial crisis, 2000 2

first funerary revolution 81

Flood Relief Fund 187

Florin, Bénédicte 157, 161, 163

food market 21–23; community food stations 22; street stalls 22–23; vegetable markets 21–22

food-purchasing "location choice" 26–31; current 26–30; future 30–31

foreign direct investment 4

Foucault, M. 77, 83

fringes 87–92

Fritz, J. 4

Funeral Interment Service (FIS) 87–90

Gamba, F. 91, 92

Gao, J. 93

gender: gendered binary division 37; impact on residents *28*

gentrification 59, 60, 71, 158

Ghertner, D. A. 159, 191

Gini coefficient 6

global inequality 3

globalization 2–4, 7, 8; visibility of 5, 6

globalization-led inequality 4

global urbanization 153

Goffman, Erving 60

Goldberg, Alan 55

Goldberg, Chad Alan 1, 7, 10, 55, 79

Gonzalez-Vicente, R. 3, 5

Goods and Services Tax 167

Google mapping 104, 111, 114, 120

Google Maps 104
graves, public interest 83
Green Form Certificate 144n1
Green Form Subsidised Home Ownership
  Scheme (GSH) 144n1
Gu, J. 87
guerrilla operations 22
guerrilla selling 32

Hanser, A. 42
Henriot, C. 92, 94n5
Ho, David Yau-Fai 96n30
Ho, Willis 137
Home Ownership Scheme (HOS) 142,
  145n2
Hong Kong: radicalized identity politics
  101–124; tourism-driven spatial change
  111–113
Hong Kong-China conflict 104, 117, 119
Hong Kong communities: analysis
  110–111; Google Maps 104; interview
  104–105; participants 110; three border
  communities 105, *106–109*
Hong Kong Special Administrative
  Government (HKSAR) 126, 134
humane approach 142
"hygienist" movement 154

identity politics 103, 104, 120
income 27; impact on residents *29*; share 3
in-depth field interviews 10
Indian nationalism 5
industrial evolution 33
industrial workers 36
"informal" actors 153
Integrated Child Development Service
  181, 182
intellectual significance 121
Interim Housing 145–146n5
international trade 4
interviewees, profile **127**
invisibilization 75–77, 87, 92
irreversible resilience 143
irreversible resistance 126–146

Jérôme, Tadié 77
Jianhua, Gao 82

Kannagi Nagar resettlement colony 184,
  187–189
Kannagi Nagar Welfare Association 189
Kim, A. 5
Kuan, H. 142
Kwong, K. M. 123n3

labor market 42–44, 46, 48
"lagging" groups 49
Land Justice League 137
Land Rehabilitation Scheme 144
land saving grave *84*
Lau, S. 142
legitimate activity, de-marginalizing:
  economic need 168–170; environmental
  contribution 167–168
lilongs 55–58, 70, 71n5
linear management paradigm 154–155
living distance: impact on residents *29*
living-in-the-margins 2–3, 7
localism 123, 137
localist 102–105, 110, 122–123
Longhua 75
low-end industries 33
lower-skilled population: Beijing 17–33; in
  mega-cities 18
Lu Duanfang 60
Lung Fung Group 114

Ma, N. 135
mainlandization 119
marginality 55, 154, 162, 178; defining 1
marginalization 82, 154, 171; of
  cemeteries 77; of "non-modern"
  practices 157; of "waste workers" 153
marginalized people 6–7
marginal man concept 1, 2, 7, 36, 49, 55,
  79, 127, 153, 177, 178; tenants
  as 190
market integration 2
Marxist theory 171
Mass Rapid Transport System (MRTS)
  176
Mass Transit Railway Corporation Ltd
  (MTRL) 133
mega-cities 17, 18, 23
micro-sociologists 8
migrant vendors 31, 32; employment
  status *23*
Modernisierungsverlierer 5
modernization 60; "ideology" 157; of
  infrastructures 159; waste 156–159
modernization campaign 49
Modi, N. 2
monumental stones *88*
moral mediation 137
multiple marginalizations 126–146

nativism 7
Ningxia *41*, 44
nostalgia 10, 12, 49, 121–124

198 *Index*

objectionable slums 12, 183, 184, 187
O'Brien, Kevin J. 7
occupancy urbanism 182
official urban planning policy 17
Olympic Games, 2008 9
otherness 10, 38

Park, R. E. 1, 7, 127, 177
Park, Robert 55
peaceful resilience 136
The People's Daily 31, 82
poor populations stigmatization 158–159
populism 3, 5
populist 3, 5, 7, 182
post-structural feminists 37
poverty 4–6
power 118–120; modes 111
protectionism 5
protectionist trade policies 4
public grievances 11
public space 33
PVC market 167

Qingming 88, 89

racial prejudice 1
radicalized identity politics 101–124
radicalized politics: estranged space
    120–122
Raman, N. 176
real estate market 76
recrimination 65
recycling 155
recycling chain 162–165; professional
    sector 163–165; waste workers
    162–163
Reddy, R. N. 157
Regional Express Line 132
rehabilitation 158, 177
renovated graves, black material *85*
residents' preference: vegetables and fruits
    30
residents' responses, demolishment 26–31;
    food-purchasing "location choice"
    26–31
resident welfare associations (RWAs) 158
resistance 7, 38, 66, 89, 121, 136–144,
    165, 185
"Robert Park's Marginal Man: The Career
    of a Concept in American Sociology" 1
Roces, M. 128
Ruiz-Junco, N. 128
rural *dama* 10, 36–50

Safai Sena 172n3
sanitary ideal 157
Secondary Market Scheme 145n3
second funerary revolution 87, 92, 93
self-determination 5
self-employed migrant vendors 18
self-employment 23–25
service economy 37
severe acute respiratory syndrome (SARS)
    101, 123n1, 135
Sewell, William Jr. 111
Shanghai: cemeteries in 75–96; dead
    from city, progressive expulsion 78–82;
    municipality of *81*; national historic city
    59; urban renovation implementation
    58–60; *see also* Tianzifang, Shanghai
Shanghainese 11
Sheung Shui 105, *106–109,* 121, 122
Shikumen 56, 58
Shui On Land 62
Simmel, G. 177, 178
social actors 60
social beautification 191
social graves 83
social groups 50
socialization 48
social marginalization 190
social movements 12, 129, 135, 139
social structures 111
social Vulnerability Index 6
social waste 158
spatial experience 114; power 118–120;
    resource 114–117; values 117–118
Sun Palace Farmers' Market 9, 10, 19–21,
    24, 27
supermarkets 30
Surplus Home Ownership Scheme: sale
    programme of 145n4
surveyed residents, socioeconomic profile
    21

Tamil Nadu Slum Clearance Board
    (TNSCB) 179, 182, 183, 187, 188
Thoraval, J. 78, 80
Tianzifang, Shanghai 11, *68, 69*; building
    usage evolution *57*; "Chinese Soho"
    61; fighting for preservation 62–63;
    groups of people saving 60–62;
    lilongs, description 55–58; residents'
    community transformation 61
tourism-driven spatial change 111–113;
    "chain-store," shops 113; shops 111,
    112, **112, 113**

touristic high spot: marginal area, transformation 70–71
traditional funerary shops 75, 76
traditional offerings, death anniversary *91*
Trump, Donald 2
Tuen Mun 105, *106–109,* 111–113, 115, 116, 121

Umbrella Movement 103
unattractive labor 42–44
unequal treaties 71n3
unproductive labor 42–44
urban capitalism 162
urban diseases 17
urban elites 157
urban hukou 20
"urban renewal" policies 158
urban sociology 37
urban strangers: displaced and rootless 47–49

Van Dijk, J. 128
vegetable markets 24
vendors' responses, demolishment 23–26; leaving Beijing 26; self-employed in Beijing 23–25; switching jobs in Beijing 25–26; unemployed in Beijing 26
victimhood conceptualization 128–130
virtual grave *90*

Wang, W. 87
waste: collection to recycling 159–161; eviction of poor 156; incineration 157; living in margins 161–162; management strategies 154; margins, Delhi 159–162; modernization, India 156–159; objects 158; pickers 9, 153, 155, 164, 168; poor populations stigmatization 158–159; in urban margins 153–172; workers 162–163
waste recovery 154; counter-discourses 165–166; legitimizing 165–167; neglected alternative 155–156; recovery workers claims 166–167; resistance movements 165–166; workers 12
Watson, J. L. 79, 80, 94n4
wealth inequality 3
Weiner, R. R. 3, 6
Western "sexist" cities 37
women 38; communal mediating roles 44; *dama* 42, 43; grouping 41; productivity 42; public positions 43; rural 36; staying at home 40
World Bank 4
Wright, M. W. 157

Xibahe 22
Xibaoxing 75
Xi Jinping 2
Xintiandi 62, 63, 65

Yinchuan *41,* 42
yitiaolong fuwu 78
Yuen Long 105, *106–109,* 111–115, 118, 121

Zhou, J. 93
Ziller, R. C. 79

Printed in the United States
by Baker & Taylor Publisher Services